ALL LOVES EXCELLING

Daily Meditation with Charles Wesley

Compiled by
Elizabeth Hart

Edited by
Gerald Hobbs
and
Pauline Webb

Preface by
Maurice Hart

Front cover illustration RSPB Images photograph by C M Gomersall

Published by Methodist Publishing House

Printed and bound in Great Britain by Hartnolls Limited, Bodmin, Cornwall

ISBN 1 85852 087 8

CONTENTS

PREFACE

The idea for this book began in correspondence between my daughter and me many years ago. Elizabeth was working as a librarian in the Vancouver School of Theology and I was living as a supernumerary Methodist minister in Devon. In our frequent letters we often quoted our favourite hymns, the hymns of Charles Wesley. Elizabeth admired Wesley as a poet and had made a thorough study of how deeply influenced he had been by the writing of John Milton. She had also written a dissertation on Susanna Wesley and the influence that gifted mother exerted on her sons. Elizabeth was fascinated by comparing the various editions of Wesley's hymns and noting how they had been changed through the years. We began to share our meditations on what Wesley's verses meant for us today, and I pointed out to her how deeply steeped they are in Scripture and how relevant their message remains for our contemporary society.

Then the idea emerged of preparing a book of daily reflections on the hymns of Wesley which would take us right through the seasons of the church's year. Elizabeth sought the help of several members of the Wesley Historical Society, of which she was an enthusiastic member. She also invited two personal friends to act as editors. The Rev Dr Gerald Hobbs, a church historian and a colleague at the Vancouver School of Theology, worked with her in Canada, and Dr Pauline Webb, a long-standing friend of the family, shared the task here in Britain. Elizabeth started work on the book with tremendous enthusiasm, eager to share her own enjoyment of Charles Wesley's hymns with a much larger company on both sides of the Atlantic.

Sadly, Elizabeth was not able to complete the work herself. In May 1993, whilst working on the manuscript, she was taken from us by an immediate and fatal illness. We were all stunned by this sudden loss, but comforted by Elizabeth's own words in one of the meditations she was writing at the time of her death, on a hymn of Charles Wesley based on the 23rd Psalm: 'There is a saying, "When in doubt, say thank you" . . . Death's vale may be dark, but it is the darkness of homecoming where fear vanishes in love and we respond in praise.'

I want to say 'thank you' to Gerald Hobbs and Pauline Webb for taking up Elizabeth's unfinished task with great sympathy and sensitivity. They were assisted in their efforts by Elizabeth's family, who managed to decipher and transcribe the mass of material already assembled in her computer. The result is a joint venture which I believe has produced a unique cycle of devotion based on both familiar and little known hymns of Charles Wesley, and firmly rooted in the biblical texts.

Maurice Hart
1997

INTRODUCTION

When Elizabeth Hart died unexpectedly on 18th May 1993, we undertook, with the blessing of her family, the completion of this book which had been so central to her work and to her spiritual life for several years. As friends whom she had asked to work with her in the project, we were familiar with much of the material in its earlier stages, and the opportunity to bring it to completion seemed a final gift we could make to a good friend. In fulfilling this task, we discovered what we could not then have anticipated, that in this manner Elizabeth would also make a lasting gift to us.

In these intervening three years the two of us have worked together and separately, at intervals as the other projects of our busy lives permitted, to bring this collection of meditations safely to birth. We inherited a version of some 320 meditations. Many of these had been through the editorial process, that is, we had each received a copy from Elizabeth and commented on the text, after which in most cases Elizabeth had done a revision. Others were in first draft, having been written in the weeks immediately preceding her death. For the remainder, Elizabeth left us a selection of some fifty further Wesley texts, from which she had evidently intended to prepare the remaining meditations.

Familiar as we were with the general concept of the book, having worked with Elizabeth as reader-critics for a number of specific texts, we nonetheless did not find it simple to reconstruct the precise principles along which she had proceeded. In the end, we believe we have been faithful to her intention, to present in a series of daily meditations, readings gathered from the vast treasury of Charles Wesley's hymns and poetry.

The reader will find here a selection that includes verses from most of the more familiar Wesley hymns, but also a great deal that, though once sung, has fallen out of modern use, as well as material from the unpublished poetry, now thankfully made accessible through the editing of Beckerlegge and Kimbrough. As befits a founding member of the Charles Wesley Society, Elizabeth had indicated in the codes at the end of each meditation the initial appearance of each hymn in print, and its place, if it occurred there, in the first large Methodist hymnal, John Wesley's 1780 *Collection of Hymns for the Use of the People Called Methodists.* For the convenience of contemporary readers, we have also given the location of the text in some modern Methodist hymnals.

Over the past two centuries, successive generations of hymnal editors – beginning with his brother John – have seen fit to introduce various changes into Charles Wesley's original texts, as language evolved and theological fashions changed: for example, few of us would quarrel with the substitution of 'mercies' for 'bowels' that has been common practice since the beginning of this century. The text printed here is sometimes the modern, familiar version; but on other occasions, we found a freshness in Wesley's original which made it seem preferable for our purposes. An asterisk (*) placed before the edition code identifies the source of our text, and any variations from that version are indicated in parentheses.

One particular matter of late twentieth-century English usage needs to be mentioned here. The Wesley brothers entered into conflict in their own day with those older views and practices within the churches that placed restrictions upon the free grace of God, and the universality of the Gospel invitation:

> Come, sinners, to the Gospel feast,
> Let every soul be Jesu's guest;
> Ye need not one be left behind,
> For God hath bidden all mankind.

In our own day, expressions like 'mankind' that were once seen as inclusive of all people (and used in this way by Wesley), have come to be understood as naming people in terms of masculine gender, a practice that is experienced by many today as exclusive. Although Wesley could not have anticipated such a linguistic shift, it is reasonable to believe that he would have had great sympathy for pastoral concern not to use language that excludes anyone from the Gospel welcome. At the same time, we recognise, in the words of the 1992 British Methodist Conference, that 'sometimes we have to accept that our literary heritage cannot always be made to share our sensitivities'. In our own interventions in the Wesley texts, we have endeavoured to balance these two considerations. Where a change could be introduced that respected the character of Wesley's own expression, we have done so; but where this would materially affect the poetic rhythm or rhyme, or alter the thought of the text, we have preferred to ask the reader's indulgence of an earlier age in leaving the original unaltered.

Like his brother John, Charles Wesley's spirit was suffused with the language of Scripture. Where he intended his text to be a meditation upon a specific biblical passage, a portion at least of that passage has been included. In other instances, a text from amongst the several reminiscences in Wesley's hymn has been chosen. These biblical passages are most frequently quoted here in the King James Version of 1611, as this was of course the translation Wesley knew almost by heart. In the Psalms, however, the Coverdale version from the *Book of Common Prayer* was equally familiar to him, and where the wording of the latter seems to have been his immediate inspiration, we have cited it. On the other hand, where a modern translation seemed to us more appropriate for the sake of drawing the reader into the text, the *New Revised Standard Version* or the *Revised English Bible* has been used.

Finally, each Wesley text with accompanying Scripture is given a short contemporary commentary, concluding with a prayer or thought for further meditation. In preparing these commentaries, Elizabeth found the 'Companions' to *Hymns & Psalms* and the *United Methodist Hymnal* a valuable resource. In our work, we have sought to respect, as much as the editorial task would allow, her words, style and thought, recognising at the same time the responsibility to which she invited us, to work with her to bring the volume to completion. In writing the missing meditations, we have sought to complement Elizabeth's own work, such that we are satisfied that the whole is faithful to the spirit in which she conceived and prepared it. It was certainly her hope that, invited by the fresh reflections and spiritual insights of one of their contemporaries, new generations might be helped to discover the rich treasures of Wesley's hymns.

It is often forgotten that Wesley's hymns were understood to be spiritual literature as well as hymns, and commended for devotional reading and prayer in addition to communal song. In a generation that is marked by a renewed interest in spirituality, *All Loves Excelling* hopes to help recover that tradition. Our volume contains 366 text selections and meditations. The format has been designed to encourage use of the book, one page at a time, as daily spiritual reading throughout a year. We have set the selections in an order which facilitates their use within the rhythm of the church year, from Advent/Christmas/Epiphany through Lent and Easter and into the long season after Pentecost. A second grouping has brought together those without an obvious seasonal application in relation to the biblical texts to which they refer, namely, as meditations on Psalms, Gospels, Acts of the Apostles and Epistles. Within the framework of the church year, the reader will find the meditations on Psalms in the weeks after Epiphany, while those on Acts, the Epistles and Gospels occur in the latter half of the volume, the season after Pentecost. For those readers who prefer to follow some other order, the index of themes and of biblical passages may be of assistance in making their selection.

A number of persons and institutions are owed an expression of gratitude. Vancouver School of Theology encouraged and supported financially the initial work by Elizabeth Hart, as well as our own; the Library staff – both those who worked under Elizabeth's direction and her successors – have greatly facilitated the completion of the book. It is fitting that benefits from the sale of the work will go to the Elizabeth Hart Fund in the VST Library. The staff at Wesley College, Bristol and at the library of Emmanuel College, Toronto gave us invaluable access to their superb Wesley collections. Oliver Beckerlegge and Paul Stanwood provided helpful advice. At Vancouver School of Theology, Susan Lamey, Gail Miller, Karen van der Meulen and Michelle Slater made their typing of successive versions of the manuscript a labour of love. Elizabeth's family and numerous friends encouraged us to persevere to the completion. There will have been others who gave assistance to Elizabeth whose names we cannot record; may the volume itself be a token of her gratitude and ours. Finally, we would express our appreciation to the board and staff of the Methodist Publishing House, particularly Mrs Susan Hibbins, who gave initial encouragement for the project, and maintained commitment to it during these three years of completion.

The spirituality of John and Charles Wesley found its anchor in the believer's personal experience of the salvation given by God in Jesus Christ. To know, to feel the forgiveness of that redeeming love is to be set free from one's bondage to fear and to guilt, and to discover the measureless resources of the Spirit for living and participating in God's new creation. It is the spiritual and poetic genius of Charles Wesley's hymns that again and again they open doors for the reader or singer into the experience of the author, inviting us to discover and celebrate with him the liberating faithfulness of God. We join with Elizabeth Hart in the hope that these pages will be such a resource for their readers.

Gerald Hobbs & Pauline Webb

London & Vancouver
1997

DAILY ARRANGEMENT

Advent Season

1 Love Divine (1)
2 Love Divine (2)
3 A Morning Hymn
4 The Morning Star
5 Thy Kingdom Come
6 The Mystery of God in Christ
7 Peace on Earth (1)
8 Peace on Earth (2)
9 An Act of Devotion
10 Waiting in Hope
11 The Strength of Mary
12 Jesus Comes
13 Dear Desire of Every Nation
14 The Dayspring from on High
15 Unto Us a Child is Born
16 And God is Born (1)
17 And God is Born (2)
18 Reconciling Extremes (1)
19 Reconciling Extremes (2)
20 See There!
21 Poverty of the Stable
22 Giving Birth
23 Angels Behold
24 Jesus is Our Flesh and Blood
25 Hymn for Christmas Day
26 The Heavenly Stranger (1)
27 The Heavenly Stranger (2)
28 Fear Not (1)
29 Fear Not (2)
30 To Follow the Star
31 Praise (1)
32 Praise (2)
33 New Year (1)
34 New Year (2)
35 Covenant Making
36 God's Covenant Love

Psalms

37 Psalm 8 (1)
38 Psalm 8 (2)
39 Psalm 8 (3)
40 Psalm 9
41 Psalm 19 (1)
42 Psalm 19 (2)
43 Psalm 19 (3)

Lent-Biblical Passages

Holy Week and Easter

The Sacrament of the Lord's Supper

Reading the Scriptures

Pentecost

Acts of the Apostles

The Epistles

The Gospels

For Special Days

LOVE DIVINE (1)

Love divine, all loves excelling,
Joy of heaven to earth come down,
Fix in us thy humble dwelling,
All thy faithful mercies crown.
Jesu, thou art all compassion,
Pure, unbounded love thou art;
Visit us with thy salvation,
Enter every trembling heart.

Breathe, O breathe thy loving spirit
Into every troubled breast,
Let us all in thee inherit,
Let us find the second rest:
Take away our love of sinning,
Alpha and Omega be,
End of faith as its beginning,
Set our hearts at liberty.

For thus says the high and lofty one who inhabits eternity, whose name is Holy: 'I dwell in the high and holy place, and also with those who are contrite and humble in spirit, to revive the spirit of the humble, and to revive the heart of the contrite.'
Isaiah 57:15 (NRSV)

The first line of the first verse states the theme developed throughout the whole of this familiar hymn, Charles Wesley's version of Purcell's popular song 'Fairest Isle, all isles excelling'. Look especially at the phrases 'all compassion', 'pure, unbounded love', and the idea that love is the 'end of faith' as well as 'its beginning'.

The second verse will be unfamiliar to many readers. Commentators seem to agree that John left it out of his 1780 hymnbook because he did not like Charles' original line five, 'take away our power of sinning'. John Fletcher of Madeley suggested 'love of sinning' as an alternative; as he said, 'Can God take away from us our power of sinning without taking away our power of free obedience?' Choice is part of the human condition; what Wesley asks for is a greater love that leaves no place for self-centredness.

PRAYER
As I am aware of my own heartbeat, so may I be aware of your love pulsing through my being. As I breathe in and out, so may I be aware of your Holy Spirit breathing upon me. As I feel the bondage of my own sins, so may I be aware of the liberation of your forgiveness. Amen.

---

*RH (1747) CH 374 RV 69 [2:5 our power of sinning] HP 267 UMH 384 VU 333

2 LOVE DIVINE (2)

Come, almighty to deliver,
  Let us all thy life receive;
Suddenly return, and never,
  Never more thy temple leave.
Thee we would be always blessing,
  Serve thee as thy hosts above,
Pray, and praise thee, without ceasing,
  Glory in thy perfect love.

Finish then thy new creation,
  Pure and sinless let us be;
Let us see thy great salvation,
  Perfectly restored in thee:
Changed from glory into glory,
  Till in heaven we take our place,
Till we cast our crowns before thee,
  Lost in wonder, love, and praise!

So if any one is in Christ, there is a new creation: everything old has passed away; see, everything has become new!

2 Corinthians 5:17 (NRSV)

This continuation of yesterday's hymn could be considered a call to participate in the transformation of personal and corporate life. The Spirit of God living in us through Jesus Christ, the life of the world, is always changing us, always bringing about a new creation.

Those of us who have sung so often this lilting, majestic hymn without really thinking of its implications may need to remind ourselves that saying 'Come' is one thing; really wanting our lives and the life of our world to be transformed is quite another. The invitation is to a transformation of our everyday lives, seeing with the insight of the Spirit, reflecting God's glory, as Paul described it to the Corinthians (2 Corinthians 3:17-18). The call 'Come' may also take us travelling along a new road of service that will enable others to enjoy that more abundant life Jesus came to bring to all.

PRAYER
Almighty God, may I praise you with my lips and my life. May I put your grace to the test in living a life of prayer and risk in your service, through Jesus, the life of the world. Amen.

---

*RH (1747) CH 374 RV 69 [1:2 1780 grace, 2:2 1780 spotless] HP 267 UMH 384 VU 333

A MORNING HYMN 3

Christ, whose glory fills the skies,
  Christ, the true, the only Light,
Sun of righteousness, arise,
  Triumph o'er the shades of night;
Day-spring from on high, be near;
Day-star, in my heart appear.

Dark and cheerless is the morn
  Unaccompanied by thee:
Joyless is the day's return,
  Till thy mercy's beams I see,
Till they inward light impart,
Glad my eyes, and warm my heart.

Visit then this soul of mine;
  Pierce the gloom of sin and grief;
Fill me, radiancy divine;
  Scatter all my unbelief;
More and more thyself display,
Shining to the perfect day.

Through the tender mercy of our God; whereby the dayspring from on high hath visited us.

Luke 1:78

Perhaps the joy of the sunrise is only truly appreciated after a long, dark, sleepless night of worry or pain. When gloom and grief and a sense of failure or loss overtake us, that too is a deep darkness of spiritual night. In this magnificent, spacious hymn Charles takes the Sun/Son images from scripture and explores them in a meditative prayer that is both a comfort and a call to hope.

Written from the 'gloom of sin and grief', the tone of the poem is still joyful, for the writer knows that Christ's light can utterly change what seems a hopelessly dark situation. It has happened before; it can happen again. The lovely day-star in the eastern sky is the first sign, then comes the piercing beam of those first rays, and finally they turn to the radiancy of full sunshine, and everything is warmed and transformed.

MEDITATION
Use this hymn as a regular start to your morning prayer for some time until you memorise it. It provides a joyous framework for all the challenges of the coming day.

---

*HSP (1740) RV 12 HP 457 UMH 173 VU 336

4 THE MORNING STAR

'See the Day-spring from afar
Ushered by the morning star!'
Haste; to him who sends the light,
Hallow the remains of night.
Souls, put on your glorious dress,
Waking into righteousness;
Clothed with Christ aspire to shine,
Radiance he of light divine;
Beam of the eternal beam,
He in God, and God in him!
Strive we him in us to see,
Transcript of the Deity.

Through the tender mercy of our God; whereby the dayspring from on high hath visited us.

Luke 1:78

Those who have a window facing the east, and wake early, will see the morning star at cloudless dawns. If, like the early Methodists, they start their devotions at that time, they will understand some of the attraction of this hymn. The idea of being dressed, not just with clothes, but with Christ himself, is an image of the radiance in which love can enclose us. It also suggests a form of protection against evil. In Romans 13:14, Paul speaks of 'putting on the Lord Jesus Christ' as a way of withstanding the temptations of the flesh.

To all this, Wesley's morning hymn adds a joyous note of urgency. 'Haste,' he says, 'Aspire to shine', for the beam of the morning star which has come in Jesus, a beam of the great light which is God, can shine in us also. This is our inner light given for our guidance, the light which can lighten everyone coming into the world.

PRAYER
Clothe me, O Lord, with the ornaments of thy heavenly grace, and cover me with the robes of righteousness. *Basil of Caesarea*

---

*HSP (1739) RV 7

Lo, he comes with clouds descending,
Once for favoured sinners slain;
Thousand thousand saints attending
Swell the triumph of his train:
Alleluia!
God appears on earth to reign.

Those dear tokens of his passion
Still his dazzling body bears;
Cause of endless exultation
To his ransomed worshippers:
With what rapture
Gaze we on those glorious scars.

Yea, amen, let all adore thee,
High on thine eternal throne;
Saviour, take the power and glory,
Claim the kingdom for thine own:
Come, Lord Jesus!
Everlasting God, come down!

All the angels stood round about the throne . . . and fell before the throne on their faces, and worshipped God, saying, Amen: Blessing, and glory, and wisdom, and thanksgiving, and honour, and power, and might, be unto our God for ever and ever. Amen.

Revelation 7:11-12

What powerful imagery the writer of Revelation gives us: words which in modern ears inevitably ring out to the accompaniment of Handel's majestic chorus in the *Messiah* oratorio. Wesley's hymn echoes something of the same exuberant glory. Sung to the splendid eighteenth century tune 'Helmsley', it too sends our imaginations soaring, so that we see Christ returning to the earth to reclaim the world for which he suffered and died. We do not know how or when that will be, but we believe he *has* come, he *does* come and he *will* come again.

The 'already but not yet' image permeates many situations. In our own lives we who are 'ransomed worshippers', freed from the power of all that can harm us, know that though earth is still our home, it is not our eternal home. We live in the now, but we live by hope in the future. The kingdom of God is within us, but it is still to come in its fullness.

PRAYER
Look up, my soul, and see thy crucified Lord all gloriously enthroned.
Behold the ragged purple now turned into a robe of light, and the scornful reed into a royal sceptre. The wreath of thorns is grown into a sparkling diadem and all his scars are polished into brightness. *John Wesley*

---

*Hymns of Intercession for all Mankind (1758) RV 92 [3:5 Jah, Jehovah] HP 241 UMH 718 VU 25

6 THE MYSTERY OF GOD IN CHRIST

With glorious clouds encompassed round,
Whom angels dimly see,
Will the Unsearchable be found,
Or God appear to me?

Will he forsake his throne above,
Himself to me impart?
Answer, thou Man of grief and love,
And speak it to my heart!

Didst thou not in our flesh appear,
And live and die below,
That I may now perceive thee near,
And my Redeemer know?

Come then, and to my soul reveal
The heights and depths of grace,
The wounds which all my sorrows heal,
That dear disfigured face.

I view the Lamb in his own light,
Whom angels dimly see,
And gaze, transported at the sight,
Through all eternity.

Clouds and darkness are round about him: righteousness and judgement are the habitation of his throne.

Psalm 97:2

The psalmist touches on the deep mystery of the nature of God. Wesley builds on this language, borrowing especially from John Milton, to create a drama of question and answer. Notice how the first verse sets the question, and the last verse answers it in almost the same terms. But there is a difference; the hidden God of verse one becomes the Lamb 'in his own light' by the final verse. In verses three-five, Christ is questioned personally: 'Is this what you did and why you did it? – then show me; come to me!'

To the common human search for God, many voices speak; many answers are proposed. This hymn reminds us that the Christian has caught in that 'dear disfigured face' of Jesus a glimpse of the eternal God who has thus revealed himself to us.

PRAYER
Lord, as I turn my eyes upon Jesus and survey his wondrous cross, help me to see my whole life more clearly in the light of his love. Amen.

FH 1767 *CH 124 HP 184 [2:2 himself to worms]

PEACE ON EARTH (1)

All glory to God in the sky,
And peace upon earth be restored!
O Jesus, exalted on high,
Appear our omnipotent Lord!
Who, meanly in Bethlehem born,
Didst stoop to redeem a lost race,
Once more to thy creatures return,
And reign in thy kingdom of grace.

When thou in our flesh didst appear,
All nature acknowledged thy birth;
Arose the acceptable year,
And heaven was opened on earth;
Receiving its Lord from above,
The world was united to bless
The giver of concord and love,
The prince and the author of peace.

O wouldst thou again be made known!
Again in thy Spirit descend,
And set up in each of thine own,
A kingdom that never shall end!
Thou only art able to bless,
And make the glad nations obey,
And bid the dire enmity cease,
And bow the whole world to thy sway.

All at once there was with the angel a great company of the heavenly host, singing praise to God: 'Glory to God in highest heaven, and on earth peace to all in whom he delights.'

Luke 2:13-14 (REB)

This is the hymn which John Wesley felt was the very best of the eighteen songs in Charles' *Hymns for the Nativity of our Lord.* The birth of Christ as the dawning of a new heaven and new earth recalls the eloquent vision of the prophet Isaiah. There a child was to usher in a peaceable kingdom, a world where justice would reign for all peoples, and even enmity in the world of nature would cease (Isaiah 11:1-9, 65:17-25).

This vision inspired too the American Quaker Edward Hicks, whose painting, *The Peaceable Kingdom*, shows a young child at play with lion, ox and leopard, while in the background native American Indians and English settlers are in amicable conversation. Wesley asks here for the gift of that spirit of peace in every human heart, that can truly mean peace for all on earth.

PRAYER
Let there be peace on earth, and let it begin with me. Amen.

---

*NH (1745) CH 11 HP 400

PEACE ON EARTH (2)

Come, then, to thy servants again,
   Who long thy appearing to know;
Thy quiet and peaceable reign
   In mercy establish below;
All sorrow before thee shall fly,
   And anger and hatred be o'er,
And envy and malice shall die,
   And discord afflict us no more.

No horrid alarum of war
   Shall break our eternal repose,
No sound of the trumpet is there,
   Where Jesus's spirit o'erflows;
Appeased by the charms of thy grace
   We all shall in amity join,
And kindly each other embrace,
   And love with a passion like thine.

And the ransomed of the LORD shall return, and come to Zion with songs and everlasting joy upon their heads; they shall obtain joy and gladness, and sorrow and sighing shall flee away.

Isaiah 35:10

As yesterday, the theme continues to be universal peace. How can this happen in a world filled with war and oppression? The very year in which Wesley wrote this hymn saw the Jacobite Rebellion, so we can understand his yearning for a time of peace. Today war seems to be everywhere, and we too yearn for world peace. But if we look beyond the headlines we may see that here and there, often in quiet ways, there are people working for reconciliation and learning to embrace even those who were once their enemies.

John was a black student from eastern Canada, who was driving with his brother David along an urban street when suddenly a shot rang out. David was hit and died in his brother's arms. There was seemingly no personal motive; it was an act of random violence against black people. Some years later, in a worshipping community John, now a theology student, told this story in a sermon on forgiveness. Deeply moved by his call to all of us to forgive our enemies as Christ has forgiven us, one of his hearers reflected on an apparent personal injustice which still held powerful control over her own life, and with God's help, was able to let it go. How powerful is the influence of peacemaking!

PRAYER
God, you came as a human being, the Prince of Peace, and you still come through the lives of those who follow him. Grant me your grace to understand how I may work for peace in the world. Amen.

---

*NH (1745) CH 211 HP 400

AN ACT OF DEVOTION

Behold the servant of the Lord!
  I wait thy guiding hand to feel,
To hear and keep thine every word,
  To prove, and do thy perfect will,
Joyful from all my works to cease,
Glad to fulfil all righteousness.

Me if thy grace vouchsafe to use,
  Meanest of all thy creatures, me,
The deed, the time, the manner choose;
  Let all my fruit be found of thee;
Let all my works in thee be wrought,
By thee to full perfection brought.

Here then to thee thine own I leave;
  Mould as thou wilt thy passive clay;
But let me all thy stamp receive,
  But let me all thy words obey,
Serve with a single heart and eye,
And to thy glory live and die.

And Mary said, Behold the handmaid of the Lord; be it unto me according to thy word.

Luke 1:38

Among some forty-five biblical texts embedded in this prayer/hymn, the dominant image is of Mary's openness to the will of God in her life. Mary waits for the coming of the child Jesus, this gift of God within her that will be born in due time. Just as Mary was receptive to this act of God in her life, so we all have the opportunity to say 'Use me' and then to allow God's purpose to come to fruition in our lives.

TO PONDER

'I don't know who – or what – put the question . . . but at some moment I did answer Yes to Someone – or Something – and from that hour I was certain that existence is meaningful and that, therefore, my life in self-surrender had a goal.'[1]
Dag Hammarskjöld

**Farther Appeal* (1745) RV 34 CH 417 HP 788

WAITING IN HOPE

In true and patient hope,
My soul on God attends,
And calmly confident looks up
Till he salvation sends;
My rock and Saviour, he
Shall answer to my call;
And while to him for help I flee
I shall not greatly fail.

Truly my soul waiteth upon God; from him cometh my salvation.

Psalm 62:1

Advent is a time of hope – hope in the winter darkness that the sun will return, hope that the Christ will come, even hope that somehow this coming will make a difference in our lives. Wesley writes of 'patient hope', something we might distinguish from the anxious variety. Patient people know that what they are looking for will eventually come, though in the darkness of the winter of our lives, that may seem a far off hope.

One of the most comforting Advent thoughts comes from John Donne, poet and Dean of St Paul's Cathedral, London. In his Christmas sermon of 1624 he speaks of the unexpected suddenness of the God-event in our lives:

> He brought light out of darkness, not out of a lesser light; he can bring thy Summer out of Winter, though thou have no Spring; though in the wayes of fortune, or understanding, or conscience, thou have been benighted till now, wintred and frozen, clouded and eclypsed, damp and benumbed, smothered and stupefied till now, now God comes to thee, not as in the dawning of the day, not as in the bud of the spring, but as the Sun at noon . . . all occasions invite his mercies, and all times are his seasons.[1]

May this be so for all of us.

PRAYER
God, in whom darkness and light are both alike, enter my darkness with your surprising light. As I wait with patient confidence for your re-entry into my life, give me eyes to see, ears to hear, and a heart that is open to receive you, through Jesus the Christ. Amen.

---

*PW 8, 135

When he did our flesh assume
    That everlasting Man,
Mary held him in her womb
    Whom heaven could not contain!
Who the mystery can believe?
Incomprehensible thou art;
    Yet we still by faith conceive,
    And bear thee in our heart.

For the Lord hath created a new thing in the earth, A woman shall compass a man.
Jeremiah 31:22

As so often, Wesley's imagination is fired by his meditation on a specific biblical text. Jeremiah predicts a new age for all Israel in which women will play a new role. Charles takes the traditional Christian reading of this verse to refer to Mary, the mother of Christ, whose own song of liberation – the Magnificat – celebrated a new age, an age of reversals, when the mighty would tumble and the poor be raised up, when the hungry would be filled with good things, and the rich would, sadly, go empty away.

If we, as the poem suggests, by faith conceive and bear Christ in our hearts, then we also are called to raise up those who are oppressed and to redress imbalances in society. Ironically, a major injustice is the fate of women all over the world. These prayers, from a recent service of worship, may help us to focus our thoughts on Mary and the witness of women.

PRAYER
We praise you, God of promise, and give you thanks this day for your servant Mary, and for all the women who have sung and danced the song of your salvation from age to age.

We remember the women who have nurtured and supported us: our mothers and grandmothers, our sisters, wives, and daughters, and our friends.

We pray for those women who are the victims of domestic violence and sexual abuse. We pray for those women who face a life of poverty and malnutrition, remembering especially our sisters in the third world.

We make our prayer through Mary's child, the first-fruits of your new creation. Amen.

---

*SH (1762) RV 160

12 JESUS COMES!

Jesus comes with all his grace,
Comes to save a fallen race:
Object of our glorious hope,
Jesus comes to lift us up.

Let the living stones cry out;
Let the seed of Abraham shout;
Praise we all our lowly King,
Give him thanks, rejoice, and sing.

He hath our salvation wrought,
He our captive souls hath bought,
He hath reconciled to God,
He hath washed us in his blood.

We are now his lawful right,
Walk as children of the light;
We shall soon obtain the grace,
Pure in heart, to see his face.

Let us then rejoice in hope,
Steadily to Christ look up:
Trust to be redeemed from sin,
Wait till he appears within.

And some of the Pharisees . . . said [to Jesus], 'Teacher, rebuke your disciples.' He answered, 'I tell you, if these were silent, the very stones would cry out.'
Luke 19:39-40 (RSV)

Like living stones be yourselves built into a spiritual house . . .
1 Peter 2:5 (RSV)

Not only 'the living stones cry out', but the poet does so too, in an exuberance of steady joy at the thought of the coming of Christ. The tone is certain, the language emphatic. Practically every line is based on words from different parts of the New Testament. The first three verses of the poem focus on Jesus and his coming; the move from 'He' (v3) to 'We' (v4) invites us to consider the meaning for ourselves.

In the Advent season, as we prepare again to celebrate the coming of Christ, Wesley reminds us of the gift of that presence, the love, joy and peace of God amongst and within us.

PRAYER
Gracious God, may I wait for your coming with an expectant heart and with eyes to see around and within me the signs of your presence. Amen.

---

*HSP (1749) [2:2 sons of Abraham] CH 388 HP 168

DEAR DESIRE OF EVERY NATION

Come, thou long-expected Jesus,
Born to set thy people free,
From our fears and sins release us,
Let us find our rest in thee.

Israel's strength and consolation,
Hope of all the earth thou art,
Dear desire of every nation,
Joy of every longing heart.

Born thy people to deliver,
Born a child and yet a king,
Born to reign in us for ever,
Now thy gracious kingdom bring.

By thine own eternal Spirit
Rule in all our hearts alone;
By thine all-sufficient merit
Raise us to thy glorious throne.

She shall bring forth a son, and thou shalt call his name Jesus; for he shall save his people from their sins.

Matthew 1:21

The name 'Jesus' is from the same root as the name 'Joshua', meaning the one who leads out into liberty a people kept captive by oppression or by sin. So it comes to mean the one who saves. This Jesus will come to liberate our world from the fears and sins that still inhibit us and hold us captive. But this Saviour came and still comes in unexpected ways, as a child whose kingdom is one of love, as a Jewish deliverer who sets all people free.

The fifteenth century theologian, Nicholas of Cusa, wrote that he had learned that the place where God is found is surrounded by 'the coincidence of contradictions'. In this time of waiting before Christmas, let us open our eyes and our hearts to see some of the contradictions – the unlikely places where Christ may be found.

PRAYER
Lord, who surprises us by your coming into our world, save us from our sins, free us from our fears, and deliver us from all that would do us harm. For your name's sake. Amen.

NH (1745) *HP 81 UMH 196 VU 2

THE DAYSPRING FROM ON HIGH

Stupendous height of heavenly love,
  Of pitying tenderness divine;
It brought the Saviour from above,
  It caused the springing day to shine;
The Sun of Righteousness to appear,
And gild our gloomy hemisphere.

God did in Christ himself reveal,
  To chase our darkness by his light,
Our sin and ignorance dispel,
  Direct our wandering feet aright,
And bring our souls, with pardon blest
To realms of everlasting rest.

Come then, O Lord, the light impart,
  The faith that bids our terrors cease;
Into thy love direct my heart,
  Into thy way of perfect peace;
To cheer my soul, of death afraid,
And guide me through the dreadful shade.

Answer thy mercy's whole design,
  My God incarnated for me;
My spirit make thy radiant shrine,
  My light and full salvation be;
And through the darkened vale unknown
Conduct me to thy dazzling throne.

Through the tender mercy of our God; whereby the dayspring from on high hath visited us, to give light to them that sit in darkness and in the shadow of death, to guide our feet into the way of peace.

Luke 1:78-79

This hymn is based on the last verses of the Benedictus – the psalm of thanksgiving spoken by Zechariah the priest, after the birth of his son John. In Wesley's hymn, the theme is of darkness giving way to light; salvation is come for all in verses 1-2, while in verses 3-4 he celebrates personal salvation. The darkness of sin and ignorance, terrors, and the fear of death are overcome by the birth of Christ, the Sun (Son) of Righteousness. Hope is reborn in our hearts as we sense the rising sun overcoming the darkness of night.

PRAYER
Come, Lord Jesus, shine with your dazzling ray and direct my heart into your way of love. Amen.

---

*MS Luke RV 109 [4:5 dreary vale] HP 462

UNTO US A CHILD IS BORN 15

To us a child of royal birth,
    Heir of the promises, is given;
The invisible appears on earth,
    The Son of man, the God of heaven.

A Saviour born, in love supreme
    He comes our fallen souls to raise;
He comes his people to redeem
    With all his plenitude of grace.

The Christ, by raptured seers foretold,
    Filled with the eternal Spirit's power,
Prophet, and Priest, and King behold,
    And Lord of all the worlds adore.

The Lord of hosts, the God most high,
    Who quits his throne on earth to live,
With joy we welcome from the sky,
    With faith into our hearts receive.

For unto us a child is born, unto us a son is given.

Isaiah 9:6

Isaiah prophesied to the people of Israel in the time of their defeat that one day light would shine upon their darkness, and there would arise among them a descendant of King David who would be known not only as a wise King and Counsellor, but as the mighty God, the Prince of Peace. For Christians, this Messianic prophecy points to the Christ who came down to earth as the Son of man coming from the God of heaven.

In this hymn celebrating Christ's nativity, it is his royal lineage and divine vocation that Charles Wesley emphasises. There is nothing here of the romantic Christmas scene. The whole hymn is a robust reminder that Christ is the fulfilment of the prophecies. He has come not just to rescue Israel but to rescue all of *us* – a pronoun that is given special emphasis by being placed at the very beginning of the hymn. In the child Jesus the invisible God becomes visible to us, and the event we commemorate at Christmas takes on cosmic significance.

PRAYER
O God who joins both earth and sky, we welcome the Christ as one of us and worship him as coming from you. May he who comes to earth for our sakes raise our hearts to heaven this day and for all eternity. Amen.

MS Luke *PW 11, 117 MHB 141

16 AND GOD IS BORN (1)

Glory be to God on high,
   And peace on earth descend;
God comes down, and bows the sky,
   And shows himself our friend!
God the invisible appears;
   God the blest, the great I AM,
Sojourns in this vale of tears,
   And Jesus is his name.

Him the angels all adored,
   Their maker and their king;
Tidings of their humbled Lord
   They now to mortals bring.
Emptied of his majesty,
   Of his dazzling glories shorn,
Being's source begins to be,
   And God himself is born!

Jesus . . . though he was in the form of God, did not regard equality with God as something to be exploited, but emptied himself . . .

Philippians 2:6-7 (NRSV)

Only a brave poet would write a line like 'Being's source begins to be'. Charles Wesley, stunned by the amazing significance of God's becoming a human being, could find no better way to express it.

The poem interweaves the nativity story from Luke with the hymn in Paul's letter to the Philippians on the meaning of the self-emptying God. Once, Wesley's hymns were being used to illustrate Protestant spirituality to a group of Catholics who were on a spiritual direction course. It was this hymn that impressed them most. 'May I have a copy?' a dozen voices asked.

Psalm 144:5 has the line, 'Bow thy heavens, O Lord, and come down: touch the mountains and they shall smoke.' Wesley begins with this image of power but links it with the birth of Christ. God comes down, not in majesty, but as our friend. The exclamation mark says it all. Friends are partners, they share love, they share joy and tears. This is a picture of God with possibilities that most of us have hardly begun to explore.

MEDITATION

Ponder a while the image of friendship. Think back to childhood perhaps, to the security of a 'best friend' recollect teenage friendships and loyalties, those in and out of marriage, woman-woman and man-man friendships, woman-man, old age and youth friendships. Remember that God is neither male nor female, but can be known as either. How do you see God as friend?

---

*NH (1745)

AND GOD IS BORN (2) **17**

See the eternal Son of God
  A mortal son of man,
Dwelling in an earthly clod
  Whom heaven cannot contain!
Stand amazed ye heavens at this!
  See the Lord of earth and skies;
Humbled to the dust he is,
  And in a manger lies!

We, the sons of men, rejoice,
  The Prince of Peace proclaim;
With heaven's host lift up our voice,
  And shout Immanuel's name:
Knees and hearts to him we bow;
  Of our flesh and of our bone,
Jesus is our brother now,
  And God is all our own!

When Laban heard the tidings of Jacob, his sister's son, he ran to meet him, and embraced him, and kissed him, and brought him to his house . . . and Laban said to him, Surely thou art my bone and my flesh!

Genesis 29:13-14

The 'flesh and bone' imagery of Laban's story, recalled here by Wesley, implies all the complexity of family bonding. Our humanity is honoured, not in the abstract but in reality, as God comes to be 'all our own'. This is such an extraordinary event that even the heavens 'stand amazed', and we join with the heavenly host in a shout of praise.

Sometimes it is very hard for us who are women to break through the poetic parallels made here between the legitimate but one-sided 'son of man'/'sons of men' imagery. We are not 'sons of men', we are daughters of women and men. Men are not just 'sons of men' either; they too have mothers, and we are brothers and sisters of one another, sharing a common human flesh. The Christ-child, born of Mary, calls women his sisters, just as we, men and women, call him our brother.

PRAYER
Loving Word of God, you have shown us the fullness of your glory in taking human flesh. Fill us, in our bodily life, with your grace and truth; that our pleasure may be boundless, and our integrity complete, in your name. Amen. *Elaine Morgan*

---

*NH (1745)

RECONCILING EXTREMES (1)

Let earth and heaven combine,
  Angels and men agree,
To praise in songs divine
  The incarnate Deity,
Our God contracted to a span,
Incomprehensibly made man.

He laid his glory by,
  He wrapped him in our clay,
Unmarked by human eye,
  The latent Godhead lay;
Infant of days he here became,
And bore the loved Immanuel's name.

See in that infant's face
  The depths of deity,
And labour while ye gaze
  To sound the mystery;
In vain; ye angels gaze no more,
But fall, and silently adore.

Therefore the LORD himself shall give you a sign; Behold, a virgin shall conceive, and bear a son, and shall call his name Immanuel.

Isaiah 7:14

Social historians comment on the eighteenth century as a bleak time for the popular celebration of Christmas. It may seem surprising then that Charles Wesley's eighteen poems in *Hymns for the Nativity of our Lord* went through some twenty-six editions in his lifetime. But his was no sentimental picture of the baby in the manger, such as became fashionable later on Victorian Christmas cards. Charles emphasises the tough, paradoxical incomprehensibility of the God-with-us event. The eternal God comes in the form of a human infant – the Jesus who is both human and divine. The last two lines of the first verse of this hymn say it perfectly, but the whole hymn is central to Wesley's theology.

Only in art or poetry can we grasp mystery at an intuitive level where reason can go no further. In an echo of 1 Peter 1:12, the hymn describes how even angels cannot see into the depths of mystery. Speechless worship is the only proper response of the angels, and of those to whom the gospel has been revealed.

PRAYER
God, our beloved, born of a woman's body: you came that we might look upon you, and handle you with our own hands. May we so cherish one another in our bodies that we may also be touched by you. Through the word made flesh, Jesus Christ. Amen.
Elaine Morgan

---

*NH (1745) HP 109

Unsearchable the love
That hath the Saviour brought,
The grace is far above
Mortal or angel's thought;
Suffice for us that God we know,
Our God is manifest below.

He deigns in flesh to appear,
Widest extremes to join,
To bring our vileness near,
And make us all divine;
And we the life of God shall know,
For God is manifest below.

Made perfect first in love,
And sanctified by grace,
We shall from earth remove,
And see his glorious face:
His love shall then be fully showed,
And we shall all be lost in God.

And the word was made flesh and dwelt among us.

John 1:14

Yesterday, the word for the incarnation was 'incomprehensible'; today in the continuation of this hymn, the word for the love of God is another negative: 'unsearchable'. Charles Wesley, sharing a long mystical tradition of those who could only approach the mystery of God through negative concepts, now ponders a series of 'widest extremes' which are indeed 'joined' because of the God-with-us event.

The extremes in the hymn are earth/heaven, human/God, mortality/divinity, and the marvellous vision that, in spite of our imperfection, we shall be like God and know the life of God, starting now and leading on beyond our mortal death. See how the poem gradually resolves itself as we move to the place where we are lost in God. A proper humility will discern holiness in others more easily than in ourselves. Even so, thinking of the 'saints' around us reminds us that God is still very much with-us, and that we too are on the way of holiness.

MEDITATION
Think for a while of other 'widest extremes' which are being (or could be) reconciled. Differences of opinion, class and race conflicts, employed/unemployed, female/male, youth/age. Others? Now reflect on your own conflicts with others and within yourself. Read verse two again.

*NH (1745) [1:4 Or man or 3:6 And man] HP 109

SEE THERE!

Where is the holy heaven-born child,
Heir of the everlasting throne,
Who heaven and earth hath reconciled,
And God and man rejoined in one?

Shall we of earthly Kings enquire,
To courts or palaces repair?
The nation's hope, the world's desire,
Alas! we cannot find him there.

Shall learning show the sinner's friend,
Or scribes a sight of Christ afford?
Us to his natal place they send,
But never go to see their Lord.

Then let us turn no more aside,
But use the light himself imparts,
His Spirit is our surest guide,
His Spirit glimmering in our hearts.

When [Herod] had gathered all the chief priests and scribes of the people together, he demanded of them where Christ should be born . . . And he sent [the wise men] to Bethlehem and said: Go and search diligently for the young child . . .

Matthew 2:4,8a

Neither the king nor the courtiers in Herod's palace went themselves to see the Christ child. They claimed to know where he would appear, but they sent others to look for him. What they knew in their minds never moved their hearts, hands or feet.

Yet the ray of light pointed to the one who came, as John said, to illuminate every human life. Not to see that light shining upon everyone we meet is to miss the Christ-event ourselves.

PRAYER
Lord, help me to search diligently and sincerely for the Christ-child in everyone I meet, that I may give due worship and homage too. Amen.

---

*NH (1745) PW 4, 123-5

O mercy divine;
How could'st thou incline
My God, to become such an infant as mine?

He comes from on high,
Who fashioned the sky,
And meekly vouchsafes in a manger to lie.

Our God ever blest,
With oxen doth rest,
Is nursed by his creature, and hangs at the breast.

The shepherds behold
Him promised of old,
By angels attended, by prophets foretold.

The wise men adore,
And bring him their store;
The rich are permitted to follow the poor.

To the inn they repair,
To see the young heir;
The inn is a palace, for Jesus is there.

And she brought forth her firstborn son, and wrapped him in swaddling clothes, and laid him in a manger.

Luke 2:7

The story is told that during Charles' childhood, Samuel and Susanna Wesley and their children never sat down to their own Christmas meal until they were certain that all the villagers of Epworth had been fed. Perhaps this was in the mind of Charles as he wrote with delicate irony that in God's wisdom the rich wise men 'are permitted to follow the poor' shepherds.

More than just a telling of the nativity story, this personal response in a dancing, carol rhythm gets to the heart of the meaning of the birth. Both simple and wise, poor and rich are welcome at the manger, but the simple get there first!

MEDITATION
Like him I would be;
My Master I see
In a stable, a stable shall satisfy me. *Charles Wesley*

---

*NH (1745) PW 4, 122-3

GIVING BIRTH

Happy the place, but happier still
  The heart where Christ is born;
The heart which he vouchsafes to fill
  Need neither sin nor mourn.
No city could with Bethlehem share
  The honour of his birth,
But every soul by faith may bear
  The Lord of heaven and earth.

[Herod] demanded of them where Christ should be born. And they said unto him, In Bethlehem of Judea, for thus it is written by the prophet.

Matthew 2:4-5

A neatly balanced poem comparing favourably our potential for giving birth to Christ within our lives with the famed importance of the city of Bethlehem.

Giving birth is a hard, painful process: the months of gestation, the self-discipline of diet, the gradual body changes until the mother feels the child has taken over her whole life. Happily married to Sally Gwynne and the devoted father of many children, Charles Wesley knew at first hand what it meant to welcome and nurture a newborn child. He compares the experience of birth to that of welcoming the Christ-child.

We might imagine many heart-changes in such a process: the gestation may be long, there is the self-discipline of prayer and the means of grace, there are demands that Christ makes in how we will live our lives in tune with his will. Others will be our midwives, indeed, they may have already been so and we have hardly noticed what has been going on! And what joy attends the birth, as we recognise the blessing Christ brings into our lives.

POINT TO PONDER
Though Christ our Lord a thousand times in Bethlehem be born
And not in thee, thy soul remains eternally forlorn. *Johann Scheffler*

---

*PW 10, 142

ANGELS BEHOLD! 23

Let angels and archangels sing
  The wonderful Immanuel's name,
Adore with us our newborn king,
  And still the joyful news proclaim,
All earth and heaven be ever joined
To praise the Saviour of mankind.

Angels behold that infant's face
  With rapturous awe the Godhead own:
'Tis all your heaven on him to gaze,
  And cast your crowns before his throne;
Though now he on his footstool lies,
Ye know he built both earth and skies.

By him into existence brought
  Ye sang the all-creating word;
Ye heard him call our world from nought:
  Again, in honour of your Lord,
Ye morning-stars, your hymns employ,
And shout, ye sons of God, for joy.

When the morning stars sang together, and all the sons of God shouted for joy.
Job 38:7

Following the tradition of Milton's poem, 'On the Morning of Christ's Nativity', Charles raises up the cosmic significance of the birth of Christ. Most of this poem is actually addressed to the angels. But we are the ones who are present also. We invite the angels, we are already adoring this newborn king. It is all happening *now*. This cosmic God who is born of a woman is now with us in all our humanity. Whatever we think of angels – a poetic image that takes us into another realm of thought - the truth still stands: earth and heaven, that is, all creation, are joined forever in the birth of the child Jesus.

PRAYER
With angels and archangels and with all the company of heaven, we laud and magnify thy glorious name, evermore praising thee and saying: Holy, holy, holy, Lord God of hosts, Heaven and earth are full of thy glory.
Book of Common Prayer, Eucharistic Preface

*NH (1745) PW 4, 118-9

JESUS IS OUR FLESH AND BONE

Lo! he lays his glory by,
Emptied of his majesty!
See the God who all things made,
Humbly in a manger laid.

Cast we off our needless fear,
Boldly to his crib draw near;
Jesus is our flesh and bone,
God-with-us is all our own.

Will his majesty disdain
The poor shepherds' simple strain?
No; for Israel's Shepherd, he
Loves their artless melody.

He will not refuse the song
Of the stammering infant's tongue;
Babes he hears humanely mild,
Once himself a little child.

Let us then our Prince proclaim,
Humbly chant Immanuel's name,
Publish at his wondrous birth
Praise in heaven and peace on earth.

And he shall be called Emmanuel, a name which means 'God is with us.'
Matthew 1:23 (REB)

The 'artless melody' of the shepherds' song and the lisping voice of the infant are represented here by the simple rhythm and rhyming couplets of this nativity hymn. But the ideas contained within it are profound. There is the echo of the creation story, where Adam greeted Eve as 'bone of my bone, and flesh of my flesh' (Genesis 2:23). Now it is God himself who has become our flesh and bone. The shepherds worship the one who has come himself as the Good Shepherd. A child himself, he is a lover of children. And we who hail the coming of the Prince of Peace discover him to be one of us.

POINT TO PONDER
The best of all is – God is with us! *(said to be John Wesley's dying words)*

---

*NH (1745) PW 4, 117-8 [2:2 to his cratch]

Hark how all the welkin rings!
'Glory to the King of kings,
Peace on earth, and mercy mild,
God and sinners reconciled!'
Joyful, all ye nations, rise,
Join the triumph of the skies;
Universal nature say:
'Christ the Lord is born today!'

Christ, by highest heaven adored,
Christ, the everlasting Lord,
Late in time behold him come,
Offspring of a Virgin's womb.
Veiled in flesh, the Godhead see,
Hail, the incarnate Deity!
Pleased as man with men to appear
Jesus! our Immanuel here!

Hail the heavenly Prince of Peace!
Hail the Sun of Righteousness!
Light and life to all he brings,
Risen with healing in his wings.
Mild he lays his glory by,
Born that man no more may die,
Born to raise the sons of earth,
Born to give them second birth.

Unto you that fear my name shall the Sun of righteousness arise with healing in his wings . . .

Malachi 4:2

It comes as quite a shock to read the original words of this very familiar Christmas hymn, 'Hark! the herald angels sing'. The versions known to most of us are the result of reworking by numerous editors, including Charles' brother John. The original emphasised that not only the angelic host but 'universal nature' joins in the welcome to the Christ-child. This cosmic vision has new meaning for us today, as we begin to comprehend how much we are all interdependent parts of universal nature. Can we dare to pin our hopes on Malachi's healing vision of the rising Sun of righteousness? Can that vision come true in the Son Jesus who is born in us to make the whole earth one?

PRAYER
Almighty God, who hast poured upon us the new light of your Incarnate Word; grant that the same light enkindled in our hearts may shine forth in our lives; through Jesus Christ our Lord. Amen. *Mass of Christmas at Dawn, Sarum Rite*

---

*HSP (1739) HP 106 UMH 240 VU 48

THE HEAVENLY STRANGER (1)

Join all ye joyful nations
The acclaiming hosts of heaven!
  This happy morn
  A child is born,
To us a Son is given;
The messenger and token
Of God's eternal favour,
  God hath sent down
  To us his Son,
A universal Saviour!

Go, see the King of Glory,
Discern the heavenly Stranger,
  So poor and mean,
  His court an inn,
His cradle is a manger;
Who from his Father's bosom
But now for us descended;
  Who built the skies,
  On earth he lies,
With only beasts attended.

For unto us a child is born, unto us a son is given.

Isaiah 9:6

The nativity story has inspired artists of many different centuries and cultures. So, as in this hymn, we can imagine people of all nations gathered around the infant Christ. But at the centre is a scene of sublime simplicity which moves the heart of even the most sophisticated. As Thomas Hardy, the sceptical English poet, wrote:

We pictured the meek mild creatures where
They dwelt in their strawy pen,
Nor did it occur to one of us there
To doubt they were kneeling then.[1]

PRAYER
Lord of all creation, we bow before your crib;
Lord of all nations, we greet you in the stranger;
Lord of all heaven, we rejoice to find you here on earth –
in Christ our Lord. Amen.

---

*NH (1745) PW 4, 110-1

Whom all the angels worship,
Lies hid in human nature;
Incarnate see
The Deity,
The infinite creator!
See the stupendous blessing
Which God to us hath given!
A child of man,
In length a span,
Who fills both earth and heaven.

Gaze on that helpless object
Of endless adoration!
Those infant hands
Shall burst our bands,
And work out our salvation;
Strangle the crooked serpent,
Destroy his works forever,
And open set
The heavenly gate
To every true believer.

When you became man to set us free, you did not shun the Virgin's womb. You overcame the sting of death and opened the kingdom of heaven to all believers.
from the Te Deum

The first verse boldly expresses the paradox of the incarnation – the hidden God made visible, the Creator becoming a creature. As we gaze on the helpless child, Charles Wesley dramatically points to the strength disguised in that apparent weakness – the hands that can break our bonds, strangle the serpent, swing wide the gates of heaven. The mystery of the incarnation is seen in the miracle of God coming in human form to partake of our weakness and to share his strength.

PRAYER
God, I thank you for the mystery of your becoming human in all the poverty and pain of a peasant woman giving birth in a stable. As I bring to you such gifts as I have, help me to treasure the gifts you have bestowed upon me, and to recognise that your strength is available to me in my weakness. Amen.

*NH (1745) PW 4, 111-2

FEAR NOT (1)

Angels speak, let all give ear;
    Sent from high,
    They are nigh,
And forbid our fear.

News they bring us of salvation,
    Sounds of joy
    To employ
Every tongue and nation.

Welcome tidings! to retrieve us
    From our fall,
    Born for all,
Christ is born to save us.

Born his creatures to restore,
    Abject earth
    Sees his birth,
Whom the heavens adore.

And the angel said unto them, Fear not: for behold, I bring you good tidings of great joy, which shall be to all people.

Luke 2:10

'Forbid our fear'! What more important message is there in the world than that? Fear, psychologists tell us, is the cause of much of the evil in the world. It leads to war and domestic violence; it poisons the workplace; it kills potential friendships, leads to selfishness and greed and racism and homophobia.

On 6th December 1989 a terrible tragedy happened in Montreal, Canada. A lone gunman entered the engineering building of the university, made his way to a classroom, and killed fourteen women students. It all happened so suddenly that no-one could stop him. And the reason? He feared women were taking jobs that he thought should be his. An act of insanity, yes, but a reminder too of the destructive power of unresolved fear.

PRAYER
Compassionate God, as I remember all who are the victims of other people's fears, help me to recognise when fear drives my own actions. When I am afraid, forbid my fear and drive it out by the good news of your love. Amen.

---

*NH (1745) [1:1 let men] PW 4, 107-8

Simple shepherds, us he raises,
Bids us sing
Christ the King,
And show forth his praises.

We have seen the King of glory
We proclaim
Christ his name,
And record his story.

Sing we with the host of heaven,
Reconciled
By a child
Who to us is given.

Glory be to God the giver;
Peace and love
From above
Reign on earth for ever.

And the shepherds returned, glorifying and praising God for all the things they had heard and seen.

Luke 2:20

The story of the shepherds is our story too; we are the shepherds. The angels come to us, and to the whole 'abject earth' and so the message is timeless, or rather, it is for all time, for *now*. Wesley's style suits the song of country shepherds with its simple words and dance metre, echoing medieval carols.

Look at the action in these verses. As shepherds 'poor and nothing knowing' we kneel before the Christ-child, but in that act, we are lifted up. With joy we tell others of a new harmony between heaven and earth – a new peaceable kingdom where love replaces fear.

PRAYER
O God, give me the humility of the shepherds and the vision of the angels, to see your love at work in the world around me. Replenish your well of love in my heart, that today I may see with your eyes of compassion, and live out this Christmas story. Amen.

*NH (1745) PW 4, 107-8

TO FOLLOW THE STAR

Mine eyes have seen his orient star,
And sweetly drawn I come from far,
Leaving the world behind;
His Spirit gently leads me on,
A stranger to a land unknown,
The newborn king to find.

The word of all-preventing grace
Marks out the Saviour's natal place;
And, follower of the word,
I keep his glimmering star in sight,
Which by its sure unerring light
Conducts me to my Lord.

Behold, there came wise men from the east to Jerusalem, saying, Where is he that is born King of the Jews? for we have seen his star in the east and are come to worship him.

Matthew 2:1-2

In the days of relative calm after the bustle of the festive season, this brief poem carries a personal message for the year ahead. The rush of obligations and expectations is stilled, the commercial fuss has died down. Like the wise men, it is time for us to follow the star.

The words 'sweetly' and 'gently' set the tone. This is no anxious or compulsively worrying journey. I am not forced to go. Rather, I am 'drawn' towards something mysterious and wonderful. As a stranger in a strange land I am courteously conducted to the place where, with true hospitality, God's grace is already there to welcome me.

How strong is the image of pilgrimage in our story! Just when we think we are comfortable, something pulls us out of our rut and beckons us on. But it is only if we take time to look up in wonder that we will see the star.

MEDITATION
Make time to be quiet, letting go of immediate preoccupations and worries and tension. If it is a clear evening or early morning, look up for one star and imagine that is the star that draws you to the Christ. Now reread the poem, thinking ahead to the unknown journey of this new year. End with a prayer of confidence that this star will always lead you to a loving God.

---

*PW 10, 142

Meet and right it is to sing,
  In every time and place,
Glory to our heavenly King,
  The God of truth and grace:
Join we then with sweet accord,
  All in one thanksgiving join;
Holy, holy, holy Lord,
  Eternal praise be thine.

Thee the first-born sons of light,
  In choral symphonies,
Praise by day, day without night,
  And never, never cease;
Angels and archangels all
  Sing the mystic Three in One,
Sing, and stop, and gaze, and fall
  O'erwhelmed before thy throne.

It is very meet, right, and our bounden duty, that we should at all times, and in all places, give thanks unto thee, O Lord, Holy Father, Almighty, Everlasting God. Therefore with Angels and Archangels and with all the company of heaven, we laud and magnify thy glorious name, evermore praising thee, and saying, Holy, holy, holy, Lord God of hosts, heaven and earth are full of thy glory: Glory be to thee, O Lord most High.

Book of Common Prayer, Service of Holy Communion

Although this hymn for Watchnight has its roots in the words of the Communion Service, its imaginative flights of tone and language – particularly in verse two – are borrowed from *Paradise Lost,* a poem Wesley knew almost by heart. In the Garden of Eden before the Fall, Adam and Eve rejoice in a hymn of praise to God, the 'Parent of Good' whom, though invisible, they can perceive through all that is around them. In contrast, the angels – the 'sons of light' in heaven – can see God directly and so 'with songs/And choral symphonies, day without night,/Circle his throne rejoicing' (*PL* V, 160-5).

Though some of us may no longer live comfortably with imagery of angels and all the architecture of a tangible heaven, we still require a language of praise which goes beyond our own resources. This hymn sings the wonder of the God whose fullness is beyond anything we can possibly imagine: it takes us through the very gates of heaven.

PRAYER
Glory be to you, Ground of all Being, Source of all Strength, Giver of all Power. Amen.[1]

*HSP (1749) RV 82 CH 212 [2:6 praise the mystic] HP 501

Vying with that happy choir,
Who chant thy praise above,
We on eagles' wings aspire,
The wings of faith and love:
Thee they sing with glory crowned,
We extol the slaughtered Lamb;
Lower if our voices sound,
Our subject is the same.

Father, God, thy love we praise,
Which gave thy Son to die;
Jesus, full of truth and grace,
Alike we glorify;
Spirit, Comforter divine,
Praise by all to thee be given,
Till we in full chorus join,
And earth is turned to heaven.

They that wait upon the LORD shall renew their strength; they shall mount up with wings as eagles; they shall run, and not be weary, and they shall walk, and not faint.
Isaiah 40:31

Yesterday's reflection on the first two verses of this hymn centred on angelic worship, suggesting that there are levels of creation above and beyond us whose being pulses with the rhythm of praise. Today, we join in their song, not just as our 'meet, right and bounden duty', but with the delight of true worship. Faith and love are the wings of the eagle on which we rise and float in effortless thanksgiving. Notice how in the last two lines this union of heaven and earth makes us one with the angels.

MEDITATION
Remember in your mind's eye the flight of an eagle or seagull when it floats on wind currents. Imagine yourself being supported like that by the love of God, and try to send your thoughts soaring beyond the immediate dimensions of time and space into those eternal realms where our voices are joined with all those who have gone before us.

PRAYER
Parent God, protecting and providing for us, nursing and nurturing us, upholding us and letting us go, give us the confidence to put our trust in you as we try out our wings and aspire to the heights to which you call us, through your love for us. Amen.

---

*HSP (1749) RV 82 CH 212 HP 501

NEW YEAR (1) 33

Come, let us anew
Our journey pursue,
Roll round with the year,
And never stand still till the Master appear.
His adorable will
Let us gladly fulfil,
And our talents improve,
By the patience of hope and the labour of love.

We give thanks to God always for you all, making mention of you in our prayers; remembering without ceasing your work of faith, and labour of love, and patience of hope in our Lord Jesus Christ.

1 Thessalonians 1:2-3

This is the first verse of a hymn written for New Year's Day 1750. It is still sung by many Methodists, either at their Watchnight service or very early in the new year. The rollicking tune Derby, generally used today, is the one that was used in the eighteenth century, apparently at John Wesley's suggestion.

The theme is a journey, with the undercurrent of the parable of the talents (Matthew 25:14-30). What could appear to be the serious and even tedious tasks ahead of us are faced with enthusiasm as we become caught up in the exuberant joy of the dance rhythm, and experience a sense of gladness in fulfilling the will of God.

Having committed ourselves to the journey, we find it is one of discipleship. To fulfil God's will gladly ('adorable' is kin to the word 'adoration') is both a gift and a challenge. Our daily prayer 'Thy will be done' (Matthew 6:10) is not only given to us by Jesus, but Jesus himself tested its limits in the garden of Gethsemane when he faced imminent suffering and death: 'O my Father . . . not as I will, but as thou wilt' (Matthew 26:39). Because God is our good parent, we shall never be taken beyond the limit of endurance. God's will for us is always 'adorable', worthy of our praise and our glad obedience.

PRAYER
Adventurous God, you have been with me in all the journeys of my life and you still walk beside me whether I am aware of your presence or not. Help me to step joyfully into this new year, and to walk gladly in the way you have chosen for me. With Jesus Christ our Lord. Amen.

Hymns for New Year's Day (1749) RV 88 *CH 45 HP 354

Our life is a dream,
Our time as a stream
Glides swiftly away,
And the fugitive moment refuses to stay,
The arrow is flown,
The moment is gone;
The millennial year
Rushes on to our view, and eternity's here.

O that each in the day
Of his coming may say:
'I have fought my way through,
I have finished the work thou didst give me to do!'
O that each from the Lord
May receive the glad word:
'Well and faithfully done;
Enter into my joy, and sit down on my throne!'

For a thousand years in thy sight are but as yesterday when it is past, and as a watch in the night. Thou carriest them away as with a flood; they are as a sleep: in the morning they are like grass which groweth up . . . in the evening it is cut down, and withereth.

Psalm 90:4-6

These verses end the New Year hymn which yesterday started with the glad urgency of doing God's will.

Wesley's words echo those of Shakespeare's *Tempest*: 'We are such stuff/As dreams are made on.' He captures too the psalmist's concept of the speedy passage of time, not just in the words of the second verse, but in the whole rhythm of the hymn. There is a sense that all our time – past, present and future – is contained in the 'now' while rushing on and sliding behind us.

Trying to measure time is an illusive task. Women of Guatemala speak of time as circular, like the ribbons in their hair. Old people's memories of forty years ago seem like yesterday; to people in a hurry, time may drag, while for the fearful, it may fly. Wesley stresses the urgency of time, warning us to use every moment faithfully and well.

MEDITATION
Because the use of time is a spiritual question, ponder how you spend your time. What does it mean to see each moment in the light of eternity?

---

*Hymns for New Year's Day (1750) [2:5 his lord] RV 88 CH 45 HP 354

Come, let us use the grace divine,
And all with one accord
In a perpetual covenant join
Ourselves to Christ our Lord;
Give up ourselves, through Jesus' power
His name to glorify,
And promise in this sacred hour
For God to live and die.

The covenant we this moment make
Be ever kept in mind;
We will no more our God forsake,
Or cast his words behind.
We never will throw off his fear
Who hears our solemn vow;
And if thou art well-pleased to hear,
Come down, and meet us now.

Come, and let us join ourselves to the LORD in a perpetual covenant that shall not be forgotten.

Jeremiah 50:5

This hymn, originally published in 1762 as a meditation based on the words to the Israelites in exile in Babylon, became part of the Methodist Covenant service, and is still in use today. John Wesley had instituted this service for his Societies in 1757, and from 1762 onwards it was used every New Year's Day. At the Conference in Dublin he records in his Journal for 12th July 1778, 'After I had several times explained the nature of . . . [the Covenant service] we solemnly renewed our covenant with God. It was a time never to be forgotten.'

Charles' hymn applies the urgency of Jeremiah's words to the covenant of the believer with Christ. It calls for the response of the whole person in commitment to him. It is not only a personal response; it is a corporate action: 'we all with one accord' give up all things for Christ for all time. The vow 'to live and die' for God is no empty phrase for those who still today face persecution for their faith. For us all, it is the challenge to make all of life a reflection of the new creation.

PRAYER
Generous God, you give me life and reason; give me also the grace to commit them both to you, that I might understand your will, and do it. Amen.

---

*SH (1762) UMH 606 HP 649

36 GOD'S COVENANT LOVE

The hills and mountains may depart,
But deeper rooted in my heart,
  From hence thou never shalt remove;
I will not take my Spirit away,
But always with my people stay,
  The covenant-God of endless love.

For the mountains shall depart, and the hills be removed; but my kindness shall not depart from thee, neither shall the covenant of my peace be removed, saith the LORD that hath mercy on thee.

Isaiah 54:10

'Nothing stays the same forever', says folk wisdom. There have been human societies marked by great social stability. That is not the world we know. We experience how rapidly tools and equipment change, as new technologies make obsolete what seemed only yesterday so new and vital and lasting. Institutions we thought of as permanent are profoundly modified, even destroyed, by the forces of social change. Our relationships too suffer the consequences of life in a constantly moving universe; friendships, marriages that seemed enduring dissolve under the stress. Impermanence often seems like the one sure thing in our way of life.

In contrast, mountains communicate to us, as they did to ancient peoples, an aura of durability, of unchanging certainties. So it was natural for the Hebrew prophet, when he wished to bring a word of encouragement to his people in exile, to cite them as an illustration of the dependable faithfulness of God. The Jews in Babylon were living with a sense of broken covenant with God, that the disasters that had overwhelmed their lives were punishment for their unfaithfulness; they had failed to keep their end of the covenant bargain, so God had cancelled all obligations and closed their account. Rather like a marriage or a friendship that betrayal has ended. But that, says the prophet, is not the nature of God, nor is God's covenant conditional. Could we imagine the uprooting of the great mountains? Still less is it conceivable that we be torn from the heart of 'the covenant-God of endless love'!

PRAYER
Teach me to trust, loving God, your unfailing love that does not falter when I do. Let it be the bedrock on which I can build my life. Amen.

---

*SH (1762)

PSALM 8 (1)

Sovereign, everlasting Lord
  How excellent thy name!
Held in being by thy word,
  Thee all thy works proclaim;
Through this earth thy glories shine,
  Through those dazzling worlds above,
All confess the Source divine
  The almighty God of love.

Thou, the God of power and grace
  Whom highest heavens adore,
Callest babes to sing thy praise,
  And manifest thy power;
Lo! they in thy strength go on,
  Lo! on all thy foes they tread,
Cast the dire Accuser down,
  And bruise the serpent's head.

O LORD our Lord, how excellent is thy name in all the earth! who hast set thy glory above the heavens. Out of the mouth of babes and sucklings hast thou ordained strength because of thine enemies, that thou mightest still the enemy and the avenger.
Psalm 8:1-2

How often Wesley finds the one word which paints the vivid picture! Here the 'dazzling worlds' of the heavens reflect the glory of God. Typically Charles Wesley develops the sense of what the psalmist is saying. Not only do the heavens speak of the majesty of God's universe, they speak too of its cosmic cohesion. All is held in being by God's word, an echo of the epistle to the Hebrews (1:3). Similarly, in the second verse of the hymn, Charles expands the psalmist's imagery by his own vivid picture of the casting down of the 'dire Accuser' and the bruising of the serpent's head, the promise given Eve in the Garden (Genesis 3:15).

PRAYER
God of the whole universe, we thank you for every glimpse we have of your glory, whether it be reflected in the dazzling stars above, or in the twinkling eyes of a little child. May we too shine in the light of your presence and irradiate with your love the darkness of our world. For your name's sake. Amen.

---

*CPH (1743) RV 119

Yet when I survey the skies
And planets as they roll,
Wonder dims my aching eyes,
And swallows up my soul.
Moon and stars so wide display,
Chant their Maker's praise so loud,
– Poor, insufferable day! –
And draw me up to God!

What is man, that thou, O Lord,
Hast such respect to him!
Comes from heaven the incarnate Word
His creature to redeem;
Wherefore would'st thou stoop so low?
Who the mystery shall explain?
God is flesh, and lives below,
And dies for wretched man.

When I consider thy heavens, the work of thy fingers, the moon and the stars, which thou hast ordained; What is man, that thou art mindful of him? and the son of man, that thou visitest him?

Psalm 8:3-4

It is puzzling to know how to read the question that rises to the psalmist's lips – 'What is man, that thou art mindful of him?' Is it asked in scepticism, like Hamlet's ironic 'What a piece of work is man!' Or is it a gasp of wonder at the marvel of the human creation?

Wesley, with what has been called 'a pessimism of nature and an optimism of grace' makes the question an occasion for proclaiming once more the gospel of the incarnation. The whole of humankind may seem to be in a wretched state, but it has been ennobled by the redeeming love of Christ, who himself took on human flesh and thus made it possible even for us to attain to the glory of heaven.

PRAYER
When I am tempted to despair of human nature, as I see the inhumanity in the world around me, help me to remember that Christ himself has shared our humanity and so made it possible for our sins to be forgiven and for our nature to rise to the heights of heaven; for his name's sake. Amen.

*CPH (1743) RV 119

Jesus, his Redeemer dies,
  The sinner to restore,
Falls that man again may rise,
  And stand as heretofore;
Foremost of created things,
  Head of all thy works he stood,
Nearest the great King of Kings,
  And little less than God.

Sovereign, everlasting Lord,
  How excellent thy name,
Held in being by thy word
  Thee all thy works proclaim;
Through this earth thy glories shine,
  Through those dazzling worlds above,
All confess the Source divine,
  The almighty God of love.

Yet you have made them a little lower than God, and crowned them with glory and honour. You have given them dominion over the works of your hands.
Psalm 8:5-6 (NRSV)

Here, the psalm has become a hymn of praise to Christ the Lord who has restored humanity to its original glory. The view of what it means to be human, expressed in this hymn, could hardly be excelled. Human beings are called to assume again their original place of dominion over all creation. In these days of our greater understanding of the importance of the proper care of the earth and of all its resources, this ecological responsibility becomes all the more urgent.

As does the psalm, Wesley repeats in his last verse the eulogy expressed in the first. Again he wonders at the marvels of this dazzling universe. The final word, however, is an addition to the psalmist's acclamation of the excellence of God. For Wesley, the last word is that this God is a 'God of love'.

PRAYER
Lover of the world and of all created things, set in our hearts a love like yours for all that you have made. Make us more worthy of the responsibility you have entrusted to us for the care of this planet of ours, that we and all your creatures may indeed fulfil your purposes for our lives and proclaim your glory now and evermore. Amen.

---

*CPH (1743) RV 119

PSALM 9

Thee will I praise with all my heart,
And tell to all how good thou art,
    How marvellous thy works of grace;
Thy name I will in songs record,
And joy and glory in my Lord,
    Extolled above all thanks and praise.

The Lord will save his people here;
In times of need their help is near
    To all by sin and hell oppressed;
And they that know thy name will trust
In thee, who, to thy promise just,
    Hast never left a soul distressed.

The Lord is by his judgements known;
He helps his poor afflicted one,
    Whose sorrows all he bears in mind;
The mourner shall not always weep,
Who sows in tears in joy shall reap,
    With grief who seeks with joy shall find.

The LORD also will be a refuge for the oppressed, a refuge in times of trouble . . . The needy shall not alway be forgotten: the expectation of the poor shall not perish forever.

Psalm 9:9,18

These verses, selected from a paraphrase of Psalm 9, were never published in Wesley's lifetime. The psalm is a paean of praise to the God who has delivered the author from the foes who menaced life itself. Charles captures this joyous note of thanksgiving. He is grateful for the grace of Christ that sets people free from sin.

He also echoes the psalmist's praise of the God of justice who cares for those who are downtrodden and oppressed. So in his verse, Psalm 9 becomes a poem of praise and comfort for all who are going through difficult times, physical as well as spiritual. Moved by the psalmist's concern for the plight of the needy, he adds the hopeful words from Psalm 126:5: 'They that sow in tears shall reap in joy.'

PRAYER
Give me the grace, O God, to show your goodness to all those who feel that they have been forgotten. Amen.

PW 8, 17-19 *HP 41 [1:2 tell mankind 3:3 His sorrows]

Our souls the book of nature draws
To adore the First eternal Cause;
The heavens articulately shine,
And speak their Architect divine;
And all their orbs proclaim aloud
The wisdom and the power of God.

See, in yon glorious azure height
The sovereign, uncreated Light!
That vast expanse of liquid air
Doth his immensity declare,
And every influence from above,
His bounteous, universal love.

The sure-succeeding night and day
His providential care display;
Who bade them to their bounds retire,
And stand, as choir to answer choir,
His knowledge infinite to tell,
And show the Great Invisible.

The heavens declare the glory of God; and the firmament sheweth his handiwork. Day unto day uttereth speech, and night unto night sheweth knowledge.
Psalm 19:1-2

Readers familiar with the earlier eighteenth century poet, Joseph Addison, will see similarities in metre and style between this Wesley paraphrase and Addison's hymn based on the same psalm, beginning:

The spacious firmament on high,
With all the blue ethereal sky,
And spangled heavens, a shining frame,
Their great Original proclaim. (HP 339)

Wesley's concern is to include us, the reader/singers, in the picture. The framework for that is in the first two lines, where we are drawn by nature to copy her praise of God. In the words of the idiom, we are taking a page out of her 'book'.

PRAYER
God of the immensities, and yet of boundless, universal love, you show your care for the universe in ways that astound our knowledge. As we catch a glimpse of the amazing order and complexity of the environment, give us humility to have reverence for your handiwork. Amen.

*PW 8, 35-36

PSALM 19 (2)

The book of covenanted grace
Its heavenly origin displays;
Strong characters of love divine
Throughout the sacred volume shine;
Jehovah, by his word, is show'd
The glorious legislative God.

The statutes of the Lord are right;
His laws and equity unite;
Reason divine in all is show'd,
Adjusted to his creatures good;
They bring us peace, and power impart,
When written on the obedient heart.

The Lord's command is plain, and free
From darkness and impurity;
It purges and restores the sight,
Guides, by a clear, unerring light,
The sinner in the paths of peace,
Convinced of sin and righteousness.

The law of the LORD is perfect, converting the soul: the testimony of the LORD is sure, making wise the simple. The statutes of the LORD are right, rejoicing the heart: the commandment of the LORD is pure, enlightening the eyes.

Psalm 19:7-8

In this second meditation on Psalm 19, Wesley moves from the psalmist's celebration of the glory of God in nature to the parallel glories of the divine Word. Christians have too often allowed a misunderstanding of Paul to cast a shade over the Torah, or Law of Israel. Wesley is very true to the spirit of the psalm in singing of the joy the child of God finds even in the letters of the Law, these 'strong characters of love divine'.

Far from finding them a curse and a burden, Wesley celebrates them as gifts of the 'covenanted grace' of 'the glorious legislative God'. These words of the Law promote peace because of their source in divine justice and equity. They give insight of divine wisdom where human vision is failing, so that by their guidance we can find the same 'paths of peace'. With the prophets Jeremiah and Ezekiel, Wesley attests to the freeing power that comes as the desire to live by God's law comes from within ourselves, 'written on the obedient heart'.

PRAYER
Give me to know, this day, a moment of that joy that sings in an obedient heart. Amen.

---

*PW 8, 36-7

How precious all thy sayings are!
No treasure can with these compare.
Thy sayings are the soul's repast,
Sweeter than honey to the taste;
They drop like manna from above,
Or flow in streams of joy and love.

Thy words are my delight and guide,
And warn me, lest I start aside:
Thrice happy are thy servants, Lord;
Obedience is our great reward;
We own to whom the grace is given,
To do thy will on earth – is heaven.

O might my every thought arise
Well-pleasing in thy glorious eyes;
My every word advance thy praise,
The strength of thy redeeming grace;
And all I have, and all I am,
Extol the power of Jesus' name.

The judgements of the LORD are true and righteous altogether. More to be desired are they than gold, yea, than much fine gold: sweeter also than honey and the honeycomb. Moreover by them is thy servant warned: and in keeping of them there is great reward. Let the words of my mouth, and the meditation of my heart, be acceptable in thy sight, O LORD, my strength, and my redeemer.

Psalm 19:9-11,14

The final verses of this poem stay close to the order and language of the Psalm. The discipline required of Wesley in keeping to this focused form of poetry, rather than reinterpreting it through the Christian story, is almost sustained to the end, but not quite! In the final lines the name of Jesus appears. This is hardly surprising, for the Hebrew Lord as Redeemer is for Wesley revealed in the redeeming grace of Jesus Christ.

PRAYER
The whole psalm itself can be our prayer for today.

---

*PW 8, 38-9

PSALM 23 (1)

O gentle shepherd, hear my cry,
And harken as thou passest by
To a poor wandering sheep;
Relieve me with thy tender care,
Behold my want of help; draw near
And save me from the deep.

Come, lead me forth to pastures green,
To fertile meads, where all serene
Invites to peace and rest;
Near the still water let me lie,
To view them gently murmur by,
Then bless the Ever-blest.

O God, thy promised aid impart,
Convert my soul and change my heart,
And make my nature pure;
Come, change my nature into thine;
Still lead me in the path divine,
And make my footsteps sure.

The LORD is my shepherd; I shall not want. He maketh me to lie down in green pastures: he leadeth me beside the still waters. He restoreth my soul: he leadeth me in the paths of righteousness for his name's sake.

Psalm 23:1-3

If you are fortunate enough to have been in sheep country at lambing time, the first verse of the poem is a reminder of the plaintive cries of sheep and lambs calling to each other when they are lost. I can remember a lamb grazing by the side of the road, who, on seeing me, was panic-stricken and rushed to its mother for safety. I felt like a wolf rather than the gentle shepherd I would have liked to be.

The plea in the third verse for personal change into the likeness of God is not part of the psalm, but is suggested by the phrases 'restoreth my soul', and 'leads me in the paths of righteousness for his name's sake'.

PRAYER
Receive me, O my Saviour, as a sheep that is gone astray, but would now return to the great Shepherd and Bishop of my soul. *John Wesley*

---

*UPCW 2, 441-42

When through the gloomy shade I roam,
Pale death's dark vale, to endless home,
O save me then from fear;
Vouchsafe with love my soul to fill,
That I in death may fear no ill,
And only praise declare.

Though foes surround, before their face
Prepare a table decked with grace,
Thy food, O Lord, impart;
With sacred oil anoint my head,
And let thy mighty love o'erspread
With joy my willing heart.

Yea, though I walk through the valley of the shadow of death, I will fear no evil: for thou art with me; thy rod and thy staff they comfort me. Thou preparest a table before me in the presence of mine enemies: thou anointest my head with oil; my cup runneth over.

Psalm 23:4-5

Continuing the personal prayer to the Shepherd, Wesley anticipates the final line of verse 6 in the psalm. Death's vale may be dark, but it is the darkness of homecoming where fear vanishes in love, and we respond in praise.

Joy in the presence of adversity is an unpredictable gift of God. Looking back on difficult times, we can usually remember that flash of light when pain lifted and laughter broke through. God seems very close at such moments, and Wesley's image rings true: that some mighty love has been spread over us. It is good to remember that as an antidote to fear.

PRAYER SUGGESTION
Read these verses slowly, aloud if possible, pondering the images and remembering times in your life when you have put your trust in God to get you through. Spend some time thinking of what you dread in the future, then read the verses again.

*UPCW 2, 442

46 PSALM 23 (3)

A pilgrim whilst on earth I rove,
O let me all thy goodness prove;
Let mercy end my days;
Admit at last my wandering feet
Thy courts to enter, thee to greet
With everlasting praise.

Surely goodness and mercy shall follow me all the days of my life: and I shall dwell in the house of the LORD for ever.

Psalm 23:6

Taking just the last verse of the 23rd Psalm – so memorable to so many people – reminds us more clearly that life is a pilgrimage, a journey. Some of us who change addresses every so often, or take extensive trips might well agree that we 'rove' on earth, but there is also a deeper emotional roving that we can see as we look back on our own journey. We may remember times of exhilarating joy, devastating loss, humdrum boredom. Sometimes we have felt trapped; at others, there has been freedom. Often we have lived with problems we did not choose; at other times we imposed them on ourselves.

There is a saying 'When in doubt, say thank you.' Some people seem to have a response to life that allows them to thank God for whatever comes, and see the goodness of God all around. They see the cup half-full, rather than the cup half-empty. The goodness and mercy of God are constant companions on their journey. One day our feet will wander home to the God who tells us that our homecoming will be something to delight us, not to make us fearful.

PRAYER
Teach us, O Lord, to use this transitory life as pilgrims returning to their beloved home; that we may take what our journey requires, and not think of settling in a foreign country. *John Wesley*

---

*UPCW 2, 442

PSALM 27

My Lord my great salvation is,
My life and health, my joy and peace,
   My light, my comfort, and my power;
Whom shall I now submit to fear?
Though hell, the world, and sin are near,
   They never shall my soul devour.

When left by all and void of hope,
Surely my God shall take me up,
   And guide me in the perfect way;
Hell, earth and sin my course oppose;
Bear me, O God, through all my foes,
   Nor suffer them my soul to slay.

My spirit utterly had failed,
Had not the almighty God upheld,
   And wrought a patient hope in me;
Hope against hope to obtain God's grace,
To see on earth God's glorious face,
   God's face in holiness to see.

The LORD is my light and my salvation; whom shall I fear? the LORD is the strength of my life; of whom shall I be afraid?

Psalm 27:1

Christians who have difficulty putting into words what they feel within have been helped to sing their faith experience by the hymns of Charles Wesley. We may be surprised to discover, as here, that Wesley was fond of paraphrasing the Psalms. But what more natural than that the great poet of evangelical faith experience should have enjoyed the Psalms, for they are the language of the biblical faith experience. In them the ancient Hebrews spoke the full range of their relationship with God, singing their praises, lamenting their griefs; yes, and reproaching God when they felt abandoned.

In our own day, when voices rightly reproach the poverty of our language about God, our tendency to limit our expression to a few well-known images like King and Father, one of the treasures the Psalms can give us is their richness of names for God. Wesley appreciated this quality; notice how he takes the opening three from the psalm and expands the list, so that the singer has no fewer than eight names by which to voice his or her trust in God. In the confident presence of such a God, 'whom indeed shall I now submit to fear'?

PRAYER SUGGESTION
Offer to God a simple affirmation of trust, using one of the names from the opening lines of this hymn.

---

*PW 8, 53-55

PSALM 37

Fret not thyself in vain
At evil folk's success,
Nor envy them the fatal gain
Of prosperous wickedness;
For all their pomp shall pass,
Their glory, wealth and power,
Cut down and withered as the grass,
And fleeting as an hour.

Trust in the Lord, and still
Thy faith by works approve;
So shall he stablish thee, and fill
With blessings from above.
Delight thee in thy God,
And God himself shall give;
Shed in thy heart his love abroad,
And there forever live.

Fret not thyself because of evildoers, neither be thou envious against the workers of iniquity. Trust in the LORD and do good; so shalt thou dwell in the land, and verily thou shalt be fed.

Psalm 37:1,3

In the acquisitive society in which we live, it is hard not to be envious of those who are much better off than we are. Every week we hear of people becoming instant millionaires simply because their numbers come up in a lottery, and even those of us who would never buy a part in such games of chance sometimes find ourselves idly speculating on what we would do with such great wealth if we had it. It is even more galling when we see people rising to the top of the ladder of success, having climbed there on the backs of others whom they have cheated or exploited. The psalmist knew what it was like to feel this kind of frustration at the apparent injustice of the world. But he turns to a different set of values. The blessings God gives are not necessarily those of wealth or prosperity, but the gift of God's love outlasts all other benefits and is the source of our deepest joy.

Although Charles Wesley himself lived a reasonably comfortable life, he regarded wealth as a temporary possession and said of himself, 'I have coveted no man's silver, or gold, or apparel.' His greatest delight was to make known to others the unfailing love of God.

PRAYER
O God, save me from envy of those who possess more than I do. Help me to measure the success of my life not by how much material reward I get, but by how many spiritual blessings I receive and am able to share with others. Amen.

---

*PW 8, 80-81 [1:2 evil men's]

PSALM 40 (1)

Patient I waited for the Lord,
Who heard and answered to my cry;
Out of the pit of sin, abhorr'd,
He brought, and set me up on high;
Out of the mire and clay he took
And fixed my feet upon a rock.

The Lord hath made my goings strong,
And stablished me with gospel grace;
Put in my mouth the joyful song,
The new, unceasing song of praise.
Many the deed divine shall see,
And fear, and trust in God, like me.

Blessed is the one that dares confide
In my redeeming God alone.
O Lord, thy works are multiplied,
The wondrous works which thou hast done!
Thy thoughts of grace to us surmount
The power of numbers to recount!

I waited patiently for the LORD; and he inclined unto me, and heard my cry. He brought me up also out of an horrible pit, out of the miry clay, and set my feet upon a rock, and established my goings. And he hath put a new song in my mouth, even praise unto our God.

Psalm 40:1-3

This is not just a psalm paraphrase. Wesley characteristically makes the psalm a reflection on his own experience, emphasised by the personal phrase 'like me'. For the Hebrew poet, the 'pit' may refer to some experience of physical danger and distress. Wesley makes it clear that he is referring to the pit of sin from which he personally has been rescued. Now he stands on firm ground and shares the good news with all who will hear and see what God has done for him. 'Count your blessings', says the old chorus. For Wesley that is impossible – like the psalmist, he has known so many blessings that they are innumerable.

PRAYER
Your goodness to us, O God, is without limit. Teach us to live with a corresponding generosity. Amen.

---

*PW 8, 91-3 [3:1 the man]

PSALM 40 (2)

I cannot all thy love declare;
No, nor the smallest part express;
Worthless my noblest offerings are,
Unfit the holy God to please;
But thou dost unto me impart
A hearing ear, and loving heart.

No shadowy form thou dost require,
No legal sacrifice approve;
Thou seek'st the contrite heart's desire
The offering of obedient love;
And lo! I come to do thy will,
And all thy law in love fulfil!

Thy welcome will concerning me,
I in the sacred volume read;
'Tis there my rule of life I see,
And in thy ways delight to tread;
While, by thy love's divinest art,
Thy law is written on my heart.

Then said I, Lo, I come: in the volume of the book it is written of me, I delight to do thy will, O my God: yea, thy law is within my heart.

Psalm 40:7-8

The paraphrase of Psalm 40 continues in these verses. They still follow closely the framework of the psalm itself, but Wesley interweaves strands from other parts of the Bible. Like the psalmist, he brings to his meditation both a hearing ear and a loving heart.

Love permeates the whole poem. It is the poet's 'heart's desire' (Psalm 21:2) to do the will of God according to the law of love. From Paul's letter to the Romans (13:10) comes the thought that love which results in just dealings with one's neighbour is the love that fulfils the law.

Verses 2 and 3 are a poetic commentary on the psalm seen through the eyes of the writer of the book of Hebrews (10:1-10). The psalmist and the letter-writer know that joyous and loving obedience, rather than sacrificial offerings, is the heart of God's law.

PRAYER
Lord, have mercy upon us and write these thy laws in our hearts, we beseech thee. Amen. *Book of Common Prayer*

---

*PW 8, 91-3

Thine everlasting righteousness,
Thou know'st I to thy church have showed;
Nor hid within my heart the grace
And goodness of my pardoning God;
Nor shunned in open thanks to approve
The truth of thy redeeming love.

The great salvation thou hast wrought
I have with joy to all declared;
Ah! gracious Lord! forsake me not,
But let thy tender mercies guard;
Thy faithful love my soul defend,
And save and keep me to the end.

I have not hid thy righteousness within my heart; I have declared thy faithfulness and thy salvation. I have not concealed thy lovingkindness and thy truth from the great congregation.

Psalm 40:10

Still within the context of Psalm 40, Wesley's style becomes that of the preacher as well as of the poet. Like the psalmist, he has felt compelled to share with others the joy of knowing the pardoning love of God.

It sounds almost as though there were a bargain being set up between the preacher and God. The writer has done his best for God, and now prays for help in return. He senses that troubles are about to overtake him.

Wesley also feels the need of the continuing protection of God's presence with him. He cannot give up preaching. He *has* to tell others in the church, the countryside, and anywhere people will listen. He has preached all his life and will keep on doing it, but only with the assurance of God's continuing love, that will enable him to hold out 'to the end'.

PRAYER
Pardoning God, as your faithful love has defended me all my days, so may my life portray a confidence that nothing in life or in death can separate me from that love. Amen.

---

*PW 8, 91-3

PSALM 45

My heart is full of Christ, and longs
  Its glorious matter to declare!
Of him I make my loftier songs,
  I cannot from his praise forbear;
My ready tongue makes haste to sing
  The beauties of my heavenly King.

Fairer than all the earth-born race,
  Perfect in comeliness thou art;
Replenished are thy lips with grace,
  And full of love thy tender heart:
God ever blest! We bow the knee,
  And own all fullness dwells in thee.

My heart overflows with a goodly theme; I address my verses to the king: my tongue is like the pen of a ready scribe. You are the most handsome of men; grace is poured upon your lips; therefore God has blessed you forever.

Psalm 45:1-2 (NRSV)

'An ode for a royal wedding in the Kingdom of Israel', says the commentary on this psalm. If we read the whole seventeen verses of the psalm we find that the poet addresses both the bride and the groom. He praises the groom's grace and love of justice; he celebrates the bride's beauty and generosity of heart.

Wesley's hymn turns the psalm into a paean of praise for Christ: an allegorical reading traditional in the church. He burns with the desire of a lover to celebrate the 'beauties' of the beloved, whose gracious words express a loving heart. If such a love poem seems an extravagant form of language in a hymn, it should remind us that Charles the preacher and theologian was also the bard of the divine love.

PRAYER
Praise be to you, O Christ, whose kingship is like that of no earthly ruler. Praise be to you, the wounded one with the tender heart full of love for all your creation. Praise be to you, whose grace is sufficient for all our needs. Amen.

CPH (1743) *HP 799 [1:6 The glories]

Great is our redeeming Lord
  In power and truth and grace;
Him by highest heaven adored,
  His Church on earth doth praise:
In the city of our God,
  In his holy mount below,
Publish, spread his name abroad,
  And all his greatness show.

Zion's God is all our own,
  Who on his love rely;
We his pardoning love have known,
  And live to Christ, and die:
To the new Jerusalem
  He our faithful Guide shall be;
Him we claim, and rest in him,
  Through all eternity.

Great is the LORD, and greatly to be praised in the city of our God, in the mountain of his holiness.

Psalm 48:1

Zion was an ancient name for the Canaanite fortress that David captured about 1000 BCE and made into Jerusalem, the capital city of the Hebrew kingdom. Several of the Psalms are hymns of Zion; they celebrate the pride and the confidence felt by the city's inhabitants, owing to the presence in their midst of the Temple of God. In later Jewish and in Christian thought, the name Zion came to be taken for the people itself, and even for the heavenly city of God, the destiny of humanity.

Here Wesley paraphrases the psalm as a hymn for the church. In our day, when the church's structures are faced with the need for radical change, and the upkeep of its older buildings is a financial burden, our churches may seem anything but glorious, and the triumphal language of the psalm may feel quaint and outdated. But look more closely. Wesley is reminding us that the glory belongs to 'Zion's God', that the rock on which we build is the 'pardoning love' made known in Christ, and that we are a people on the move, living with the vision of a city yet to be, a 'new Jerusalem'.

PRAYER
God of the human story, in a time when it is easy to feel discouragement, let me find joy in singing your praises for what you have already done, and for what you yet call us to be; in the name of Christ who loved the church, and gave himself for it. Amen.

AM (1797) PW 8, 111 *MHB 699

Thee in the watches of the night
  Do I not, Lord, remember still,
And meditate with calm delight
  On the dear counsels of thy will?

My God, I wake to call thee mine,
  To think on all thy love,
To taste the graciousness divine,
  And further blessings prove.

Have I not remembered thee in my bed: and thought upon thee when I was waking?
Psalm 63:7 (BCP)

Rereading the whole of Psalm 63 is a good background to this meditation. These two short poems by Wesley, in different metres, form as it were bookends to the experience of night. There is a tone of mystical 'calm delight' in the presence of God, but also a real need to feel safe. Even the act of thinking about God in the night implies being awake – perhaps disturbingly so – when the rest of the world is asleep.

Dietrich Bonhoeffer, imprisoned and later executed during the Second World War, had every reason to know the uncertainties of night in the prison camp. This is a night-time prayer he wrote in 1943:

PRAYER
O Lord my God, I thank you for bringing this day to a close. Thank you for giving me rest in body and soul. Your hand has been over me, and has guarded me and preserved me.

Forgive my lack of faith and any wrong that I have done today, and help me to forgive all who have wronged me.

Let me sleep in peace underneath your protection, and keep me from all the temptations of darkness. Into your hands I commend my loved ones, and all who dwell in this household. I commend to you my body and soul. O God, your holy name be praised. Amen.[1]

---

*SH (1762)

All praise to him who dwells in bliss,
Who made both day and night,
Whose throne is darkness, in the abyss
Of uncreated light.

Whom thou dost guard, O King of kings,
No evil shall molest;
Under the shadow of thy wings
Shall they securely rest.

Thy angels shall around their beds
Their constant stations keep;
Thy faith and truth shall shield their heads
For thou dost never sleep.

May we, with calm and sweet repose
And heavenly thoughts refreshed,
Our eyelids with the morn's unclose,
And bless the Ever-blessed.

My mouth shall praise thee with joyful lips: When I remember thee upon my bed and meditate on thee in the night watches. Because thou hast been my help, therefore in the shadow of thy wings will I rejoice.

Psalm 63:5-7

Night ends with praise; morning begins with praise. John Cosin, the seventeenth century Church of England divine, collected sayings from the Bible and also from the early Church Fathers on the value of prayer at various times of the day. The following is his somewhat challenging morning advice from Chrysostom:

> It behoveth us therefore to RISE before the Sun be up . . For tell me, with what face can we behold the Sun, unless we worship him first, that hath made so glorious a light for us?[1]

PRAYER
May your presence accompany me in darkness, and lighten each morning with the joy of new opportunity. Amen.

CPH (1741) *PW 2, 27-8 MHB 934

Through labour exhausted and pain,
Will Christ from his servant depart,
Or with me in weakness remain
The strength and the joy of my heart?
His power I in weakness shall prove,
Confiding in Jesus's name,
The God of unchangeable love,
For ever and ever the same.

Cast me not off in the time of old age; forsake me not when my strength faileth.
Psalm 71:9

Psalm 71 is the lament of an elderly person. Discouraged by a weakening body, afflicted with loneliness and a feeling of persecution, the writer pours out this cry, pleading not to be abandoned by God as well. As we accompany ageing parents or friends toward their end, as we sense in ourselves the increasing burden of mortality, we can sympathise with such fears. Death may indeed be 'the last enemy' to be overcome (1 Corinthians 15:26); there can also be something terribly demoralising to the spirit in the petty indignities of old age.

Perhaps at a time of his own deep weariness and physical suffering, Charles Wesley helps us identify with the painful question of the psalmist: as my body weakens, as my mental powers diminish, will I finally experience also the ultimate betrayal, the loss of the sense of the presence of Christ? He finds encouragement for himself and for us all in the words of the apostle Paul, who in a time of personal suffering learned to trust in a deeper way the One whose undergirding strength becomes most known to us in our times of greatest weakness (2 Corinthians 12:9). Held in this 'unchangeable love', we shall find strength and joy even at the last.

PRAYER
Tarry thou with me, O Lord, for it is toward evening with me, and the day is far spent of this my toilsome life. Let thy strength be made perfect in my weakness.[1]
Bishop Lancelot Andrewes

---

*SH (1762) PW 9, 308

PSALM 71 (2)

Thou who from infancy to age
Hast been my never-failing Friend,
Support through life's extremest stage,
And bring me to my journey's end,
And bid me live, to sing thy praise,
An age of everlasting days.

Thou art my hope, O LORD God: thou art my trust from my youth . . . Let my mouth be filled with thy praise . . . forsake me not when my strength faileth.

Psalm 71:5,8-9

Charles Wesley was in his early fifties when he wrote this verse, and was to live almost another thirty years. His prayer to his 'never-failing friend' was answered, for he was active and singing the praise of God almost to the end of his days. After the age of eighty his preaching lost some of its vigour, but gained some music, as he interspersed his sermons with hymns in order to save his energy.

These days, medical and social support makes old age less of a material menace than in the days of Wesley, but we still fear isolation, loss and pain. One woman, in writing of growing old gracefully, says:

> We can spend our energies regretting, fighting, resenting our losses, or we can grieve them, learn from them and celebrate them as having given us gifts of vision, insight and empathy. This is the task of transformation and transformation means to take the life that comes to us and reshape those experiences into meaning and the kind of knowing that comes of living fully and well. This task calls us to give up the need to control, to be in charge, to carve life . . . into a thing of our own design.[1]

This writer also speaks of getting involved in causes 'that are greater than ourselves', so that life stays 'alive, vital and full of hope'. Such wisdom, such living is to sing the praise of our life's Friend to journey's end.

PRAYER
Lord, when the signs of age begin to mark my body (and still more when they touch my mind) . . . grant that I may understand that it is you who are painfully parting the fibres of my being in order to penetrate to the very marrow of my substance and bear me away within yourself into your eternity.[2] *Teilhard de Chardin*

---

*SH (1762) PW 9, 308

O what shall I do my Saviour to praise,
So faithful and true, so plenteous in grace,
So strong to deliver, so good to redeem
The weakest believer that hangs upon him!

How happy are they whose hearts are set free,
The people that can be joyful in thee;
Their joy is to walk in the light of thy face,
And still they are talking of Jesus's grace.

For thou art their boast, their glory and power;
And I also trust to see the glad hour,
My soul's new creation, a life from the dead,
The day of salvation, that lifts up my head.

Blessed is the people, O LORD, that can rejoice in thee; they shall walk in the light of thy countenance. Their delight shall be daily in thy Name; and in thy righteousness shall they make their boast.

Psalm 89:16-17 (BCP)

The God to whom the Hebrew people sang songs of praise and confidence is also the God of all people. Remembering also Christ's life and death, we too are confident that this is a God to be trusted.

This hymn, which is part of a longer one, is a complex weaving of Old and New Testament texts. The players in the story are Christ, others ('the people') and I myself ('I also'). So I too am an inheritor of this great tradition of thanksgiving and trust. The lilting rhythm emphasises the spirit of joy making us almost want to dance as we walk and talk together in the presence of Jesus.

PRAYER
Generous God, set our hearts free from false weights: the opinions of others, the power of resentment, the fruitless worry about someone we love, the fear of the future, the guilt for what we have done, or have failed to do. Grant us newness of life and your grace to know ourselves loved and forgiven, that we may walk joyfully in the light of the face of Jesus Christ. Amen.

HSP (1742) *CH 190 [2:1 How happy the man whose heart is] HP 569

What shall I render to my God
For all his mercy's store?
I'll take the gifts he has bestowed,
And humbly ask for more.

The sacred cup of saving grace
I will with thanks receive,
And all his promises embrace,
And to his glory live.

My vows I will to his great name
Before his people pay,
And all I have, and all I am,
Upon his altar lay.

What shall I render unto the LORD for all his benefits toward me? I will take the cup of salvation, and call upon the name of the LORD. I will pay my vows unto the LORD now in the presence of all his people.

Psalm 116:12-14

Each of these three verses of a longer hymn starts with one of the sentences of Psalm 116, which Wesley expands into the last two lines of each verse. The unusually simple rhythm and rhyme echo the earlier metrical psalms or the hymns of Isaac Watts.

To take gifts and ask for more seems contrary to what we were taught at our mother's knee. Certainly, society assumes that we pay for what we get, and those who do not pay, do not receive. But that assumes a world that is like a Christmas shopping list where we try to match exactly the value of gifts given to us. This hymn/psalm says that God's extravagant bounty becomes our bounty of extravagance too, and we give to God, in return for all his gifts to us, the gift of our whole lives.

PRAYER
Generous God, forgive my careful measuring of my goods, my moments of meanness, and my tidy judgements about who deserves to receive from me or from others. Help me to accept humbly, to live boldly, and to give generously. Amen.

PH (1743) *HP 703

PSALM 116 (2)

Thy hands created me, thy hands
  From sin have set me free;
The mercy that has loosed my bands
  Has bound me fast to thee.

The God of all-redeeming grace
  My God I will proclaim,
Offer the sacrifice of praise,
  And call upon his name.

Praise him, ye saints, the God of love,
  Who has my sins forgiven,
Till, gathered to the church above,
  We sing the songs of heaven.

O LORD, truly I am thy servant; I am thy servant, and the son of thine handmaid: thou hast loosed my bonds. I will offer to thee the sacrifice of thanksgiving, and will call upon the name of the LORD.

Psalm 116:16-17

The theme continues the psalm of praise. These verses add the overtone of redemption – the idea of a slave being set free by a price being paid for him or her. This comes not solely from the psalm but from a New Testament perspective added by Wesley. The whole of this psalm was used as part of the Anglican Churching of Women service; that is, the thanksgiving of women after childbirth. It is also the psalm that appears in the lectionary on Maundy Thursday, the eve of Christ's betrayal and of his suffering in the Garden of Gethsemane. Thus liberation and bondage, sacrifice and praise, pain and deliverance are twin experiences of God's mercy at work in our lives. Our first and last response must always be of thanksgiving.

PRAYER
Make me a captive, Lord,
And then I shall be free.
Amen. *George Matheson*

PH (1743) *HP 703

Ye nations, who the globe divide,
Ye numerous nations scattered wide,
To God your grateful voices raise;
To all his boundless mercy shown,
His truth to endless ages known
Require our endless love and praise.

To him who reigns enthroned on high,
To his dear Son, who deigned to die
Our guilt and errors to remove;
To that blest Spirit who grace imparts,
Who rules in all believing hearts,
Be ceaseless glory, praise and love.

O praise the LORD, all ye nations: praise him, all ye people. For his merciful kindness is great toward us: and the truth of the LORD endureth forever. Praise ye the LORD.

Psalm 117

One of the shortest psalms in the Psalter catches Charles Wesley's eye and inspires in him the vision of a world united in the praise of God. In the compass of two verses he spans all the nations of the earth. God's mercy knows no bounds; God's praise should know no limits.

In his day, the psalmist would have had in mind above all the nations of the Mediterranean and Middle East. Wesley's global knowledge would have been considerably more extensive. Today, in a universe vaster than even he could have envisaged, we can still affirm the sovereignty of God and acknowledge that all peoples owe their allegiance to the One who created the heavens and the earth.

PRAYER

In our prayer today let us bring before God particularly all those organisations which we know of that are striving to bring the nations together in justice and peace. We pray for the United Nations Organisation and all its agencies; for the World Council of Churches and all its member churches; for the Roman Catholic Church and all worldwide communions; for the media who now span the globe and by satellite and cable are able to let nation speak to nation. May their words be words of peace, their works be works of justice, and their worship be worthy of the God of earth and heaven. Amen.

---

*HSP (1739) PW 1, 124

Good thou art, and good thou dost,
Thy mercies reach to all,
Chiefly those who on thee trust,
And for thy mercy call;
New they every morning are;
As fathers when their children cry,
Us thou dost in pity spare,
And all our wants supply.

Mercy o'er thy works presides;
Thy providence displayed
Still preserves, and still provides
For all thy hands have made;
Keeps with most distinguished care
The one who on thy love depends,
Watches every numbered hair,
And every step attends.

Thou art good, and doest good; teach me thy statutes.

Psalm 119:68

Like as a father pitieth his children, so the LORD pitieth them that fear him.

Psalm 103:13

To comprehend the goodness of God requires more than a lifetime of experience, but this hymn for children sets them on the right path. God's own, good world is still being lovingly cared for by the One who preserves and nourishes all. The parent image from Psalm 103, and the 'numbered hair' image from the Sermon on the Mount speak of a personal God – the God of mercy.

'I have often repented of judging too severely, but very seldom of being too merciful,' wrote John Wesley. And he – the man who seemed to be always busy – also advocated being merciful to ourselves: 'When our mind is hurried, it is hardly possible to retain either the spirit of prayer or thankfulness' and at another time: 'You are no more at liberty to throw away your health than to throw away your life.'[1]

PRAYER

Merciful God, forgive me as I forgive others; like a father, pity my foolishness; like a mother, rock me in your arms, that I may love myself as you love me, through Jesus Christ, our forgiving Saviour. Amen.

HC (1763) *CH 236 [2:6 The man who 2:8 all his steps] MHB 59

PSALM 121 (1)

To the hills I lift mine eyes,
  The everlasting hills;
Streaming thence in fresh supplies,
  My soul the Spirit feels.
Will he not his help afford?
  Help, while yet I ask, is given:
God comes down, the God and Lord
  That made both earth and heaven.

Faithful soul, pray always; pray,
  And still in God confide;
He thy feeble steps shall stay,
  Nor suffer thee to slide;
Lean on thy Redeemer's breast;
  He thy quiet spirit keeps;
Rest in him, securely rest,
  Thy watchman never sleeps.

Neither sin, nor earth, nor hell
  Thy keeper can surprise;
Careless slumber cannot steal
  On his all-seeing eyes:
He is Israel's sure defence;
  Israel all his care shall prove,
Kept by watchful providence
  And ever-waking love.

I will lift up mine eyes unto the hills, from whence cometh my help.

Psalm 121:1

Metrical psalms, especially in the 'Old Version' of Sternhold and Hopkins, were the usual form of congregational praise in Wesley's day. Here, like his contemporary Isaac Watts, Wesley is turning his poetic skill to a new paraphrase of Psalm 121, verses 1-4; and like Watts, he turns the psalmist's words into an expression of Christian experience. Modern translations follow the Hebrew in making the first verse of the psalm into a question. But Wesley knows the Prayer Book and King James translations by heart; and so he looks to the 'everlasting hills' as a symbol of the very dwelling place of God, from which come ever new supplies of the refreshing Spirit. Notice how other eloquent adjectives emphasise the words of the psalm: 'feeble steps', 'all-seeing eyes', 'watchful providence', 'ever-waking love'.

PRAYER
May the peace of God, which passes all understanding, keep guard over our hearts and minds, through Christ Jesus. Amen.

---

*PH (1743) PW 8, 235 MHB 497

PSALM 121 (2)

See the Lord, thy keeper, stand
  Omnipotently near!
Lo! He holds thee by thy hand,
  And banishes thy fear;
Shadows with his wings thy head;
  Guards from all impending harms:
Round thee and beneath are spread
  The everlasting arms.

Thee in evil's scorching day
  The sun shall never smite;
Thee the moon's malignest ray
  Shall never blast by night;
Safe from known or secret foes,
  Free from sin and Satan's thrall,
God, when flesh, earth, hell oppose,
  Shall keep thee safe from all.

Christ shall bless thy going out,
  Shall bless thy coming in;
Kindly compass thee about,
  Till thou art saved from sin;
Like thy spotless Master, thou,
  Filled with wisdom, love, and power,
Holy, pure and perfect now,
  Henceforth, and evermore.

The LORD is thy keeper: the LORD is thy shade upon thy right hand.

Psalm 121:5

Read verses 5-8 of the psalm itself and then read Wesley's hymn. Notice how he expands the psalmist's thoughts by references to other passages of scripture and particularly by reference to Christ himself.

In the first verse, the mingled images of God's sheltering wings and embracing arms echo other verses from the Old Testament. They are words which have brought comfort and reassurance to many in time of trouble.

PRAYER
O God, in the first moments of our lives you embrace us through the arms of a mother. Help us to be conscious of your encircling arms protecting us all the days of our lives and waiting to welcome us at our last homecoming. Amen.

---

*PH (1743) PW 8, 236 MHB 497

O disclose thy lovely face!
 Quicken all my drooping powers;
Gasps my fainting soul for grace,
 As a thirsty land for showers;
Haste, my Lord, no more delay,
Come, my Jesus, come away!

Well thou know'st I cannot rest
 Till I fully rest in thee,
Till I am of thee possessed,
 Till, from every sin set free,
All the life of faith I prove,
All the joy and heaven of love.

With me O continue, Lord!
 Keep me, or from thee I fly;
Strength and comfort from thy word
 Imperceptibly supply;
Hold me till I apprehend,
Make me faithful to the end.

I stretch forth my hands unto thee: my soul gaspeth unto thee as a thirsty land.
Psalm 143:6 (BCP)

Many of Charles Wesley's hymns are like love lyrics, where he seems to be addressing a human person with all the impatience of a passionate lover. In this hymn-poem he is both the pursuer and the pursued. Like Francis Thompson's 'Hound of Heaven', this poem expresses the experience that it is not simply our seeking after Christ that leads us to him, but rather his seeking after us. It is not our hold on him that matters in the long run, but his hold on us, however imperceptible that may be. That is what will keep us faithful to him in the end.

PRAYER
Ah! foolish, blindest, weakest,
I am he whom thou seekest,
Thou dravest love from thee
who dravest me. *Francis Thompson*

HSP (1740) *PW 1, 254-5 [1:5 no longer stay] MHB 545

Celebrate the eternal God
  With harp and psaltery,
Timbrels soft and cymbals loud
  In his high praise agree:
Praise him every tuneful string;
  All the reach of heavenly art,
All the powers of music bring,
  The music of the heart.

Him, in whom they move and live,
  Let every creature sing,
Glory to their Maker give,
  And homage to their King:
Hallowed be his name beneath,
  As in heaven on earth adored;
Praise the Lord in every breath,
  Let all things praise the Lord.

Praise him with the sound of the trumpet: praise him with the psaltery and harp . . . Let every thing that hath breath praise the LORD.

Psalm 150:3,6

This poem is rather longer than Wesley's other meditation on the same psalm. Here, keeping close to the exuberant mood of the psalm, he calls for praise with an orchestra of sound – brass, percussion and stringed instruments – and, in a line typical of Wesley, he adds, 'the music of the heart'.

But making music is not just a human activity. All creation – 'every thing that hath breath' in the psalmist's words – joins in the praise. After centuries of a world view centred upon human beings, modern science may help us understand the larger interconnection of all life. If so, we will come closer to the poetry of the Hebrew tradition, where trees clap their hands and valleys sing to the God 'in whom they move and live' – a phrase Wesley borrows from Paul's address to the Athenians (Acts 17:28).

Finally, by including words from the Lord's Prayer (2:5-6) the poem reminds us that the praise of all creation is included within the prayer that Jesus taught the men and women who were his followers.

PRAYER
God, you continue to create your good world. Let me be one of the many voices in the orchestra of your creatures who praise you. Amen.

P&H (1743) *HP 55

CREATION'S PRAISE – PSALM 150

Breathe in praise of your creator
    Every soul his honours raise
Magnify the Lord of nature
    Magnify the God of grace
        Hallelujah,
Fill the universe with praise!

Let every thing that hath breath praise the LORD. Praise ye the LORD.

Psalm 150:6

As a meditation on the psalm, this may seem a little short. After all, where are the trumpets, the timbrels, strings and pipes, the lute and harp, the loud clashing cymbals? Where is the dance?

For listeners who know the psalms, the instruments are all there in the imagination; this little poem is a condensed doxology. How simple it is, and what more needs to be said? The opening word requires little skill, for breathing is the very core of our being. Focusing on breathing is part of most meditative traditions, a calming, steadying process – yet here our breath is used as praise. It is as if the whole body is one with the universe and with God the creator of all things, God who by grace continues to give us life and love.

One of the tasks of our generation is to see ourselves as part of nature, not as superior to it. All life is interdependent and interwoven; not just animals but trees and plants breathe too. A tree thoughtlessly cut down, a river polluted, the extinction of a species threatens us all. All nature breathes in praise of God; all nature is sacred.

MEDITATION
An Indian schoolboy said, 'I do not know what to say when I am asked to make up a prayer. It is like being told to breathe.'

PRAYER
Creator God, you give breath to all life; show me what this means in my life. Give me insight to discern my role in your continuing creation. Where I have influence to nurture the world, give me strength to use it, and to share in creation's praise of you. Amen.

---

*SH (1762)

Author of every work divine
Who dost through both creations shine,
The God of nature and of grace,
Thy glorious steps in all we see,
And wisdom attribute to thee,
And power and majesty and praise.

Thou didst thy mighty wings outspread,
And brooding o'er the chaos, shed
Thy life into the impregn'd abyss,
The vital principle infuse,
And out of nothing's womb produce
The earth and heaven, and all that is.

That all-informing breath thou art
Who dost continued life impart,
And bidd'st the world persist to be;
Garnished by thee yon azure sky
And all those beauteous orbs on high
Descend in golden chains from thee.

And the earth was without form, and void; and darkness was upon the face of the deep. And the Spirit of God moved upon the face of the waters.

Genesis 1:2

Not published in a hymnbook since 1785, this poem makes a splendid contribution to our ecological age, for we need to be reminded that God's breath continues to create the world and is in all living things. It has been suggested that verse 1 owes its inspiration to a passage from the *Aeneid* where Virgil speaks of all the elements of earth and sky which 'exist through inward spirit'. 'Their total mass/by mind is permeated . . ./From mind and spirit comes life' (VI 726-8).

The second verse borrows language from *Paradise Lost* to portray the image of the dove brooding at creation and impregnating the vast abyss with the gift of life. Milton, addressing the Spirit, says:

. . . thou from the first
Wast present, and with mighty wings outspread
Dovelike sat'st brooding on the vast abyss
And mad'st it pregnant. (*PL* I, 19-21)

PRAYER
God our Creator, you have made us one with this earth, to tend it and bring forth fruit; may we so respect and cherish all that has life from you, that we may share in the labour of all creation to give birth to your hidden glory, through Jesus Christ. Amen.[1]
Janet Morley

---

*Hymns of Petition and Thanksgiving for the Promise of the Father [Hymns for Whitsunday] (1746) RV 127

Thou dost create the earth anew,
Its maker and preserver too,
By thine almighty arm sustain:
Nature perceives thy secret force,
And still holds on her even course
And owns thy providential reign.

Thou art the Universal Soul,
The plastic power that fills the whole,
And governs earth, air, sea, and sky:
The creatures all thy breath receive,
And who by thy inspiring live,
Without thy inspiration die.

Spirit immense, eternal Mind,
Thou on the souls of lost mankind
Dost with benignest influence move,
Pleased to restore the ruined race,
And new-create a world of grace
In all the image of thy love.

These wait all upon thee . . . thou openest thine hand, they are filled with good. Thou hidest thy face, they are troubled: thou takest away their breath, they die, and return to their dust. Thou sendest forth thy spirit, they are created: and thou renewest the face of the earth.

Psalm 104:27-30

Yesterday's emphasis on creation is expanded in these three verses. Readers today will be struck by this use of the word 'plastic' to describe the Creator's power. It originally meant 'moulding', as a potter moulds the clay. That recalls Jeremiah's image of God shaping human lives (Jeremiah 18). But, like moulded clay on the wheel, human lives can become misshapen. Wesley sees God's new creation as the restoration of the original design, in the image of divine love.

MEDITATION
Apprehend God in all things, for God is in all things. Every single creature is full of God and is a book about God. Every creature is a word of God. If I spent enough time with the tiniest creature – even a caterpillar – I would never have to prepare a sermon. So full of God is every creature. *Meister Eckhart*

*Hymns of Petition and Thanksgiving for the Promise of the Father (1746) RV 127

Long o'er my formless soul
The dreary waves did roll;
Void I lay and sunk in night.
Thou, the overshadowing Dove,
Call'dst the chaos into light,
Bad'st me be, and live and love.

Thee I exult to feel,
Thou in my heart dost dwell;
There thou bear'st thy witness true,
Shed'st the love of God abroad;
I in Christ a creature new,
I, ev'n I, am born of God!

And the earth was without form, and void; and darkness was upon the face of the deep. And the Spirit of God moved upon the face of the waters.

Genesis 1:2

This story of rebirth is so anchored to the cosmic imagery of the first creation story that it makes all personal new birth a part of the creation of all things new. The language of the brooding, overshadowing dove comes from Milton, but the concept is a traditional blending of the dove as representing the Spirit, with the same Spirit of God creating the world.

The aboriginal Nisga'a people of northern British Columbia, Canada, have their own story of the Spirit creating the world. They wear red and black ceremonial robes to symbolise light coming out of darkness, but unlike the Genesis story, they believe that when light came it showed their ancestors already alive, waiting to emerge from the darkness.

Jesus' words to Nicodemus, that one must be born of water and the spirit to enter the kingdom of God (John 3:3), have often been 'spiritualised' by a Greek concept of a body and spirit division. Wesley brings us back firmly to the Hebrew world, to the tangible reality of creation where the Spirit moves in all things, and continues to bring light out of chaos; out of death, new life and love.

PRAYER
Spirit of life and light, take me out of the darkness that I may know and feel your love, and be born again into the newness of your creation. Amen.

---

*HSP (1739) RV 4

Not on the whirlwind's wings he flies
Not in the thunder's voice he speaks,
But that the fallen one may rise,
The Lord his ruined creature seeks.
Not in the burning blaze of day,
(For fury hath no place in him)
But placid as the evening ray,
He comes to sentence, and redeem.

They heard the voice of the LORD God walking in the garden in the cool of the day.
Genesis 3:8

For the Son of man is come to seek and to save that which was lost.
Luke 19:10

The setting for this brief verse is the primeval Garden, where earth's first human inhabitants have been set by their Creator (Genesis 2-3). They are given a relationship with God, responsibility for the care of the garden earth, companionship of one another; but after an act of disobedience they run and hide, fearful as they await the punishment of their wrongdoing.

Meditating on this story, Wesley recalls another troubled man, the prophet Elijah, who in running away encountered God not in whirlwind, earthquake or fire, but as 'a still small voice' (1 Kings 19:9-12). So he depicts this scene quite differently from how we might have imagined it. This is not a God who hurls thunderbolts from a distant heaven, but the One who comes in search of the creature who is lost. The meeting is not some high noon confrontation, but an encounter in the quiet of the evening, where God's word of justice is tempered by the will to save.

We are given freedom by our Maker, and we live with the consequences of our choices. But in quiet moments, in unexpected encounters, we too discover the God who comes in search of us, whose final will is our good, whose last best word is love.

PRAYER
As you have found me, gracious God, so help me this day to speak your gentle word of peace to those who live in fear of judgement. Amen.

*SH (1762) [3 fallen man]

WRESTLING JACOB (1)

Come, O thou Traveller unknown,
 Whom still I hold, but cannot see!
My company before is gone,
 And I am left alone with thee;
With thee all night I mean to stay,
And wrestle till the break of day.

I need not tell thee who I am,
 My misery, or sin declare;
Thyself hast called me by my name;
 Look on thy hands, and read it there:
But who, I ask thee, who art thou?
Tell me thy name, and tell me now.

And Jacob was left alone; and there wrestled a man with him until the breaking of the day.

Genesis 32:24 (read to verse 32)

The story of Jacob's fearful return to his home country and the brother whom he had wronged is one of the great dramas of the Hebrew Scriptures. Having sent his flocks and people on ahead, Jacob is left alone and wrestles all that night with an unknown assailant.

In the next three days, we meditate on Wesley's 'Wrestling Jacob'; a drama within the original drama. Taking the wrestling image, Charles makes it a metaphor for his own struggle to know the name and nature of God. But the poem is not just *about* wrestling with God; one *feels* too the harrowing experience, the loneliness of the inner spiritual struggle.

This may be Wesley's finest hymn. Certainly Isaac Watts, the hymnwriter, said it was worth all the hymns he had written. Today, it is one of the few Wesley poems which survives in literary anthologies. Space does not permit a full commentary here, but observe that in these two verses there is a hint that Isaiah's promise, 'I have graven thee on the palms of my hands' (Isaiah 49:16), is blended with the wounds in Christ's hands. Here too he asks for the first time the anxious question, 'But who are you?'

PRAYER
O God, with whom we wrestle until the break of day, make us long to seek your face beyond the limits of our strength, that in our wounds we may remember you, and in your blessing we may find ourselves, through Jesus Christ. Amen.[1]
Janet Morley

---

*HSP (1742) RV 25 CH 136 HP 434 UMH 386-7

WRESTLING JACOB (2)

In vain thou strugglest to get free;
  I never will unloose my hold!
Art thou the Man that died for me?
  The secret of thy love unfold:
Wrestling, I will not let thee go,
Till I thy name, thy nature know.

Wilt thou not yet to me reveal
  Thy new, unutterable name?
Tell me, I still beseech thee, tell;
  To know it now resolved I am:
Wrestling, I will not let thee go,
Till I thy name, thy nature know.

'Tis all in vain to hold thy tongue,
  Or touch the hollow of my thigh:
Though every sinew be unstrung,
  Out of my arms thou shalt not fly;
Wrestling, I will not let thee go,
Till I thy name, thy nature know.

What though my shrinking flesh complain,
  And murmur to contend so long?
I rise superior to my pain,
  When I am weak, then I am strong;
And when my all of strength shall fail,
I shall with the God-Man prevail.

And Jacob asked him, and said, Tell me, I pray thee, thy name.

Genesis 32:29

Now we have the gradual build-up of tension as question piles on question, the same request with slight variations but demanding insistence. Still there seems no answer. The last verse here explores the paradox of strength in weakness, summed up in the couplet at the end of verse four. This is a turning point in the spiritual struggle – a moment of certainty, though the struggle is not yet won. Look at 2 Corinthians 12:9 for Paul's reference to discovering strength in weakness.

PRAYER
Lord, help me to acknowledge my weakness so that I might know your strength. Amen.

---

*HSP (1742) RV 25 CH 136 HP 434 UMH 386-7

WRESTLING JACOB (3)

My strength is gone, my nature dies,
    I sink beneath thy weighty hand,
Faint to revive, and fall to rise;
    I fall, and yet by faith I stand,
I stand, and will not let thee go,
Till I thy name, thy nature know.

Yield to me now, for I am weak,
    But confident in self-despair;
Speak to my heart, in blessings speak,
    Be conquered by my instant prayer;
Speak, or thou never hence shalt move,
And tell me, if thy name is Love.

'Tis Love! 'Tis Love! Thou diedst for me!
    I hear thy whisper in my heart;
The morning breaks, the shadows flee,
    Pure, universal love thou art;
To me, to all, thy mercies move:
Thy nature and thy name is Love.

My prayer hath power with God; the grace
    Unspeakable I now receive;
Through faith I see thee face to face,
    I see thee face to face, and live!
In vain I have not wept and strove,
Thy nature and thy name is Love.

And Jacob called the name of the place Peniel: for I have seen God face to face, and my life is preserved.

Genesis 32:30

The struggle of the soul is above all the struggle to know a God of love. Wesley knows from experience that, however agonising the struggle, however doubtful the outcome may seem, it is a struggle of faith, not despair. When the moment of discovery comes, then, how fitting that the 'whisper' in the heart is in the language of love poetry: 'My beloved is mine, and I am his . . . until the day break, and the shadows flee away' (Song of Songs 2:16-17). He has caught a life-sustaining glimpse of the face of God, and that face is love.

PRAYER
For your Spirit, who does not cease to struggle within us, we praise you, God of love. Amen.

---

*HSP (1742) RV 25 [3:5 thy bowels] CH 136 HP 434 UMH 386-7

WRESTLING JACOB (4) 75

I know thee, Saviour, who thou art,
Jesus, the feeble sinner's friend;
Nor wilt thou with the night depart,
But stay and love me to the end;
Thy mercies never shall remove,
Thy nature and thy name is Love.

The Sun of Righteousness on me
Hath risen with healing in his wings;
Withered my nature's strength, from thee
My soul its life and succour brings;
My help is all laid up above:
Thy nature and thy name is Love.

Contented now upon my thigh
I halt, till life's short journey end;
All helplessness, all weakness I
On thee alone for strength depend;
Nor have I power from thee to move:
Thy nature and thy name is Love.

Lame as I am, I take the prey,
Hell, earth, and sin with ease o'ercome;
I leap for joy, pursue my way,
And as a bounding hart fly home,
Through all eternity to prove
Thy nature and thy name is Love.

Then the lame shall leap like a deer, and the tongue of the speechless sing for joy.
Isaiah 35:6 (NRSV)

After the earlier verses of agonising struggle, these last sparkle with exultant joy. Again and again they echo the refrain that is the liberating discovery: 'Thy nature and thy name is love.' The image of the bounding deer leaping for joy is caught up in the metre which now seems to rush along, as the traveller with new confidence picks up the journey, knowing the companion and the destination is God.

Every one of these verses could be a source of profound meditation: the constancy of God who does not leave us when the day dawns, the sun of righteousness bringing spiritual health, our wounds a reminder of our need of God, and finally, the image of the hart bounding homeward.

PRAYER
For the wrestling of the Spirit within us, pleading for us and for the whole of creation, waiting expectantly for God's love to be revealed, we praise you, O God. Amen.

---

*HSP (1742) RV 25 CH 136 HP 434 UMH 386-7

Shepherd divine, our wants relieve
In this our evil day,
To all thy tempted followers give
The power to watch and pray.

The Spirit of interceding grace
Give us in faith to claim;
To wrestle till we see thy face
And know thy hidden name.

I will not let thee go, unless
Thou tell thy name to me,
With all thy great salvation bless,
And make me all like thee.

Then let me on the mountain-top
Behold thine open face,
While faith in sight is swallowed up,
And prayer in endless praise.

And Jacob called the name of the place Peniel: for I have seen God face to face and my life is preserved.

Genesis 32:30

When Charles Wesley wrote this hymn, the people called Methodists were suffering persecution, often from those in church and society who might have protected them. The first two lines of the hymn, calling on the 'shepherd divine', bring to mind by way of contrast Ezekiel's reference to the false shepherds of Israel who devoured their flock instead of caring for it (Ezekiel 34:11-19).

In the struggles of daily life, we too wrestle in prayer that we might be conscious of God's power and presence with us. Wesley gives two biblical illustrations of the way in which we may catch a glimpse of this presence. We must be as earnest as Jacob who wrestled with the angel of God, demanding to know the name of the Saviour. We may also expect the occasional 'mountain-top' experience, such as that enjoyed by the disciples on the Mount of Transfiguration, when they caught a glimpse, however fleeting, of Christ's full glory (Matthew 17:5-8).

PRAYER
Mysterious Spirit of God, hold on to me as I struggle to understand who you are. Give me your grace to make me aware of your presence in my life and in the world this day. Amen.

---

*HSP (1749) CH 288 HP 558

Captain of Israel's host, and Guide
Of all who seek the land above,
Beneath thy shadow we abide,
The cloud of thy protecting love;
Our strength, thy grace; our rule, thy word;
Our end, the glory of the Lord.

By the unerring Spirit led,
We shall not in the desert stray;
We shall not full direction need,
Or miss our providential way;
As far from danger as from fear,
While love, almighty love, is near.

The LORD went before them by day in a pillar of cloud, to lead them the way; and by night in a pillar of fire, to give them light; to go by day and night.

Exodus 13:21

In their journey from Egypt to the promised land, the Israelites had unfamiliar and difficult terrain to cross. But as they left Egypt for lands unknown, they discerned before them visible signs to mark the way: a pillar of cloud by day, and at night a pillar of fire, directions provided by the God who journeyed with them.

Wesley assures us that on our pilgrimage through life we too shall not lack direction. God's love and Word are our guides; God's Spirit draws us on in the path marked out by love.

This hymn has been a kind of valedictory anthem for British Methodists. It is always sung at the conclusion of the annual Methodist Conference, and was often sung as a farewell hymn for missionaries setting out on their journey overseas.

PRAYER
Lord, guide us through our earthly pilgrimage, that we wander not aimlessly in the wilderness, but keep steadily to the path you mark out for us until we reach your promised land. Amen.

SH (1762) [1:2 that land 2:1 thine 2:3 The light of man's direction need] *CH 317 HP 62

Omnipotent Redeemer,
Our ransomed souls adore thee:
Our Saviour thou,
We find it now,
And give thee all the glory.
We sing thine arm unshortened,
Brought through our sore temptation;
With heart and voice
In thee rejoice,
The God of our salvation.

Thine arm hath safely brought us
A way no more expected,
Than when thy sheep
Passed through the deep,
By crystal walls protected.
Thy glory was our rearward,
Thine hand our lives did cover,
And we, ev'n we,
Have walked the sea,
And marched triumphant over.

And Moses stretched out his hand over the sea; and the LORD caused the sea to go back by a strong east wind all that night, and made the sea dry land, and the waters were divided. And the children of Israel went into the midst of the sea upon the dry ground: and the waters were a wall unto them on their right hand, and on their left.
Exodus 14:21-22

This hymn was 'written after a deliverance from a tumult': probably the Wednesbury riots of October 1743 when both John and Charles Wesley were in danger of their lives. Charles records it as having been sung after the fierce riots of 1747 in Devizes: 'We joined in hearty praises to our deliverer . . .' The hymn recalls the Exodus story, which is still a powerful inspiration for oppressed peoples as they struggle and look for deliverance.

PRAYER
God my deliverer, I thank you for rescuing me in times of danger, for being my support in dark days, and for bringing me to a safe place. May I trust you as I walk my journey, and know you will always be with me, whatever the future may bring. Amen.

RH (1747) *HP 574

Forward? But whither shall we go?
The desert is on either side,
Behind us the Egyptian foe,
Before, the interposing tide!
Yet while we thy command obey,
Our road impassable pursue,
The ocean yields an open way,
And lets thy ransomed people through.

And the LORD said unto Moses, Wherefore criest thou unto me? speak unto the children of Israel, that they go forward.

Exodus 14:15

Being caught between the devil and the deep blue sea is a familiar inner experience. The ancient legend of the menacing rocks of Scylla and Charybdis threatening sailors whichever direction they took struck the same note as this verse of Charles Wesley's. He imagines the Israelite slaves as they flee Egypt feeling similarly threatened whichever way they move. But the verse catches another familiar experience of those who go forward in faith. That which seems the most threatening prospect so often proves to be the path into a whole new future.

A retired minister was once asked by a young woman for advice about a decision she had to make about her future career. One path, she explained, looked straightforward, leading to almost certain success. The other involved a risk and required her to give up her worldly prospects for the sake of Christian service. 'Whenever you have that kind of decision to make,' said the wise old minister, 'take the one with the risk. That way you will throw yourself on the mercy of God.'

MEDITATION
Ye fearful saints, fresh courage take;
The clouds ye so much dread
Are big with mercy and will break
In blessings on your head. *William Cowper*

---

*SH (1762)

80 FORGIVENESS HEALS

Physician of the sin-sick soul,
  Thou heal'st us when thou dost forgive;
Thy mercy makes, and keeps us whole,
  In perfect health it bids us live.
In perfect holiness renewed,
  And filled with all the life of God.

I am the LORD that healeth thee.

Exodus 15:26

The starting point for this short poem is an incident recounted in the book of Exodus. Having safely crossed the Red Sea, the Israelites have experienced their first three days without fresh water. Their joy at deliverance turns to murmuring against Moses their leader. In response to his prayer, God shows him a certain tree that will 'heal' or sweeten the bitter water.

In the poem, Jesus, the great physician, comes with the healing of forgiveness. As recorded in Mark 2:17, Jesus says to his critics, 'They that are whole have no need of a physician, but they that are sick: I came not to call the righteous, but sinners to repentance.'

Current medical research is discovering ever new evidence of the effect of the mind/spirit on bodily health and disease. Doctors can help in many ways, but when we feel guilty, or 'sin-sick' as Charles puts it, we can be healed only by a more powerful sense of a cleansing forgiveness. Christians experience this in worship, in private prayer, or through many other unexpected means, but thousands have only a vague belief in a judgemental God and find the church an alien place. The good news of God's forgiving love is urgently needed, and only we, as we know ourselves forgiven, can be the hands and feet of Christ to bring this kind of healing to our neighbours.

PRAYER
Our Lord Jesus Christ, present with me now in risen power, enter into my body, mind and spirit, protecting me from all that harms, and filling me with healing and his peace, for your name's sake. Amen.[1]

---

*SH (1762)

ON EAGLES' WINGS 81

As an eagle cleaves the air,
   Whose wings support her young,
Jesus doth his people bear,
   As swift, as smooth, as strong!
Saviour, urge thy rapid flight,
   Soar to that sublime abode,
Bear us far above all height,
   And bring us home to God.

I bare you on eagles' wings, and brought you unto myself.

Exodus 19:4

'You are the wind beneath my wings,' sings Bette Midler in the moving film *Beaches*. It is the story of two friends, one of whom plays a supporting role throughout the career of a successful singing star. It is only when the friend is dying that the star realises how much she has depended on the love and loyalty of that woman, who has been 'the wind beneath her wings'. In the story of almost every person who has reached the heights, there is someone in the background who has made it possible for him or her to take wing and fly.

In this verse Wesley takes hold of the biblical image of one person being borne up by another to describe what it is like to allow Jesus not only to bear us up but even to carry us along on his wings, so that we move at his pace, in his peace and with his power – 'swift, and smooth and strong'. There are times when even young people grow weary or lose heart, but, says the prophet Isaiah, 'they that wait upon the Lord shall renew their strength; they shall mount up with wings as eagles; they shall run and not be weary; they shall walk and not faint'.

PRAYER
Spirit of God, who broods over us like a mother sheltering her young, who teaches us to fly like an eagle, who bears us up as the wind beneath our wings, help us to soar ever upwards, trusting in your power to carry us to the heights, for your name's sake. Amen.

---

*SH (1762)

GOD – GRACIOUS AND LONGSUFFERING

Thy ceaseless, unexhausted love,
Unmerited and free,
Delights our evil to remove
And help our misery.
Thou waitest to be gracious still;
Thou dost with sinners bear,
That, saved, we may thy goodness feel,
And all thy grace declare.

The LORD passed by before him, and proclaimed, The LORD, The LORD God, merciful and gracious, long suffering, and abundant in goodness and truth, keeping mercy for thousands, forgiving iniquity . . .

Exodus 34:6-7a

In the passage from Exodus on which Wesley bases this hymn, Moses has come before the Lord in fear and trembling. He knows that his people have sinned grievously, disobeying the laws of God. Now that Law is to be engraved on two new tablets of stone. God speaks to Moses again in the hidden silence of the mountain, assuring him that though the gravity of the people's sin will affect the community for many generations, the Lord is compassionate and merciful, and forgives iniquity.

It is always God's nature to have mercy, however little we merit it. God 'delights' in showing an unbroken love that never tires of us, as a parent delights in loving even a wayward child and will wait patiently for the child to recognise the error of its ways and respond to that forbearing love.

PRAYER
Lord, we come to you trusting in your mercy and not in any goodness of our own . . . it is your nature always to have mercy, and on that we depend. Amen.[1]
Methodist Service Book

SH (1762) [1:1 Thy causeless] CH 241 *HP 48

GOD – ABUNDANT IN GOODNESS ABUNDANT IN TRUTH

Thy goodness and thy truth to me,
  To every soul, abound,
A vast, unfathomable sea,
  Where all our thoughts are drowned.
Its streams the whole creation reach,
  So plenteous is the store
Enough for all, enough for each,
  Enough for evermore.

Faithful, O Lord, thy mercies are,
  A rock that cannot move;
A thousand promises declare
  Thy constancy of love.
Throughout the universe it reigns,
  Unalterably sure;
And while the truth of God remains
  The goodness must endure.

[Moses] said, I beseech thee, show me thy glory. And [God] said, I will make all my goodness pass before thee.

Exodus 33:18-19

Yesterday, the first stanza of this poem set the scene: the ceaseless, free, unexhausted, unmerited love of God. Today, these two stanzas explore further this love in two biblical metaphors: the sea and the rock. The language is exultant – there are no limits to this love; hence the continuing use of the negatives: 'unfathomable' and 'unalterably'. Words such as 'abound', 'whole', 'vast', 'universe', and the repetition of 'all' encourage us to feel the unlimited extent of the constant love that is God's glory.

Ponder for a moment the sea imagery. God's goodness is like the 'unfathomable' ocean out of which all the continents have emerged, and which unceasingly flows around our whole human habitation. This vast love of God is not just for me – it is for all and for always.

The rock gives another image. We feel its safety and strength; we can rely totally on the promises of God's love, which remains constant through all ages and for all people.

PRAYER
Unbounded God, whose will is that your children should live confidently and joyfully in your love; help me to lose my self-absorption in the ocean of your love for all people; to ground my life on this sure foundation. Amen.

SH (1762) CH 241 *HP 48

O gracious Father! why to man,
So thankless since the world began,
Hast thou thy goodness shown?
Why dost thou help us to believe?
Why dost thou bid us look, and live?
The secret, now, make known!

Or, if thou wilt not yet reveal
What only thy great self canst tell,
Still let us here abide!
Let us thy goodness keep in view,
And let thy goodness keep us true,
Lest from thy ways we slide.

And he [Moses] said, I beseech thee, show me thy glory. And [God] said, I will make all my goodness pass before thee . . . but my face shall not be seen.
Exodus 33:18-19,23 (read verses 9-23)

All of us have moments when the little knowledge of which we feel certain seems quite inadequate for the challenges that we are encountering. At such times, we can sympathise with the story from the life of Moses, to which Wesley's poem makes allusion. Moses had discovered just how tough a task the leadership of his people through the wilderness could be. Looking with alarm at the uncertainties of the road ahead, he asked God for a face-to-face encounter, something that would give him the sort of confidence he was lacking. But this could not be; no mortal can ever receive the full revelation of God. What he was given instead was a glimpse of God's goodness; he was permitted to see where God had been.

Wesley's prayer suggests that this can be enough. The mysteries of life are not ours fully to understand. Nor can we, any more than Moses, or Jesus' disciples on the Mount of Transfiguration, remain always on the privileged mountain-tops of the spirit. But we may ask to carry with us down the paths of life a sustaining memory of the vision of God's goodness.

MEDITATION
Recall an occasion in which, in an unexpected way, you caught a sense of the fundamental goodness of God, and think of the ways in which that experience has helped keep you true.

*UPCW 2, 440

A CHARGE TO KEEP 85

A charge to keep I have:
A God to glorify;
A never-dying soul to save,
And fit it for the sky;
To serve the present age,
My calling to fulfil;
O may it all my powers engage
To do my Master's will!

Arm me with jealous care,
As in thy sight to live;
And O, thy servant, Lord, prepare
A strict account to give!
Help me to watch and pray,
And on thyself rely,
Assured, if I my trust betray
I shall for ever die.

Keep the charge of the LORD, that ye die not.

Leviticus 8:35

One of the most simple, memorable and always contemporary phrases of Charles Wesley, 'to serve the present age', arises from this short meditation on a verse in Leviticus. The original context is part of an ordination ceremony for Aaron as high priest, where the charge was to stay inside the tent for seven days on penalty of death. When Wesley was working on this meditation, he had Matthew Henry's biblical commentary at his side and wrote two verses based on the Puritan writer's words. In modern hymnbooks, this has become a four-stanza hymn. In the 1983 British *Hymns & Psalms,* the final two lines read: 'So shall I not my trust betray, Nor love within me die.'

PRAYER
Lord, grant that my commitment to your service may strengthen my commitment to social responsibility, and help me to see contemporary issues in the light of eternal values. Amen.

*SH (1762) CH 309 HP 785 UMH 413

THE YEAR OF JUBILEE

Blow ye the trumpet, blow!
The gladly solemn sound
Let all the nations know,
To earth's remotest bound:
The year of jubilee is come!
Return, ye ransomed sinners, home.

Jesus, our great high priest,
Hath full atonement made;
Ye weary spirits rest,
Ye mournful souls be glad:
The year of jubilee is come!
Return, ye ransomed sinners, home.

The gospel trumpet hear,
The news of heavenly grace,
And saved from earth, appear
Before your Saviour's face:
The year of jubilee is come!
Return to your eternal home.

Then shalt thou cause the trumpet of the jubilee to sound . . . And ye shall hallow the fiftieth year, and proclaim liberty throughout all the land unto all the inhabitants thereof.

Leviticus 25:9-10

The vision that all work should cease and all Hebrew slaves be liberated at the completion of seven sabbaths of years (forty-nine) is part of the Priestly Code. At the declaration of the Year of Jubilee the slaves return home. Charles Wesley applies this image to Jesus, the great high priest, who died to liberate us from the consequence of our sin. As freed slaves we come home to God. The repetition of the last couplet in each verse adds a solemn ceremonial tone to the whole poem.

This coming home as forgiven people sets us free from old resentments to forgive others as we have been forgiven.

PRAYER
O Christ, you hold open the gate of forgiveness so that I may walk through it. May I return my slaves to their freedom, and live joyfully in your year of jubilee. Amen.

HNYD (1750) PW 6, 12-3 *UMH 379

The eagle fond her charge awakes
  Where in the nest they doze,
And while her fluttering plumes she shakes,
  The way to fly she shows;
She spreads her wings, her young to bear,
  Before their own they try,
And takes them up and cleaves the air,
  And soars above the sky.

'Twas thus in nature's sleep I lay,
  When Christ his Spirit shed;
His Spirit stirred me up to pray,
  And hovered o'er my head,
Infusing the first gracious hope
  He spread his wings abroad,
And trained his infant-pupil up
  To seek the face of God.

As an eagle stirreth up her nest, fluttereth over her young, spreadeth abroad her wings, taketh them, beareth them on her wings: so the LORD alone did lead [Jacob], and there was no strange god with him.

Deuteronomy 32:11-12

Though these verses do not reach the sublime heights of much of Wesley's poetry, they are worth noting for the striking use he makes of the image. The story is of Israel being driven on its way through the wilderness like a young eaglet being forced out of its nest and taught to fly.

Those who live in eagle country often marvel at the great wingspan of these large birds, flying with apparent ease. Yet even their young have to learn how to fly, and are supported by the mother bird until they take wing themselves.

Wesley ingeniously compares that phenomenon to his own experience of learning to pray and to soar up spiritually to the heights of heaven. Maybe he is recalling here how his own mother had, with eagle-like devotion, trained him as an 'infant-pupil'; he recognises in her care the work of Christ's own Spirit, stirring us up to pray.

PRAYER
Grace gives us faith to fortify our reason;
and heaven itself shall be conquered by us. *John Wesley*

---

*SH (1762) PW 9, 108

None is like Jeshurun's God,*
So great, so strong, so high;
Lo! he spreads his wings abroad,
He rides upon the sky:
Israel is his first-born son;
God, the almighty God, is thine;
See him to thy help come down,
The excellence divine.

Thee the great Jehovah deigns
To succour and defend;
Thee the eternal God sustains,
Thy Maker and thy Friend:
Sinner, what hast thou to dread?
Safe from all impending harms,
Round thee and beneath are spread
The everlasting arms.

There is none like unto the God of Jeshurun, who rideth upon the heaven in thy help, and in his excellency on the sky. The eternal God is thy refuge, and underneath are the everlasting arms.

Deuteronomy 33:26-27

Here are two strong models of God. One is as an eagle, carrying us on its wings, the other is of God holding out arms to catch us if we fall. Both have the tangible reality of Hebrew images; both speak to us of the security of parental love.

In a book written in 1896, William Cornaby, a scholar of Chinese culture and a Methodist missionary there tells of a dialogue he had with a native woman. He likened her devoted care for her child to the sacrificial care of the great 'Father-Mother God'. 'Would you rather suffer than let your child suffer?' Yes, she would. 'And do you know that is the same with our good Father-Mother above?'[1] And so on. This image of God loving us with a mother's care seems so natural that one wonders why it should now be cause for controversy.

PRAYER
Eternal God, strong Mother and Father, Maker and Friend, sustain me in all the trials of life; nourish me, defend me, and if I fall, hold out your loving arms to receive me, through Jesus Christ. Amen.

HSP (1742) *CH 395 MHB 68

---

* Jeshurun is an ancient name for Israel.

That thy stock may never cease,
That thy little may increase,
Gladly of that little give,
Poor thyself, the poor relieve;
The great prophet entertain,
Sure eternally to gain
All the infinite reward,
All the glory of thy Lord.

For thus saith the LORD God of Israel, The barrel of meal shall not waste, neither shall the cruse of oil fail, until the day that the Lord sendeth rain upon the earth.
1 Kings 17:14

The setting for this verse is the story of the unnamed widow – a non-Israelite from Sidon – who nourishes the refugee prophet Elijah with her last food and drink. To get the most from the story, read the whole of 1 Kings 17. The woman who, in a time of famine, is prepared to share the little she has finds that the promise of the prophet comes true, and she has enough food to supply herself and her son until the rains come.

This miracle story recalls another, the story of Jesus feeding the five thousand. There, too, one person shares the little he has (and perhaps encourages others to do the same). In Christ's hands the little becomes enough to feed the multitude. Look at the emphasis Wesley places on the generosity of the woman. The line 'poor thyself, the poor relieve' speaks volumes about giving. Very often a person who knows hardship – whether it is hunger, loss, or loneliness – is the first person to reach out to others in need. Those who have much often do not see or understand the needs of those who have little. Those who give even the little they have receive great blessing in return.

MEDITATION
What hardship in my own life could be used to bless others? How can I understand the suffering of those who have to cope with hardships that I have not experienced? Perhaps the secret is in creative listening and being open to receive help from others myself.

PRAYER
Lord, may I, who have never known what it is to be really hungry, never cease to minister to the needs of those who have never known what it is to be really full. Amen. *Nadir Dinshaw*

---

*SH (1762)

Be it my only wisdom here
To serve the Lord with filial fear,
With loving gratitude;
Superior sense may I display,
By shunning every evil way,
And walking in the good.

O may I still from sin depart!
A wise and understanding heart,
Jesus, to me be given;
And let me through thy Spirit know
To glorify my God below,
And find my way to heaven.

Behold, the fear of the LORD, that is wisdom; and to depart from evil is understanding.
Job 28:28

The real question for Job – and for us also – is: 'Where shall wisdom be found?' (Job 28:12). After an imaginative hunt for wisdom in all the places and precious things of the earth, finally God gives Job the answer: fear (or reverence) God and avoid evil. Jesus has shown, moreover, that our relationship to God is one of 'filial fear' – the respect of a child for a loving parent. Finally, the hymn reminds us of the plea of Solomon, who, at the beginning of his reign asks for 'a wise and understanding heart' (1 Kings 3:12).

For Wesley, true wisdom is the gift of the Holy Spirit. It is the love of God, empowering us not just to avoid evil, but also to 'walk in the good'. This is our 'only wisdom' – the sure foundation for today and all the days of our lives.

PRAYER
O Christ, my Master and Lord, grant that I may see thee more clearly, love thee more dearly, and follow thee more nearly day by day. Amen. *Richard of Chichester*

---

*SH (1762) CH 311 HP 786

Thou to me, O God, hast sent,
Food and raiment and content;
Yet for farther grace I sue,
For poverty and riches too.
Both, and both at once, I want:
Poverty of spirit grant,
And fill me, Father, from above
With all the riches of thy love.

Give me neither poverty nor riches; feed me with the food convenient for me.
Proverbs 30:8

This poem, inspired by the passage in Proverbs, quickly moves away from the original literal meaning, a request for a simple but sufficient standard of living. 'Blessed are the poor in spirit, for theirs is the kingdom of heaven,' says Jesus (Matthew 5:3); this poverty Wesley invites us to pray for, along with the riches of God's love.

Jean Vanier, founder and sustainer of l'Arche at Trosly-Breuil in France, and other similar homes for mentally disabled persons, speaks eloquently about the gifts of those who are poor in spirit:

> I have seen the most extraordinary progress in grace and love in people who are very poor humanly and psychologically, who can hardly talk, who always live on the verge of some crisis or other. I have seen Raphael, radiant with joy. One feels his presence in the group and yet he is severely handicapped . . . They have taught me more about the gospel and even about human relationships than all the great psychological and philosophical concepts; or rather, they have allowed me to catch a glimpse of what should be true theology . . . I have discovered Jesus in them . . .[1]

PRAYER
Creator God, you love all your creation; you speak through those who allow your love to flow through their lives. Grant me the grace to let down my defences and live in the simplicity of poverty of heart and life. So may I be open to share the riches of your love with all those whom I meet. Amen.

---

*SH (1762) RV 157

92 TRUE WISDOM (1)

Happy the one who finds the grace,
The blessing of God's chosen race,
The wisdom coming from above,
The faith that sweetly works by love.

Happy beyond description we
Who know 'The Saviour died for me',
The gift unspeakable obtain,
And heavenly understanding gain.

Wisdom divine! Who tells the price
Of wisdom's costly merchandise?
Wisdom to silver we prefer,
And gold is dross compared to her.

Happy are those who find wisdom, and those who get understanding, for her income is better than silver, and her revenue better than gold.
Proverbs 3:13-14 (NRSV) (read to verse 18)

This is the first half of a hymn in praise of wisdom. For the Hebrew people, true wisdom was rooted in a right relationship with God. Wesley takes a passage from Proverbs, and weaves into it Christian insights from the words of Paul and Peter.

His fondness for the word 'happy' (see also the last verse of tomorrow's reading) reminds us that for Israel, happiness was the characteristic of a life lived in wisdom. The 'chosen race' (verse 1:2) alludes to God's calling of Israel to be God's people, a call which Peter extends to the Gentiles (1 Peter 2:9). Paul situates the heart of right living in 'faith that works by love' (Galatians 5:6), in the 'unspeakable gift' of God (2 Corinthians 9:15).

PRAYER
Generous God, of your great bounty you have given us all things. We ask for one more gift: the wisdom of heavenly understanding, that we may discern your will, walk in your way of simplicity, and find our happiness, through Jesus Christ our Lord. Amen.

Redemption Hymns (1747) *CH 14 [1:1 the man who 2:1-4 he . . . knows . . . obtains . . . gains]
HP 674

TRUE WISDOM (2) 93

Her hands are filled with length of days,
True riches, and immortal praise,
Riches of Christ, on all bestowed,
And honour, that descends from God.

To purest joys she all invites,
Chaste, holy, spiritual delights;
Her ways are ways of pleasantness,
And all her flowery paths are peace.

Happy are they who wisdom gain;
Thrice happy who this guest retain;
They own, and shall forever own,
Wisdom, and Christ, and heaven are one.

Length of days is in her right hand; and in her left hand riches and honour. Her ways are ways of pleasantness, and all her paths are peace.

Proverbs 3:16-17

Continuing yesterday's poem, Wesley's subject is wisdom, personified as a woman whose wise teaching enriches the lives of those who follow her. For those accustomed to the traditional portrayal of sages and teachers as men, it can be refreshing to discover that in Hebrew tradition, wisdom is a feminine figure. Hers is the insight of the created world; she invites us to the goodness of life in covenant with God. This is not at all a sombre, joyless life. Feasting with friends, flowers on pleasant and peaceful paths – life with divine wisdom knows its share of delights.

Jesus' first followers, as Jews, were of course familiar with this tradition. It is not surprising, then, that they identify Jesus, the teacher and the giver of eternal life, with the Wisdom of God (1 Corinthians 1:23-24) In this hymn, Wesley weaves together themes from Hebrew and Christian traditions, celebrating the richness of life as he knows it in Christ, and inviting all the world to receive this wise guest, to discover indeed that 'wisdom and Christ and heaven are one'.

PRAYER
Gracious God, you remind me of what is really important in life. Call me back to where I belong, that I may find my happiness in the true riches of Christ. Amen.

Redemption Hymns (1747) *CH 14 [3:1 the man who . . . gains 3:2 who his guest retains 3:3 He owns] HP 674

WATCH IN ALL THINGS

Jesus, my Saviour, Brother, Friend,
  On whom I cast my every care,
On whom for all things I depend,
  Inspire, and then accept my prayer.

If I have tasted of thy grace,
  The grace that sure salvation brings,
If with me now thy Spirit stays,
  And hovering hides me in his wings:

Still let him with my weakness stay,
  Nor for a moment's space depart,
Evil and danger turn away,
  And keep till he renews my heart.

When to the right or left I stray,
  His voice behind me may I hear:
Return, and walk in Christ thy way;
  Fly back to Christ, for sin is near.

Uphold me, Saviour, or I fall;
  O reach me out thy gracious hand!
Only on thee for help I call,
  Only by faith in thee I stand.

Thine ears shall hear a word behind thee, saying, This is the way, walk ye in it, when ye turn to the right hand, and when ye turn to the left.

Isaiah 30:21

At its root, the word 'friend' is related to the word 'freedom'. It suggests a relationship we are free to choose, and a relationship in which we are free to be ourselves. But because the relationship depends on such free choice, it has to be nurtured by regular communication and by common pursuits. One should never take one's friends for granted, but cherish their companionship.

Jesus bestowed the title 'friends' upon his disciples when he felt that they understood enough of the way he was walking to go with him. He promised them his constant presence, even when he was no longer visible to them. So, in this hymn, we pray for the awareness of that presence throughout our own life's journey.

PRAYER
Don't walk before me,
I may not follow;
Don't walk behind me,
I may not lead;
Just walk beside me
And be my friend. *Source unknown*

HSP (1742) *CH 303 MHB 478

Welcome as the water-spring
To a dry, barren place,
O descend on me, and bring
Thy sweet refreshing grace!
O'er a parched and weary land
As a great rock extends its shade,
Hide me, Saviour, with thine hand,
And screen my naked head.

First and last in me perform
The work thou hast begun;
Be my shelter from the storm,
My shadow from the sun;
Weary, parched with thirst, and faint,
Till thou the abiding Spirit breathe,
Every moment, Lord, I want
The merit of thy death.

Each will be like a hiding place from the wind, a covert from the tempest, like streams of water in a dry place, like the shade of a great rock in a weary land.

Isaiah 32:2 (NRSV)

The prophecy of Isaiah, promising the coming of just rulers who will protect their people, becomes a prayer of petition in these verses of Wesley. Hebrew images of unrelenting heat and drought, so familiar to those living in arid regions, now have more meaning for us, as global climate change affects formerly fertile lands. Now we are struck by the emotional power of these words: water which springs up to quench deep thirst, the rock as shelter from the sun's unrelenting blaze, and as safety in the storm; a crevice in the rock as a place in which to hide.

The efficacy of prayer is proved in experience. Charles Wesley could recall times when he had known God's care, protection and love. It had happened before; let it happen again.

PRAYER
Rock of ages, cleft for me,
Let me hide myself in thee. *Augustus Toplady*

HSP (1742) CH 283 * MHB 459

ISAIAH THIRTY-FIVE

Lo! for us the wilds are glad,
All in cheerful green arrayed;
Opening sweets they all disclose,
Bud and blossom as the rose.

Hark! the wastes have found a voice!
Lonely deserts now rejoice,
Gladsome hallelujahs sing,
All around with praises ring.

See these barren souls of ours
Bloom, and put forth fruits and flowers,
Flowers of Eden, fruits of grace,
Peace, and joy, and righteousness.

Blind we were, but now we see;
Deaf – we harken now to thee;
Dumb – for thee our tongues employ;
Lame – and lo! we leap for joy!

The wilderness and the solitary place shall be glad for them; and the desert shall rejoice, and blossom as the rose.

Isaiah 35:1 (read verses 1-10)

Isaiah's glowing vision of hope and transformation for the exiled people of Israel is the foundation of these selections from a twenty-verse poem. Wesley adds another transformation as he makes it personal to the reader or singer. 'The wilderness . . . shall be glad,' says Isaiah; 'Lo! for us the wilds are glad,' says Wesley. 'Then shall the lame man leap as an hart . . .' says Isaiah; 'lo! we leap for joy!' says Wesley. His own once barren life has burst into bloom as the result of the heart-warming experience of God's grace in May 1738. Now it is as though the whole earth shares his joy, a joy which we too can share.

PRAYER
Come to my dry and parched life, and water it with the streams of your grace, O God, that my desert may blossom and produce good fruits of peace and joy and righteousness. Amen.

HSP (1740) *CH 339

Head of thy church triumphant,
We joyfully adore thee;
Till thou appear,
Thy members here
Shall sing like those in glory.
We lift our hearts and voices
With blest anticipation,
And cry aloud,
And give to God
The praise of our salvation.

While in affliction's furnace,
And passing through the fire,
Thy love we praise,
Which knows our days
And ever brings us nigher.
We clap our hands exulting
In thine almighty favour;
The love divine
Which made us thine
Shall keep us thine for ever.

Thus saith the LORD that created thee . . . Fear not, for I have redeemed thee . . . when thou walkest through the fire, thou shalt not be burned; neither shall the flame kindle upon thee.

Isaiah 43:1-2

This hymn was originally written for the 'time of tumult' in 1745 when, in the national crisis of the Jacobite uprising, Methodists were suspected of treason. The hymn recalls miracles by which God's people have been saved in times of great affliction. For example, in the story in Daniel 3, the Hebrew slaves, who were cast into the fiery furnace for their refusal to bow down before the gods of Babylon, were protected by the divine presence of one who appeared beside them. So we too, when we are passing through a time of trial, can be assured that God is keeping watch over us.

PRAYER
O God, in all our dangers keep us aware of your protecting presence, and in all the changing scenes of life may we know we are always in your care. Amen.

HTT (1745) RV 33 *HP 818

Enlarge thy dwelling-place, extend
Thy pale to earth's remotest end,
  Within no narrow bounds confined.
With cords of everlasting love,
With stakes of truth that cannot move,
  Spread out thy tent for all mankind.

Enlarge the place of thy tent, and let them stretch forth the curtains of thine habitations: spare not, lengthen thy cords, and strengthen thy stakes.

Isaiah 54:2

In times of stress, the natural reaction of a community is to look inward; we are tempted to preoccupy ourselves with the life of the group we feel we can trust, to operate on a scale we can manage. In contrast, in the fifth century before Christ, the Jewish prophet called on his people exiled in Babylon not to let themselves be caught in a narrow religious nationalism, but rather to expand the horizons of the spirit in embracing their calling as a 'light to the nations'. Similarly, John and Charles Wesley preached the renewal of their own Church of England in a breaking down of old élitisms. Their mission in the public streets and fields of England was a real bursting of 'narrow bounds', a spreading of the gospel tent to welcome the whole human race.

In our day, the ecumenical vision pushes at the confining borders of our religious loyalties, challenging us to 'enlarge our dwelling place' to include the whole inhabited earth. Where God's house is extended on 'cords of everlasting love', it will have a place for all who seek the truth that sets us free.

PRAYER

Eternal God, whose image lies in the hearts of all people,
We live among peoples whose ways are different from ours, whose faiths are foreign to us . . .
Help us to remember that you love all people with your great love, that all religion is an attempt to respond to you, that the yearnings of other hearts are much like our own and are known to you.
Help us to recognise you in the words of truth, the things of beauty, the actions of love around us. Amen.[1] *World Council of Churches*

*SH (1762)

Ho! every one that thirsts, draw nigh,
('Tis God invites the fallen race),
Mercy and free salvation buy;
Buy wine, and milk, and gospel grace.

Come to the living waters, come!
Sinners, obey your Maker's call;
Return, ye weary wanderers, home,
And find my grace is free for all.

Why seek ye that which is not bread,
Nor can your hungry souls sustain?
On ashes, husks, and air ye feed;
Ye spend your little all in vain.

In search of empty joys below,
Ye toil with unavailing strife;
Whither, ah whither would you go?
I have the words of endless life.

Ho, everyone who thirsts, come to the waters; and you that have no money, come, buy and eat! Come, buy wine and milk without money and without price. Why do you spend your money for that which is not bread, and your labour for that which does not satisfy?

Isaiah 55:1-2 (NRSV)

Wesley's imagination is caught by the prophet's cry. Like a woman at an oriental market stall offering food and drink to all comers, Isaiah's God invites his people in Babylonian exile to rediscover the riches and satisfaction of the gift of covenant relationship. The words of the prophet suggest to Wesley the evangelist many parallels from the gospels.

These were the words, too, which his brother John took as his text for one of his first ventures in open-air preaching, to colliers in a field near Bristol. There, on 8th April 1739, John discovered to his astonishment that there really was a hunger and thirst among the poor for 'the words of eternal life' (John 6:68). A lifetime mission was born.

PRAYER

I hunger and I thirst, Jesu, my manna be;
Ye living waters burst out of the rock for me. *J. S. B. Monsell*

HSP (1740) *CH 4

Eternal beam of light divine,
Fountain of unexhausted love,
In whom the Father's glories shine,
Through earth beneath, and heaven above!

Jesu, the weary wanderer's rest,
Give me thy easy yoke to bear,
With steadfast patience arm my breast,
With spotless love and lowly fear.

Be thou, O Rock of Ages, nigh!
So shall each murmuring thought be gone,
And grief, and fear, and care shall fly,
As clouds before the midday sun.

Speak to my warring passions: Peace!
Say to my trembling heart: Be still!
Thy power my strength and fortress is,
For all things serve thy sovereign will.

O death! Where is thy sting? Where now
Thy boasted victory, O grave?
Who shall contend with God: Or who
Can hurt whom God delights to save?

O LORD, my strength, and my fortress, and my refuge in the day of affliction.
Jeremiah 16:19

The title of this hymn, 'In Affliction', gives us the vantage point to understand the energy behind it. When life presents us with more than we can cope with, we search for meaning in our distress. Wesley does the same. The starting point is his urgent need for emotional calm, shown in verse four. The first line echoes Jesus' words in the storm: 'Peace, be still' (Mark 4:39); the second line draws as well on Psalm 46:10: 'Be still, and know that I am God.'

When things are in turmoil Charles literally 'recalls' Jesus, both the divine 'fountain of unexhausted love,' and the human one who invites us to come in our burdened life, and learn to share his easy yoke (Matthew 11:28-9). What more could we want for this life and the next?

PRAYER
God, you are the beginning and the end of my life, and of all things. In my distress, comfort and calm me, in my fear support me, and in my loneliness be present as a friend, for the sake of your Son Jesus, who experienced all this before me. Amen.

---

*HSP (1739) RV 6 CH 328 MHB 496

Sing, ye happy souls, that press
Toward the height of holiness,
Praise him whom in part ye know;
Freely to his goodness flow,
All his promises receive,
All the grace he hath to give.

Jointly, Lord, we come to thee,
All in one request agree:
Feed us with the living bread,
With thyself our spirits feed,
Give the unction from above,
Oil of joy, and wine of love.

For thy truth and mercy's sake,
As a watered garden make
Every soul that gasps for God,
With thine holiest love o'erflowed,
Till by just degrees we rise
In terrestrial paradise.

They shall come and sing in the height of Zion, and shall flow together to the goodness of the LORD, for wheat, and for wine, and for oil, and for the young of the flock and of the herd: and their soul shall be as a watered garden; and they shall not sorrow any more.

Jeremiah 31:12

Charles Wesley makes his own Jeremiah's vivid image of the soul as 'a watered garden': our souls, being dry, 'gasp for God'; it is God's love which overflows in us until we live as it were in an earthly paradise – a return to the Garden of Eden – a return to perfection. The wheat, wine and oil of the prosperous land envisaged by Jeremiah become metaphors of Christ, the bread of life. And, like Jeremiah, Wesley invites us to join in the songs of pilgrims on their journey to Zion, the 'height of holiness'.

PRAYER

Come to our dry hearts, O God, and pour into them your overflowing goodness, so that we may be as watered gardens – green and fruitful. Amen.

*SH (1762) *SH (1796) [3:6 Thy]

Our earth we now lament to see
 With floods of wickedness o'erflowed,
With violence, wrong and cruelty,
 One wide-extended field of blood,
Where hosts like fiends each other tear
 In all the hellish rage of war.

O might the universal Friend
 This havoc of his creatures see!
Bid our unnatural discord end,
 Declare us reconciled in thee!
Write kindness on our inward parts
 And chase the murderer from our hearts!

Who now against each other rise,
 The nations of the earth constrain
To follow after peace, and prize
 The blessings of thy righteous reign,
The joys of unity to prove,
 The paradise of perfect love!

But this shall be the covenant that I will make with the house of Israel; After those days, saith the LORD, I will put my law in their inward parts, and write it in their hearts; and will be their God, and they shall be my people.

Jeremiah 31:33

There is nothing new in war, but to each generation its monstrosity strikes with fresh horror. In our nuclear age, when we have power to destroy all life, a prevalent feeling is that of helplessness in the face of human inability to live in peace.

Reconciliation begins at home. That means starting where we are and building upon the work of others. The Taizé Community – known for its worldwide encouragement of peace – says simply:

> What characterises those who seek reconciliation is that, following Christ, they wish to fulfil more than to destroy, to understand more than to exhort.[1]

PRAYER
Reconciling God, you love your whole creation. Help me to work for peace with justice in every part of my life and in the life of the world, that we all may be one in your paradise of perfect love. Amen.

HIAM (1758) PW 6, 112-3 *UMH 449 [1:5 where men]

Physician of the sin-sick race,
Come with thy plenitude of grace
To this poor dying soul;
The oil and wine of grace pour in,
And heal the desperate wounds of sin,
And make my spirit whole.

Ah, give me, Lord, in thee to find
The spirit of an healthful mind,
The kingdom from above;
Thine utmost truth in me reveal,
Mine unbelief and misery heal
By perfect peace and love.

Thy presence doth my bliss ensure,
Thy presence is my nature's cure,
The Truth, the Peace thou art;
And thee possessing, I possess
Life – everlasting righteousness –
Perfection in my heart.

I will bring [this city] health and cure, and I will cure them, and will reveal unto them the abundance of peace and truth.

Jeremiah 33:6

One of the most poignant notes in the prophet Jeremiah is his grief over the sickness of the society in which he lived. Looking at his people's unfaithfulness to God's covenant, their greed and injustice to the poor and weak, Jeremiah likens the situation to an open sore, whose infection he feels personally (Jeremiah 8:21-2).

In his later years the prophet discovers hope in the God who brings healing to a suffering world. Wesley is moved here by the prophet's words to express his own need, and that of his world, 'the sin-sick race', for healing. God is indeed the great 'physician', whose presence, like the Good Samaritan's, brings 'the oil and wine of grace' to restore health in us, and bring healing to the nations.

PRAYER
Great Physician, by the light of your truth, show us what is unhealthy in our lives; by the medicine of your love, bring us and our world to wholeness and peace. Amen.

SH (1762) *SH (1796)

ON A JOURNEY

Come, all whoe'er have set
Your faces Zion-ward,
In Jesus let us meet,
And praise our common Lord;
In Jesus let us still walk on,
Till all appear before his throne.

Nearer, and nearer still,
We to our country come,
To that celestial hill,
The weary pilgrim's home:
The New Jerusalem above,
The seat of everlasting love.

The peace and joy of faith
We every moment feel,
Redeemed from sin and wrath,
And death and earth, and hell,
We to our Father's house repair,
To meet our elder Brother there.

The children of Israel shall come, they and the children of Judah together, going and weeping: they shall go, and seek the LORD their God. They shall ask the way to Zion.
Jeremiah 50:4-5

The image of life in Christ as a pilgrimage is vividly portrayed in *The Pilgrim's Progress* by John Bunyan, a book from his parents' generation that Charles Wesley knew well. In the first, better known part, Bunyan recounts the frequent hardships encountered by the lonely traveller, Christian, as he made his way from the City of Destruction. The second part gives the account of his wife Christiana's subsequent journey with their children. For them, the loneliness of the way is overcome by the companionship of others who join them on the journey to the Celestial City. The road is the same, but they more frequently find inns and hospitable resting places; they enjoy times of music and merriment together.

In this hymn, which may remind us of Isaac Watts' similar 'Come, we that love the Lord', Charles Wesley invites us to discover the way of Christ as a pilgrimage of companions, who walk together in the praise of God and the mutual love of friendship, who share the anticipated joy of homecoming.

PRAYER
Fix thou our steps, O Lord, that we stagger not at the uneven motions of the world, but steadily go on to our glorious home; neither censuring our journey by the weather we meet with, nor turning out of the way for anything that befalls us. For the sake of Jesus Christ our Lord. Amen. *John Wesley*

---

*HSP (1749) CH 484 MHB 606

Make our earthly souls a field
Which God delights to bless,
Let us in due season yield
The fruits of righteousness;
Make us trees of paradise
Which more and more thy praise may show,
Deeper sink and higher rise,
And to perfection grow.

And the tree of the field shall yield her fruit, and the earth shall yield her increase, and they shall be safe in their land.

Ezekiel 34:27

Injustice was rife in Israel; leaders had been tending to themselves instead of to their flock, and both land and people suffered from their selfishness and neglect. The prophet foresees a time when God will replace this misrule with an age of divine rule. Under this covenant of peace, people will experience justice; and the land itself will grow fertile again, watered by abundant showers of blessing.

This prophecy of wholeness becomes a parable for our lives in Wesley's verse. There are two metaphors within the larger one. First, our souls are the nourishing soil of the earth (both earthy and earthly), which, when blessed by God, will produce good fruit at the proper time. There are echoes of the parable of the sower here also. In the second metaphor we become trees, with strong roots sinking deeper into good earth as the tops reach to the sky. But we are not just trees – we are trees of paradise – with all that implies of the perfection of the Garden of Eden. So it is that the overriding image is none other than our reunion with the perfection of God.

MEDITATION

With these images in mind, take a walk into a wood or a forest, or if that is impossible, stand or sit under any tree and take time for reflection. How do you see yourself as being part of the wholeness of creation? How can you contribute to its harmony and well-being?

---

*SH (1796)

SLIPPING BACK

How am I healed, if still again
I must relapse with grief and pain
  Into my old disease?
If Christ with all his power and love,
Can never perfectly remove
  My desperate wickedness?

But Lord, I trust, thy gracious skill
Shall throughly my backslidings heal,
  My sinfulness of soul,
Destroy the bent to sin in me,
Cure my original malady,
  And make, and keep me whole.

I will heal their backsliding, I will love them freely: for mine anger is turned away from him.

Hosea 14:4

This is more a personal poem than a corporate hymn. Charles Wesley is very conscious of his failings. He keeps going wrong. As he says elsewhere, echoing Paul, he is not just a sinner, but the chief of sinners; his sin is more than sin, it is wickedness. And it is not ordinary wickedness but 'desperate wickedness'. The near-angry tone of the opening lines expresses his frustration.

These words of Hosea first provoke and then comfort him, as they may do others who feel trapped in some desperate, endless cycle of addiction, partial recovery and further addiction. The second verse expresses Wesley's confidence that the skill of Christ the healer can correct this 'bent to sin' and that by God's grace he can be permanently cured.

PRAYER
Wilt thou forgive that sin where I begun
Which was my sin, though it were done before?
Wilt thou forgive that sin, through which I run,
And do run still: though still I do deplore?
When thou hast done, thou hast not done,
For I have more . . . *John Donne*

---

*SH (1796) PW 10, 84-5

WHAT SHALL I GIVE? 107

Wherewith, O God, shall I draw near,
  And bow myself before thy face?
How in thy purer eyes appear?
  What shall I bring to gain thy grace?

What gifts delight the Lord our God?
  Can these wash out my guilty stain?
Rivers of oil, and seas of blood,
  Alas! they all must flow in vain.

Whoe'er to thee themselves approve
  Must take the path thy Word hath showed,
Justice pursue, and mercy love,
  And humbly walk by faith with God.

Wherewith shall I come before the LORD, and bow myself before the high God? What doth the LORD require of thee, but to do justly, and to love mercy, and to walk humbly with thy God?

Micah 6:6,8

These are the first three verses of a thirteen-verse hymn in which Wesley acknowledges that he has not met the prophet's call for justice, mercy and love. Nonetheless, he trusts that through the atoning love manifest in Christ's life and death he will be forgiven.

Can any of us hear the Micah passage without some sense of failure? We may offer to God all kinds of prayer, regular worship and many good works, but the prophet warns that these still fall short of the standard God requires of us. If in our desperately unjust world we turn a blind eye to the wrongs imposed on others; if in this callous and judgemental world we do not always act with compassion; and if we ever feel over-confident in ourselves, then we have need to ask for God's forgiveness and turn again to walk humbly in the light of his Word.

PRAYER
Righteous God, you have shown me what is good; teach me how to work for justice, to love with mercy and to walk by faith in the way of Christ. Amen.

---

*HSP (1740) CH 123 MHB 343

Jesu, lover of my soul,
Let me to thy bosom fly,
While the nearer waters roll,
While the tempest still is high;
Hide me, O my Saviour, hide,
Till the storm of life is past;
Safe into the haven guide,
O receive my soul at last!

Other refuge have I none,
Hangs my helpless soul on thee;
Leave, ah, leave me not alone,
Still support and comfort me.
All my trust on thee is stayed
All my help from thee I bring;
Cover my defenceless head
With the shadow of thy wing.

Plenteous grace with thee is found,
Grace to cover all my sin;
Let the healing streams abound,
Make, and keep me pure within.
Thou of life the fountain art;
Freely let me take of thee;
Spring thou up within my heart,
Rise to all eternity.

But thou sparest all, for they are thine, O LORD, thou lover of souls.

Wisdom 11:26

This, one of the most familiar of Charles Wesley's hymns, is also one of the most passionate. He wrote it soon after his conversion experience. It is still good medicine in times of distress and disaster. When we have failed, or done wrong and hurt others; when we feel desperately vulnerable; when we are sick, or lonely, or sad; when life is just too much for us; when we are too unhappy even to formulate a prayer, these words say it for us. Thanks be to God.

PRAYER
'Thou, O Christ, art all I want, more than all in thee I find.' Be the sure companion of all who need you this day, for the sake of your truth and grace. Amen.

---

*HSP (1740) RV 15 HP 528 UMH 749 VU 669

'This night thou shalt deny me thrice'
Is the meek Master's warning word,
'I never will,' the servant cries,
And boldly contradicts his Lord;
'Though all beside turn back and flee,
I vow to live and die with thee.'

The Saviour sad replies no more,
Nor eagerly his word defends,
But leaves it to the trying hour;
And who on his own strength depends,
Peter the confident, the proud,
Abjures his Master and his God.

Much of myself I dare not say,
Or glory in my faith unproved,
Or promise in the evil day
That I alone shall stand unmoved;
Weakest and sinfullest of all,
I fear to affirm, 'I cannot fall.'

Peter said to him, 'Even though all become deserters, I will not.' Jesus said to him, 'Truly I tell you, this day, this very night, before the cock crows twice, you will deny me three times.' But he said vehemently, 'Even though I must die with you, I will not deny you.' And all of them said the same.

Mark 14:29-31 (NRSV)

Mark, who as a scribe is closely associated with Peter, describes this incident vividly. Peter's bold declaration is full of dramatic irony. At a Maundy Thursday rereading of this story in a local church, the solemn atmosphere was broken by a hoot of laughter from a newcomer who had never heard the story before! How like human nature it all is. How real, how tragic.

Wesley uses this story as a reminder that only life and time can tell whether our actions match our words. As Christ does not argue the point with Peter, so he waits for our actions to prove our brave words. A little self-understanding that we can and do fail is a healthy antidote to pride.

MEDITATION
Read the sequel to the story in Mark 14:66-72, using it as a source of personal reflection.

---

*PW 11, 75-6

110 FALSE STRENGTH

See the strength that is in man!
  Peter by a word o'erthrown
Checks our self-presumption vain,
  Makes our utter weakness known.
Thus we feel our helplessness,
  Tremble at temptation nigh,
Own our constant need of grace,
  From ourselves to Jesus fly.

And Simon Peter stood and warmed himself. They said therefore unto him, Art not thou also one of his disciples? He denied it, and said, I am not.

John 18:25

To appreciate the irony of Peter's denial when confronted by the servant girl after the arrest of Jesus, one needs to compare it with his earlier declaration of loyalty. During what would be the last supper shared with his disciples, Jesus warned them of the coming struggle. Peter replied, in the words of Luke, 'Lord, I am ready to go with thee, both into prison, and to death.' To this Jesus replied, 'I tell you, Peter, the cock shall not crow this day, before that thou shalt thrice deny that thou knowest me' (Luke 22:33-34).

But it is not just Peter who fails Jesus. Luke reports these words after a quarrel among the disciples about who is the greatest; John records the incident after Judas has gone out to betray Jesus. Friends can betray each other, misunderstand each other, promise loyalty and fail, be competitive when they should be in community – all these experiences remind us that we too can behave like that. In Wesley's words they show our 'utter weakness, our helplessness', and our need to rely not on our own worth but on God's free grace.

PRAYER
O God, only you know the many times I fail you, fail my friends and those around me. As you forgave Peter, forgive me, and give me your grace to know my own weakness. Save me from presumptuous sin and teach me to trust only in your mercy and not in any goodness of my own. Amen.

---

*UPCW 2, 268

God of unexampled grace,
   Redeemer of mankind,
Matter of eternal praise
   We in thy passion find;
Still our choicest strains we bring,
   Still the joyful theme pursue,
Thee the friend of sinners sing
   Whose love is ever new.

Endless scenes of wonder rise
   From that mysterious tree,
Crucified before our eyes
   Where we our Maker see:
Jesus, Lord, what hast thou done?
   Publish we the death divine,
Stop, and gaze, and fall, and own
   Was never love like thine!

Never love nor sorrow was
   Like that my Jesus showed;
See him stretched on yonder cross,
   And crushed beneath our load!
Now discern the Deity,
   Now his heavenly birth declare!
Faith cries out: 'Tis he, 'tis he,
   My God, that suffers there!

Is it nothing to you, all ye that pass by? Behold, and see if there be any sorrow like unto my sorrow, which is done unto me.

Lamentations 1:12

These are the first three verses of a nine-verse poem which will be followed through the next two days, a text that takes us on a dramatic visit to the dying Christ on the cross.

From his Gestapo prison, Dietrich Bonhoeffer reflected on the mystery of a God who shares human suffering:

> People draw near to God in his distress,
> find him rejected, homeless, without bread,
> burdened with sin and weakness, nearly dead.
> Christians stand with God in his wretchedness.[1]

PRAYER
God, grant I may have the courage to be present with you as you suffer with all your creation. Amen.

---

*HLS (1745) RV 54 HP 166

Jesus drinks the bitter cup;
The wine-press treads alone,
Tears the graves and mountains up
By his expiring groan;
Lo! the powers of heaven he shakes;
Nature in convulsion lies,
Earth's profoundest centre quakes.
The great Jehovah dies!

Dies the glorious Cause of all,
The true eternal Pan,
Falls to raise us from our Fall,
To ransom sinful man:
Well may Sol withdraw his light
With the sufferer sympathise,
Leave the world in sudden night,
While his creator dies.

Well may heaven be clothed with black
And solemn sackcloth wear,
Jesu's agony partake
The hour of darkness share:
Mourn the astonished hosts above,
Silence saddens all the skies,
Kindler of seraphic love
The God of angels dies.

Now from the sixth hour there was darkness over all the land unto the ninth hour . . . Jesus, when he had cried again with a loud voice, yielded up the ghost . . . and the earth did quake, and the rocks rent . . .

Matthew 27:45,50-51

J. Ernest Rattenbury has compared this part of Wesley's poem to a Renaissance painting: 'Botticelli could have written it if he had been a poet.'[1] Like Milton, Wesley dares to draw upon classical mythology for images to express the cosmic enormity of this death. All nature, too, dresses itself in mourning, watching in awed silence as the creator dies.

MEDITATION
Read again these verses, and let silence be the voice of your contemplation.

---

*HLS (1745) [3:5 th' astonied hosts] RV 54

STOP AND GAZE (3) 113

O my God, he dies for me,
 I feel the mortal smart!
See him hanging on the tree –
 A sight that breaks my heart!
O that all to thee might turn!
 Sinners ye may love him too,
Look on him ye pierced, and mourn
 For one who bled for you.

Weep o'er your desire and hope
 With tears of humblest love;
Sing, for Jesus is gone up,
 And reigns enthroned above!
Lives our head, to die no more:
 Power is all to Jesus given,
Worshipped as he was before
 The immortal king of heaven.

Lord, we bless thee for thy grace
 And truth which never fail,
Hastening to behold thy face
 Without a dimming veil:
We shall see our heavenly King,
 All thy glorious love proclaim,
Help the angel-choirs to sing
 Our dear triumphant Lamb.

And Jesus came and spake unto them, saying, All power is given unto me in heaven and in earth.

Matthew 28:18

In the verses we read yesterday from this nine verse poem we watched cosmic events from an awed distance. In this last section of the poem Wesley dramatically plunges us into a realisation that this all happened 'for me'. Heartbreak at the sight of this innocent suffering may lead us to the recognition that our own wounds are healed by his. Then grief turns to singing as we consider the risen Lord, and invite all people to join us in telling of the 'glorious love' that brings universal liberation.

PRAYER
We thank you that you have shared the suffering of our world, so that all creation may share your glorious liberty. Amen.

---

*HLS (1745) RV 54

Would Jesus have the sinner die?
Why hangs he then on yonder tree?
What means that strange expiring cry?
Sinners, he prays for you and me:
Forgive them, Father, O forgive!
They know not that by me they live.

Dear loving, all-atoning Lamb,
Thee, by thy painful agony,
Thy bloody sweat, thy grief and shame,
Thy cross, and passion on the tree,
Thy precious death and life, I pray:
Take all, take all my sins away!

O let me kiss thy bleeding feet,
And bathe and wash them with my tears;
The story of thy love repeat
In every drooping sinner's ears;
That all may hear the quickening sound,
Since I, even I, have mercy found.

And when they were come to the place which is called Calvary, there they crucified him . . . Then said Jesus, Father, forgive them; for they know not what they do.
Luke 23:33-34

The problem of evil and suffering constantly prompts the question 'why?' It is partly answered by the classic doctrine of Christ as the second Adam who takes away the evil consequences of the sin of the first, by absorbing into himself all the suffering that evil can inflict. In verse three of this hymn, Charles turns the words of the Passiontide litany from the *Book of Common Prayer* into a poem of penitence.

Wesley then turns to the personal experience of the woman 'who was a sinner' and who bathed Christ's feet with her tears (Luke 7:37-38). She understood something of the cost of a love which can forgive sin. All who go on loving and refusing to hate, even in the face of evil and violence, prove in themselves the power of such love.

PRAYER
O let thy love my heart control, thy love for every sinner free,
That every fallen human soul may taste the grace that found out me.
(from verse five of this hymn)

HGEL (1741) *CH 32 [3:6 If I, even I] HP 185

O Love divine! what hast thou done!
The immortal God hath died for me!
The Father's co-eternal Son
Bore all my sins upon the tree;
The immortal God for me hath died,
My Lord, my Love is crucified.

Behold him, all ye that pass by,
The bleeding Prince of life and peace!
Come sinners, see your Maker die,
And say, was ever grief like his?
Come, feel with me his blood applied:
My Lord, my Love is crucified.

Is crucified for me and you,
To bring us rebels back to God;
Believe, believe the record true,
We all are bought with Jesu's blood:
Pardon for all flows from his side:
My Lord, my Love is crucified.

Is it nothing to you, all ye that pass by? Behold and see if there be any sorrow like unto my sorrow, which is done unto me.

Lamentations 1:12

Anyone familiar with Stainer's *Crucifixion* will realise that these words from the book of Lamentations have been understood by Christians as an anticipation of the sufferings of Christ. This hymn adds an extra poignancy as we, the readers, are brought face to face with Christ on the cross. It is all happening in the present moment. Gods are immortal – they do not die – yet our God is dying on our behalf. The lovely refrain, which Wesley borrows from the Early Fathers by way of the seventeenth century poet John Mason, links the Christ whom I serve as Lord, with Christ my lover, a bold yet powerful blending of different aspects of my relationship to Christ. Though intensely personal, the hymn also sounds a note of universalism – this sacrificial love brings forgiveness and life for all.

PRAYER
Highest in creation, Christ lives among the least. He journeys with the rejected and welcomes the weary. Come now, all who thirst and drink the water of life. Come now, all who hunger and be filled with good things. Come now, all who seek and be warmed by the fire of love. Amen.[1] *Iona Community*

HSP (1742) *CH 27 [2:3 Come see, ye worms 3:4 Ye all; We 1742] HP 175 UMH 287

BEHOLD THE MAN!

Arise, my soul, arise,
Shake off thy guilty fears;
The bleeding sacrifice
In my behalf appears:
Before the throne my surety stands,
My name is written on his hands.

He ever lives above,
For me to intercede,
His all-redeeming love,
His precious blood to plead;
His blood atoned for all our race,
And sprinkles now the throne of grace.

Five bleeding wounds he bears,
Received on Calvary;
They pour effectual prayers,
They strongly speak for me:
'Forgive him, O forgive!' they cry,
'Nor let that ransomed sinner die!'

My God is reconciled,
His pardoning voice I hear;
He owns me for his child,
I can no longer fear;
With confidence I now draw nigh,
And 'Father, Abba, Father!' cry.

For Christ is entered . . . into heaven itself, now to appear in the presence of God for us.

Hebrews 9:24

Biographers have written about the power of this hymn to strengthen the faith of believers; theologians have seen in it a succinct statement of the doctrine of atonement; and still others have commented on Wesley's use of the medieval devotion to the five wounds of Christ.

For each believer it has a personal message, that gazing on Christ on the cross can in itself be a mystical experience. The mystery of the atonement may be difficult to grasp, but we can understand hands. The hands on which our names are engraved are the hands pinned by the nails. How else can God show that he loves us to the end of the world – and beyond? How else is fear swallowed up in love, a love that can dare to speak 'with confidence' the beloved name – Abba, Father.

PRAYER
Abba, Father, into thy hands I commend my spirit.

---

*HSP (1742) RV 29 CH 194 HP 217

Lamb of God, whose bleeding love
We thus recall to mind,
Send the answer from above,
And let us mercy find;
Think on us, who think on thee;
And every struggling soul release:
O remember Calvary,
And bid us go in peace.

By thine agonising pain,
And bloody sweat, we pray,
By the dying love to man,
Take all our sins away;
Burst our bonds, and set us free;
From all iniquity release:
O remember Calvary,
And bid us go in peace!

Let thy blood, by faith applied,
The sinner's pardon seal,
Speak us freely justified,
And all our sickness heal;
By thy passion on the tree
Let all our griefs and troubles cease:
O remember Calvary,
And bid us go in peace.

By thine agony and bloody sweat; by thy cross and passion; by thy precious death and burial . . . Good Lord, deliver us.

Book of Common Prayer

Both the Scriptures and the prayers of his beloved Anglican liturgy prompted Wesley's pen. In this extended meditation on the Litany, the passage on Christ's passion and death inspires this prayer for personal salvation. The rhythmic nature of the original words is echoed in the repetitive last two lines of each verse of the poem, reminding people of the later words of the Litany: 'O Lamb of God, that takest away the sins of the world; Grant us thy peace.'

In verse three of this hymn Wesley reminds us also of an 'official non-believer', a Roman centurion who with great effectiveness said to Jesus: 'Speak the word only, and my servant shall be healed' (Matthew 8:8). God's will is that we all go in peace.

PRAYER
Let your peace fill our heart, our world, our universe. Peace . . . Peace . . . Peace.

---

*HSP (1745) RV 53 HP 550

All ye that seek the Lord who died,
Your God for sinners crucified,
Prevent* the earliest dawn, and come
To worship at his sacred tomb.

Bring the sweet spices of your sighs,
Your contrite hearts, and streaming eyes,
Your sad complaints and humble fears;
Come, and embalm him with your tears.

While thus ye love your souls t'employ,
Your sorrow shall be turned to joy;
Now, now let all your grief be o'er!
Believe, and ye shall weep no more.

The Lord of life is risen indeed,
To death delivered in your stead;
His rise proclaims your sins forgiven,
And shows the living way to heaven.

Haste then, ye souls that first believe,
Who dare the gospel word receive,
Your faith with joyful hearts confess,
Be bold, be Jesus' witnesses.

Now upon the first day of the week, very early in the morning, [the women] came unto the sepulchre, bringing the spices which they had prepared . . . and they found the stone rolled away from the sepulchre.

Luke 24:1-2

'Weeping may endure for a night, but joy cometh in the morning,' says the psalmist (Psalm 30:9). Wesley reminds us through this account of the women's discovery of the empty tomb that all our grief can be turned to joy. Though tears may blind our eyes for a time, the eyes of faith can still see the hope that lies beyond the empty tomb. Here there is comfort for all who are bereaved; here there is confidence for all who are afraid; here there is forgiveness for all who are contrite.

PRAYER
Pray particularly today for those who mourn the recent loss of a loved one, that they may not be ashamed to weep, but that they may also be surprised by joy.

HLR (1746) *PW 4, 129-30 HP 188

---

*Go before

Christ the Lord is risen today,
Sons of men and angels say:
Raise your joys and triumphs high;
Sing ye heavens, and earth reply.

Love's redeeming work is done,
Fought the fight, the battle won;
Vain the stone, the watch, the seal;
Christ hath burst the gates of hell!

Lives again our glorious king;
Where, O death, is now thy sting?
Once he died our souls to save;
Where's thy victory, O grave?

Sing, O heavens; and be joyful, O earth; and break forth into singing, O mountains: for the LORD hath comforted his people, and will have mercy on his afflicted.
Isaiah 49:13

O death, where is thy sting? O grave, where is thy victory?
1 Corinthians 15:55

These verses are from the first Easter hymn ever published by Wesley. It has all the energy and poetic skill released at the time of his conversion, and was one of five hymns Wesley wrote at that time for the festivals of the church year. It is apparently patterned on the anonymous *Lyra Davidica* of 1708, which has a similar format, but very different style. That earlier hymn, beginning 'Jesus Christ is risen today', is a teaching hymn in four verses recounting Christ's death and resurrection, and the benefits of his passion, concluding with a formal verse of praise.

In comparison, Charles' work is a long paean of exultation, rejoicing in both cosmic imagery and personal delight. Exclamation marks and questions abound. Quotations from many parts of the Old and New Testaments interweave themselves, and the whole has become, in one version or another, one of the most beloved of all Easter hymns.

PRAYER
Lord of all life and power, through the mighty resurrection of your Son you have overcome the old order of sin and death and have made all things new in him. Grant that we, being dead to sin and alive to you in Jesus Christ, may reign with him in glory; to whom, with you and the Holy Spirit, be praise and honour, glory and might, now and in all eternity. Amen.[1] *Methodist Service Book*

---

*HSP (1739) RV 9 HP 193 UMH 302 [1:2 Earth and heaven in chorus say] VU 157

Soar we now where Christ hath led,
Following our exalted Head;
Made like him, like him we rise;
Ours the cross, the grave, the skies!

Hail the Lord of earth and heaven!
Praise to thee by both be given:
Thee we greet triumphant now;
Hail the resurrection thou!

King of glory! Soul of bliss!
Everlasting life is this;
Thee to know, thy power to prove,
Thus to sing, and thus to love!

Therefore we are buried with him by baptism into death: that like as Christ was raised up from the dead by the glory of the Father, even so we also should walk in newness of life. For if we have been planted together in the likeness of his death, we shall be also in the likeness of his resurrection.

Romans 6:4-5

Following the opening verses declaring the power of the resurrection for both earth and heaven, Wesley's first Easter hymn now focuses on our response. Can this be for us also? Can we soar heavenward? Yes, indeed, comes the reply, 'Ours the cross, the grave, the skies.' These are signs not only of the actual resurrection after death, but also of the smaller deaths and resurrections that occur throughout our lives, as light comes out of darkness and joy out of pain.

The last two verses are addressed to the risen Christ – the eternal but new King of glory of Psalm 24. All the power of Wesley's own personal experience is in the words 'know' and 'prove' and 'love'. This is everlasting life here and now.

PRAYER

Almighty God, through Jesus Christ you overcame death and opened to us the gate of everlasting life. Grant that we, who celebrate the day of our Lord's resurrection, may, by the renewing of your Spirit, arise from the death of sin to the life of righteousness; through Jesus Christ our Lord. Amen.[1] *The United Methodist Hymnal*

HSP (1739) RV 9 HP 193 UMH 302 VU 157

More courageous than the men,
When Christ his breath resigned
Women first the grace obtain
Their living Lord to find;
Women first the news proclaim,
Know his resurrection's power,
Teach the apostles of the Lamb
Who lives to die no more.

It was Mary Magdalene, and Joanna, and Mary the mother of James, and other women which told these things unto the apostles. And their words seemed to them as idle tales, and they believed them not.

Luke 24:10-11

In an age when, as now, men held most of the power, Charles Wesley repeatedly emphasises women's place in the Christian story. This little poem remained unpublished until 1990. Like so many records of the life and wisdom of women, it became buried in time. Note how Wesley describes the women as being 'first'. As Dorothy L. Sayers once put it, 'No wonder that women were first at the cradle and last at the cross. They had never met a man like this man', a man who treated them as totally human. They were not just last at the cross, but they were the first to obtain the grace and to tell the news of the resurrection. They became the apostles to the Apostles.

Wasting or not recognising the gifts of women has been one of the far-reaching sins of the church and of our society. Yet in so many instances in the history of the church, it is the witness of women that has opened the door to the preaching of the gospel.

PRAYER
God, who created us male and female in your own image, help us to honour one another, and acknowledge each other's gifts, so that we may work together to proclaim your gospel and promote justice for all your children. Amen.

---

*UPCW 2, 207

JESUS LIVES

Who seek the Crucified,
Dismiss your needless fear;
He once for sinners died,
But lives no longer here;
This is the third triumphant day:
Come see the place where Jesus lay.

Among the dead in vain
Ye seek your heavenly Lord;
He lives! He lives again
According to his word!
Receive the power his life imparts,
And find him risen in your hearts.

The angel said unto the women, Fear not ye: for I know that ye seek Jesus, which was crucified. He is not here: for he is risen, as he said. Come, see the place where the Lord lay.

Matthew 28:5-6

Matthew's story of the resurrection appearance to the women at the tomb is told quickly. When the angel appears, the guards are so frightened they become 'as dead men'; the women hear the message and hurry off to tell the other disciples.

In this simple, but profound poem, Wesley makes us pause and holds our attention on the message of the angel; the message is not just for the two Marys but for us as well. The first verse is almost a paraphrase of the biblical text, but line three adds a gospel comment. Verse two enlarges the angel's phrase 'as he said' to 'He lives again/According to his word.' Jesus had said he would rise on the third day. The last two lines are personal and change the style from description of a past event, to a command for our own lives.

The seek/find motif starts and ends the poem. It may recall for us the words of Jesus: 'Ask and it shall be given unto you; seek and you shall find; knock and it shall be opened unto you.' But, as Wesley also reminds us, the Easter experience is of finding a treasure that far exceeds our expectations and our searching.

PRAYER
Risen Jesus, may I recognise your presence already in my heart. Amen.

---

*PW 10, 437

It is the voice of my beloved,
My fears are fled, my griefs removed,
He calls a sinner by her name,
And he is mine, and his I am!
  Jesus by a word made known
  Thee my gracious Lord I own.

My gracious Lord, I know, thou art
The lawful Master of my heart,
I feel thy resurrection's power,
And joyful at thy feet adore;
  Now I only live to prove
  Thou art God, and God is love.

Jesus saith unto her, Mary. She turned herself and saith unto him, Rabboni; which is to say, Master.

John 20:16

This is a scene of transformation. Mary's grief at the death of her friend Jesus, compounded by her distress that someone had removed his body, gradually turned to almost unbelieving joy as she recognised his voice. Literally 'by a word made known', but that word was her own name!

Wesley boldly links this to the sensuous imagery of the Song of Songs (2:8), where twice the woman hears the 'the voice of my beloved' coming to her in joy and delight. He follows here a traditional Christian reading of the Song, which took this Hebrew love song first as a portrayal of the relationship of Christ with the church, then as an image of the love between Christ and the faithful soul.

In this light, the final two lines of the hymn take on a special meaning. If God is lover as well as 'love', and 'I only live to prove' this, it means my sharing in that great love for the world that God has created and redeemed.

PRAYER
Speak to me by name, O Master,
Let me know it is to me,
Speak that I may follow faster
With a step more firm and free. *Frances Ridley Havergal*

*MS John RV 180 [1:3 his name]

Who at his cross had stood
And seen the dying God,
Happy Magdalene receives
The first visit from her Lord,
By his resurrection lives,
Finds in him her full reward.

He thus delights to approve
Her constancy of love,
Shows himself alive to her
Once by seven devils possessed,
Now his chosen messenger,
Now preferred to all the rest.

He still vouchsafes to bless
Who boldly him confess,
Prize their Saviour's grief and shame,
Will not from his cross remove;
Those he calls to bear his name,
Honours with his richest love.

Now when Jesus was risen early the first day of the week, he appeared first to Mary Magdalene, out of whom he had cast seven devils.

Mark 16:9

The men had run away – forsaken him and fled – and it was the women who had the courage to go to the cross, and to stay there until he died. Perhaps they were no more brave than the others, but it was women's traditional work to follow the body to the tomb, to go home and prepare the burial spices and bring them to the body two days later, when the Sabbath was over. Mary Magdalene is associated in the gospel with extravagant love rather than traditional care, but according to Mark, it was she who first saw the risen Christ.

In a world that often devalues women, Wesley repeatedly honours Mary, whom Christ 'preferred to all the rest'. Such 'constancy of love', he says, brings its own reward – she is chosen as the messenger of the resurrection. Women and men who share the cross that others carry and stubbornly stand by their friends whatever suffering they must bear – these too are honoured. These, like Mary, become the 'chosen messengers' of Christ and the harbingers of hope.

PRAYER

Crucified and risen Lord, in your mercy bless and nourish all those in all parts of the world who stand by others in their suffering. Be their strength, their comfort and their hope, now and always. Amen.

---

*PW 11, 93-4

Happy Magdalene, to whom
  Christ the Lord vouchsafed to appear!
Newly risen from the tomb,
  Would he first be seen by her?
Her by seven devils possessed,
  Till his word the fiends expelled,
Quenched the hell within her breast,
  All her sins and sickness healed.

Yes! To her the Master came,
  First his welcome voice she hears;
Jesus calls her by her name,
  He the weeping sinner cheers,
Lets her the dear task repeat,
  While her eyes again run o'er,
Lets her wash his bleeding feet,
  Kiss them, and with joy adore.

Jesus said to her, 'Do not hold me . . . but go to my brethren and say to them, I am ascending to my Father and your Father, to my God and your God.'

John 20:17 (RSV)

That a woman who had been so great a sinner should be the first to see the risen Christ is, to Wesley, a source of endless wonder and joy. The drama of the original story – the empty tomb – the gardener whom Mary does not recognise until he speaks her name – is even heightened by the imagined re-enacting of Mary's washing of the Saviour's feet and wiping them with her tears.

In his *Notes on the New Testament,* John Wesley points out that Jesus' words to Mary could be translated 'Do not cling to me', and he makes reference to Matthew 28:9 where it says that the disciples held him by the feet. Mary is told not to linger, but to hurry to the others with the glad news of the resurrection.

PRAYER
Lord, when I am overcome with grief or regrets, do not let my tears so blind my eyes that I cannot see you in your resurrection glory. Enable me to let go of the past, to move forward in hope into the future. Amen.

---

*HLR (1746) PW 4, 132

Who can now presume to fear,
Who despair their Lord to see?
Jesus, wilt thou not appear,
Show thyself alive to me?
Yes, my God, I dare not doubt,
Thou shalt all my sins remove;
Thou hast called a legion out,
Thou wilt perfect me in love.

Surely thou hast called me now!
Now I hear thy voice divine,
At thy wounded feet I bow,
Wounded for whose sins but mine!
I have nailed him to the tree,
I have sent him to the grave;
But the Lord is risen for me,
Hold of him by faith I have.

Here for ever would I lie,
Did'st thou not thy servant raise,
Send me forth to testify
All the wonders of thy grace.
Lo! I at thy bidding go,
Gladly to thy followers tell
They their rising God may know,
They the life of Christ may feel.

Mary Magdalene came and told the disciples that she had seen the Lord, and that he had spoken these things unto her.

John 20:18

Here Charles Wesley identifies himself with the character of Mary Magdalene, whom he imagines kneeling at the feet of the risen Christ. His fear and doubt are like hers as she approaches the tomb. Like her, he has been freed from 'a legion' of sins. He too has bowed at those feet which she had anointed with her perfume. He too feels intimately involved in all the suffering of his passion, and comes in sadness to the grave. And like her, he personally witnesses Christ's risen presence and longs to hold on to that moment forever. But, like Mary, he must go and tell others so that they too may know and feel the experience of being in the presence of the living Lord.

PRAYER
Lord, may I not only stand with Mary in awe before the empty tomb, but go with her in joy to tell the good news to others. Amen.

---

*HLR (1746) [1:2 his Lord] PW 4, 133

Christ, our living Head draw near,
At our call,
Quicken all
Thy true members here.

All thy resurrection's power,
All thy love,
From above,
On thy servants shower.

Partners of thy death and passion,
O that we
All might see
All thy great salvation.

Children of the resurrection,
Lead us on
To the crown
Of our full perfection.

We must no longer be children, tossed to and fro and blown about by every wind of doctrine . . . But speaking the truth in love, we must grow up in every way into him who is the head, into Christ.

Ephesians 4:14-15 (NRSV)

Paul's vision of the unity of members in the body of Christ pictured in Ephesians 4 is the image behind this hymn. Some might call it a carol, for its joyous, dancing rhythm fits that form. It is also a prayer to the Christ of 'resurrection power'. As 'children of the resurrection', may former childish behaviour grow into the maturity of perfect love.

PRAYER
Lord, we died with you on the cross.
Now we are raised to new life.
We were buried in your tomb.
Now we share in your resurrection.
Live in us, that we may live in you.[1]
Anglican Church of Canada

HLR (1746) *PW 4, 148

STAY WITH US (1)

Come, then, thou Prophet of the Lord,
  Thou great Interpreter divine,
Explain thine own transmitted Word;
  To teach and to inspire is thine,
Thou only can'st thyself reveal,
  Open the book, and loose the seal.

Now, Jesu, now the veil remove,
  The folly of our darkened heart,
Unfold the wonders of thy love,
  The knowledge of thyself impart;
Our ear, our inmost soul we bow,
  Speak, Lord, thy servants hearken now.

Make not as thou wouldst farther go,
  Our Friend and Counsellor and Guide,
But stay, the path of life to show,
  Still with our souls vouchsafe to abide,
Constrained by thy own mercy stay,
  Nor leave us at the close of day.

He expounded unto them in all the Scriptures the things concerning himself. And they drew nigh unto the village . . . [and] they constrained him, saying, Abide with us: for it is toward evening, and the day is far spent.

Luke 24:27-29

One of the longest and liveliest of the Easter narratives is the story of the encounter with the risen Christ on the road to Emmaus. Two disciples making their way despondently home from Jerusalem are joined on the road by a stranger who opens the Scriptures to them, loosing, as it were, the seal on the sacred book. So fascinated are they that they invite him to share the hospitality of their home, and in the 'breaking of bread' they recognise the presence of Jesus.

For us, as for them, the very familiarity of the Bible can be like a veil over our eyes. We need the presence of the Spirit to unlock the mystery of God's love to us, even in the midst of the commonplace, and to assure us that he will be with us, right to the close of life's day.

PRAYER
O Christ, you come as a stranger when we are least expecting you. You show us our way of life by interpreting your own story. Stay with us. Give us hospitable hearts, hearing ears and understanding minds, that we may not miss your guiding light. Amen.

HLR (1746) *PW 4, 136-7

Come in, with thy disciples sit,
  Nor suffer us to ask in vain;
Nourish us, Lord, with living meat,
  Our souls with heavenly bread sustain;
Break to us now the mystic bread,
  And bid us on thy body feed.

Honour the means ordained by thee,
  The great unbloody sacrifice,
The deep tremendous mystery;
  Thyself in our enlightened eyes
Now in the broken bread made known,
  And show us thou art all our own.

And it came to pass, as he sat at meat with them, he took bread, and blessed it, and brake, and gave to them. And their eyes were opened, and they knew him.
Luke 24:30-31

The wonder of this simple story of the breaking of bread in the home at Emmaus directs our thoughts to another, 'the deep tremendous mystery' of the presence of Christ in the sacrament of Holy Communion. At the Lord's Table we yearn for a glimpse of himself, our host; we would be nourished with 'living', 'heavenly', 'mystic' bread. The Emmaus story can be also for us a reminder that the risen Christ is present, even if unrecognised, in all our meals shared in love in his name.

PRAYER
Stay with us, Lord, for the day is far spent and we have not yet recognised your face in each of our brothers and sisters.
Stay with us, Lord, for the day is far spent and we have not yet shared your bread in grace with all our brothers and sisters.
Stay with us, Lord, because our very night becomes day when you are there.[1]
World Alliance of Reformed Churches

---

*HLR (1746) PW 4, 137

FOOLS AS WE ARE!

Ah! Lord, if thou indeed art ours,
If thou for us hast burst the tomb,
Visit us with thy quickening powers,
Come to thy mournful followers, come;
Thyself to thy weak members join,
And fill us with the life divine.

Thee, the great prophet sent from God,
Mighty in deed and word we own;
Thou hast on some the grace bestowed,
Thy rising in their hearts made known;
They publish thee, to life restored,
Attesting they have seen the Lord.

Fools as we are, and slow of heart,
So backward to believe the word!
The prophets' only aim thou art,
They sang the sufferings of their Lord;
Thy life for ours a ransom given,
Thy rising to ensure our heaven.

Then he said unto them, O fools, and slow of heart to believe all that the prophets have spoken.

Luke 24:25 (read verses 14-27)

Despite the reports carried by the women from the empty tomb, most of the disciples on that first Easter Day were 'mournful followers', remaining in hiding or walking sadly homeward from Jerusalem.

The story of the encounter of two of them with the living Christ on the road to Emmaus provides Wesley with a point of departure for a meditation on our own struggle for belief in the resurrection of Jesus. Like them, we have heard the story of Jesus many times. We have been attracted by his teaching; we have heard the call to be his disciples. But the harsh realities of our world and the depth of our own doubts have made 'weak members' of us and we are 'slow of heart' to believe. We need a fresh encounter, however fleeting, with the risen One who will open to us the Scriptures and restore to us our hope.

PRAYER
Lord, open your Word to us that through its pages, we too may meet the risen Christ. Amen.

---

*HLR (1746) PW 4, 134-6

Ye faithful souls who Jesus know,
If risen indeed with him ye are,
Superior to the joys below,
His resurrection's power declare,
Your faith by holy tempers prove,
By actions show your sins forgiven,
And seek the glorious things above,
And follow Christ, your Head, to heaven.

There your exalted Saviour see,
Seated at God's right hand again,
In all his Father's majesty,
In everlasting pomp to reign:
To him continually aspire,
Contending for your native place;
And emulate the angel-choir,
And only live to love and praise.

If ye then be risen with Christ, seek those things which are above, where Christ sitteth on the right hand of God. Set your affection on things above, not on things on the earth.

Colossians 3:1-2

This hymn was written as a meditation on the Colossians text. Paul's phrase describing Christ as sitting at the right hand of God allows Wesley some celestial imagery. 'Pomp' may have negative overtones today, but in Wesley's Miltonic tradition it echoed all the glory and wonder and majesty of God's presence.

Heaven may be the goal of our journey, the Christian's 'native place', but the way of following the incarnate Christ is a way that begins on the earth. Faith and works are inextricably linked (James 2:18). Christ's resurrection power is proved by 'holy tempers', while our sense of forgiveness is shown by our actions.

PRAYER
My Lord, I have nothing to do in this world, but to seek and serve thee; I have nothing to do with a heart and its affection but to breathe after thee; I have nothing to do with my tongue and pen, but to speak to thee, and for thee, and to publish thy glory and thy will. Amen. *Richard Baxter*

SH (1762) *CH 408 HP 751

See, Jesus, thy disciples see,
The promised blessing give;
Met in thy name, we look to thee,
Expecting to receive.

With us thou art assembled here;
But O thyself reveal!
Son of the living God, appear!
Let us thy presence feel.

Breathe on us, Lord, in this our day,
And these dry bones shall live;
Speak peace into our hearts, and say,
'The Holy Ghost receive.'

Whom now we seek, O may we meet!
Jesus the crucified,
Show us thy bleeding hands and feet,
Thou who for us hast died.

O ye dry bones, hear the word of the LORD. Thus saith the LORD God unto these bones; Behold, I will cause breath to enter into you, and ye shall live.

Ezekiel 37:4-5

The almost breathless tone of this hymn captures vividly the surprise of the first Easter appearances. See us, reveal yourself to us, appear to us, let us feel your presence, breathe on us, speak peace into our hearts, talk to us, meet with us, show us, commands the poet. It is clear that he is in a state of high expectancy. He is sure that as the risen Jesus showed himself to those first disciples, so he shows himself to us now. For we too are waiting to receive.

There is all the difference in the world between knowing with the mind and feeling with the heart. That is why in verse three we ask for a revelation of Jesus that lets us feel his presence. Our task is to wait expectantly; we can take comfort that the same breath that entered the dry bones of Ezekiel's vision and made them live, that moved the disciples from fear to boldness, can enliven us as well.

PRAYER
Breathe on me, breath of God. Fill me with life anew. Amen. *Edwin Hatch*

HSP (1749) *CH 474 HP 763

Words cannot prove
That thee I love,
My soul's eternal Lover;
Actions must the doubt remove,
And all my soul discover.

Filled may I be
With charity,
And carry in my bosom
The dear lambs redeemed by thee,
And rather die than lose them.

Now dearest Lord,
Let fire or sword
My soul and body sever,
Give me but that parting word,
'I love my God forever!'

When they had finished breakfast, Jesus said to Simon Peter, 'Simon son of John, do you love me more than these?' He said to him, 'Yes, Lord; you know that I love you.' Jesus said to him, 'Feed my lambs.'

John 21:15-16 (NRSV)

The risen Jesus has made breakfast on the shore for the disciples who have been fishing all night. In this conversation with Simon Peter, Jesus allows him to cancel out his earlier pre-crucifixion denials by a threefold declaration of love. Characteristically, Peter does not quite understand what is happening at the time, and is 'grieved' that Jesus asks him the same question three times, insisting that of course he loves Jesus.

In this poem Wesley catches the same tone of Peter's insistence, but also realises that what Jesus is asking of Peter, and of us, is proof of our love not only in words, but in action.

MEDITATION
Be shepherds to the flock of Christ. Hold up the weak; bind up the broken; bring again the outcasts; seek the lost. So be merciful that you are not too remiss; so minister discipline that you forget not mercy; that when the Chief Shepherd appears you may receive the never-fading crown of glory, through Jesus Christ our Lord. Amen.[1] *Methodist Service Book*

---

*UPCW 2, 280-81 RV 182

Hail the day that sees him rise,
Ravished from our wishful eyes!
Christ, awhile to mortals given,
Reascends his native heaven!

There the pompous triumph waits:
Lift your heads, eternal gates;
Wide unfold the radiant scene;
Take the King of glory in!

Him though highest heaven receives,
Still he loves the earth he leaves;
Though returning to his throne,
Still he calls our kind his own.

Ever upward let us move,
Wafted on the wings of love,
Looking when our Lord shall come,
Longing, gasping after home.

There we shall with thee remain,
Partners of thy endless reign;
There thy face unclouded see,
Find our heaven of heavens in thee!

Lift up your heads, O ye gates; and be ye lift up, ye everlasting doors; and the King of glory shall come in.

Psalm 24:7

And it came to pass, while [Jesus] blessed [the disciples], he was parted from them, and carried up into heaven.

Luke 24:51

Lectionaries, including the *Book of Common Prayer,* traditionally set Psalm 24 amongst the readings for Ascension Day. Charles' particular language of 'pompous (i.e. pomp-filled) triumph' owes much also to the magisterial language of Milton. The daringly sensual language of mysticism is here too, in words like 'ravished' and 'wishful' (verse one), and 'wafted' and 'gasping' (verse five), suggesting transformation into a bliss beyond reason. Christ not only 'loves the earth he leaves', but calls humankind 'his own', and takes us with him into heaven. He bears us up even while we are still on earth, on the wings of everlasting love, so that we may find 'our heaven of heavens' in Christ himself.

PRAYER

Everliving God, your eternal Christ once dwelt on earth, confined by time and space. Give us faith to discern in every time and place the presence among us of him who is head over all things and fills all, even Jesus Christ our ascended Lord. Amen.[1]
Laurence Hull Stookey

*HSP (1739) RV 10:1-4, 9-10 [3:4 calls mankind] HP 197 UMH 312 VU 189

Our Lord is risen from the dead!
Our Jesus is gone up on high!
The powers of hell are captive led,
Dragged to the portals of the sky.

Loose all your bars of massy light,
And wide unfold the ethereal scene:
He claims these mansions as his right;
Receive the King of Glory in!

Who is this King of Glory, who?
The Lord, that all his foes o'ercame,
The world, sin, death, and hell o'erthrew;
And Jesus is the conqueror's name.

Lo! his triumphal chariot waits,
And angels chant the solemn lay:
Lift up your heads, ye heavenly gates;
Ye everlasting doors, give way!

Who is this King of Glory, who?
The Lord, of glorious power possessed;
The King of saints, and angels too,
God over all, for ever blest!

Lift up your heads, O ye gates; and be ye lift up, ye everlasting doors, and the King of glory shall come in.

Psalm 24:7

In the Anglican calendar, Psalm 24 was a set psalm at Evensong on Ascension Day. This may have been the starting point for this hymn based on a Hebrew psalm that celebrates the entrance of the ark into the temple. Wesley answers the psalmist's question 'Who is this King of glory?' with the Christian affirmation that it is Christ, the one who has ascended into heaven. Wesley's gift for taking images and expanding them is nourished by his having memorised long passages of Milton. Here practically every non-biblical word comes directly from *Paradise Lost.*

PRAYER
O God, you withdraw from our sight that you may be known by our love; help us to enter the cloud where you are hidden, and surrender all our certainty to the darkness of faith in Jesus Christ. Amen.

CPH (1743) *CH (1831) 554 HP 206

136 THE TRUE ELIJAH (1)

All hail the true Elijah,
The Lord our God and Saviour!
Who leaves behind,
For all mankind,
The token of his favour.

Borne on his fiery chariot,
With joyful acclamation
Pursue the Lord,
To heaven restored,
The God of our salvation.

Who see their Lord at parting,
They shall on earth inherit
A double power,
A larger shower
Of his descending Spirit.

The Spirit of our Master
Shall rest on each believer,
And surely we
Our Master see
Who lives and reigns for ever.

Elisha said, I pray thee, let a double portion of thy spirit be upon me. And he said . . . If thou see me when I am taken from thee it shall be so unto thee . . . Behold, there appeared a chariot of fire, and horses of fire . . . and Elijah went up by a whirlwind into heaven.

2 Kings 2:9-11

Here Wesley draws on an ancient Christian tradition, which took Elijah's ascent in a chariot of fire for an image of the ascension of Christ. As Elisha the young prophet asked Elijah's blessing to carry on his ministry, so we modern disciples are encouraged to envision Christ entering into the glory of God's presence, and bestowing on us as benediction 'The Spirit of our Master' for our ministries in his name.

PRAYER
O Christ, who vanished from the sight of those first disciples that you might live for ever in our hearts, give us this day and every day a sense of your continuing presence. Amen.

---

*HLR (1746) PW 4, 149-50

Yes, our exalted Jesus,
By faith we now adore thee,
And still we sit
Before thy feet,
And triumph in thy glory.

In vain the flaming chariot
Hath parted us asunder,
We still through grace
Behold thy face,
And shout our loving wonder.

By faith we catch thy mantle,
The covering of thy Spirit
By faith we wear,
And gladly share
Thine all-involving merit.

We rest beneath thy shadow,
Till, by the whirlwind driven,
From earth we rise,
And mount the skies,
To grasp our Lord in heaven.

Elijah went up by a whirlwind into heaven. And Elisha saw it, and he cried, My father, my father, the chariot of Israel, and the horsemen thereof. And he saw him no more . . . He took up also the mantle of Elijah that fell from him.

2 Kings 2:11-13

These verses conclude yesterday's hymn for Ascension Day that borrows its images from the graphic story of Elijah's departure from earth in a fiery chariot.

Wesley draws a contrast between the exalted Jesus and his earthbound disciples. Though we glory in the triumph of Christ, we who have to live in this world can only clothe ourselves in his garment of humble service. But we are constantly sustained in days of discouragement by the knowledge that his kingdom cannot fail, and that one day we shall share in his final triumph.

PRAYER
Though to our earthbound eyes the forces of evil seem so strong, lift our hearts by the vision of heaven in which you reign supreme. Amen.

---

*HLR (1746) PW 4, 150

Jesus, we look to thee,
Thy promised presence claim;
Thou in the midst of us shalt be,
Assembled in thy name.

Thy name salvation is,
Which now we come to prove;
Thy name is life and joy and peace
And everlasting love.

Present we know thou art,
But O thyself reveal!
Now, Lord, let every bounding heart
The mighty comfort feel.

O may thy quickening voice
The death of sin remove;
And bid our inmost souls rejoice
In hope of perfect love!

For where two or three are gathered together in my name, there am I in the midst of them.

Matthew 18:20

The disciples, we are told in the gospels, were themselves given to singing hymns. On the night of their last supper with Jesus they sang a hymn before they went out to the Mount of Olives (Matthew 26:30). We can imagine them, therefore, singing a hymn when they gathered together again, following the sad event of the crucifixion when they hardly dared to believe the stories of the resurrection. The mood of Wesley's text catches the mood of John's account of the apostles' first shared experience of the presence of the risen Christ, as retold in John 20:19-30. Their first tentative prayer is answered by the confident awareness of Christ's real presence. Not surprisingly, this hymn is sometimes sung at the beginning of the Communion Service, as we approach expectantly our appointment with the risen Christ.

PRAYER

Lord, you know that there are times when I doubt your presence. Dispel my doubts as you did those of your first disciples, and convince me that I too can be made perfect in love. Amen.

---

*HSP (1749) [4:1 might] HP 760

Jesu, show us thy salvation,
   (In thy strength we strive with thee)
By thy mystic incarnation,
   By thy pure nativity,
Save us thou, our new Creator;
   Into all our souls impart
Thy divine, unsinning nature,
   Form thyself within our heart.

By thy first blood-shedding, heal us;
   Cut us off from every sin;
By thy circumcision seal us,
   Write thy law of love within;
By thy Spirit circumcise us,
   Kindle in our hearts a flame;
By thy baptism, Lord, baptise us
   Into all thy glorious Name.

By thy fasting and temptation
   Mortify our vain desires;
Take away what sense, or passion,
   Appetite, or flesh requires;
Arm us with thy self-denial,
   Every tempted soul defend,
Save us in the fiery trial,
   Make us faithful to the end.

By the mystery of thy holy Incarnation; by thy holy Nativity and Circumcision; by thy Baptism, Fasting, and Temptation, by thine Agony and bloody Sweat . . . Good Lord, deliver us.

Book of Common Prayer, The Litany

Both John and Charles Wesley were reared on the *Book of Common Prayer* and must have known the Litany by heart. Here, in the first part of an extended meditation on the passion, Charles devotes a whole verse to each phrase of the Litany. The repeated bidding, 'By thy . . .' and the constant response 'save us', 'seal us', 'arm us', 'make us' have a rhythmic effect that echoes the power of the Litany itself.

PRAYER
Lord Jesus Christ, Son of God, have mercy on me. Amen.

HLR (1746) *PW 4, 138-9

By that highest point of passion,
  By thy sufferings on the tree,
Save us from the indignation
  Due to all my kind, and me;
Hanging, bleeding, panting, dying,
  Gasping out thy latest breath,
By thy precious death's applying,
  Save us from eternal death.

From the world of care release us,
  By thy decent burial save;
Crucified with thee, O Jesus,
  Hide us in thy quiet grave;
By thy power divinely glorious,
  By thy resurrection's power
Raise us up, o'er sin victorious,
  Raise us up to fall no more.

By the coming of thy Spirit
  As a mighty rushing wind,
Save us into all thy merit,
  Into all thy sinless mind;
Let the perfect gift be given,
  Let thy will in us be seen,
Done on earth as 'tis in heaven:
  Lord, thy Spirit cries 'Amen!'

. . . By thy Cross and Passion; by thy precious Death and Burial; by thy glorious Resurrection and Ascension; and by the coming of the Holy Ghost, Good Lord, deliver us.

Book of Common Prayer, The Litany

In this further reflection on the Litany, Charles Wesley vividly imagines each event in the passion of Christ, so that we become ourselves, as it were, eye-witnesses of it. Even so we pray that we may receive all the benefits of his redemption.

PRAYER
May the Holy Spirit so call to our mind the events of your passion that we may indeed claim all the benefits your love has won for us. Amen.

HLR (1746) *PW 4, 139 [1:4 all mankind]

Thou Shepherd of Israel, and mine,
The joy and desire of my heart,
For closer communion I pine,
I long to reside where thou art;
The pasture I languish to find
Where all who their Shepherd obey,
Are fed, on thy bosom reclined,
And screened from the heat of the day.

'Tis there, with the lambs of thy flock,
There only I covet to rest,
To lie at the foot of the Rock,
Or rise to be hid in thy breast;
'Tis there I would always abide,
And never a moment depart,
Concealed in the cleft of thy side,
Eternally held in thy heart.

Tell me, O thou whom my soul loveth, where thou feedest, where thou makest thy flock to rest at noon.

Song of Songs 1:7

Jews and Christians alike have found in the delightful lyrics of the Hebrew love poems of the Song of Songs an entrance into mystical meditation upon God as Lover and Beloved. Wesley begins this extraordinarily fervent text with a pastoral image, exploring the rich shepherd themes of Scripture with the passion of intimate relationship; like a lamb, he would be laid on the strong Shepherd's breast (see Isaiah 40:11).

The transition to contemplation of the Crucified may seem to us abrupt. But in the words of Johann Heermann's hymn (echoing John 10:11) this 'Good Shepherd for the sheep was offered'. The adoration of the Crucified is a rich tradition in Christian mysticism. To be so identified with the Beloved, as Wesley seeks here, may be what Paul intended when he spoke of 'bearing in my body the marks of the Lord Jesus' (Galatians 6:17). It dares to speak of a love so intense and pure that it feels itself at rest, being hidden in the wounded side of the Lord, 'eternally held' in his heart.

PRAYER

Therefore, kind Jesus, since I cannot pay thee,
I do adore thee, and will ever pray thee,
Think on thy pity and thy love unswerving,
Not my deserving.
Based on Johann Heermann

SH (1762) *HP 750

Rejoice, the Lord is King!
Your Lord and King adore;
Mortals, give thanks, and sing,
And triumph evermore:
Lift up your heart, lift up your voice;
Rejoice! Again, I say: Rejoice!

Jesus the Saviour reigns,
The God of truth and love;
When he had purged our stains,
He took his seat above:
Lift up your heart, lift up your voice,
Rejoice! Again, I say: Rejoice!

His kingdom cannot fail,
He rules o'er earth and heaven;
The keys of death and hell
Are to our Jesus given:
Lift up your heart, lift up your voice,
Rejoice! Again, I say: Rejoice!

Rejoice in glorious hope;
Jesus the Judge shall come;
And take his servants up
To their eternal home:
We soon shall hear the archangel's voice,
The trump of God shall sound: Rejoice!

The LORD reigneth; let the earth rejoice.

Psalm 97:1

'Lift up your hearts,' says the presider at the Great Thanksgiving in the Communion Service. 'We lift them up to the Lord,' is the congregational response. Wesley adapts this ancient bidding – Sursum Corda – into a rhythmic chorus of praise. The Hebrew image of kingship in Psalm 97 is modified by images of Christ from Paul's writings, and the final chorus is based on 1 Thessalonians 4:16.

Though the model of Christ as king has been part of the history of the church, it can be a dangerous one if taken in a literal sense and used to justify religious imperialism. Always before us we must hold the image of true kingship: the Christ who rode on a donkey, who never claimed a worldly kingdom, but only a kingdom of love and peace.

PRAYER
God of all truth, you show me your reign of righteousness and love. May I always – at all times and in all places – give thanks and sing praise to you, through Jesus Christ the Lord. Amen.

---

*Hymns for our Lord's Resurrection (1746) RV 59 HP 243 UMH 715-6 VU 213

Jesus, we thus obey
Thy last and kindest word;
Here, in thine own appointed way,
We come to meet thee, Lord.

Thy presence makes the feast;
Now let our spirits feel
The glory not to be expressed,
The joy unspeakable.

With pure celestial bliss
Thou dost our spirits cheer;
Thy house of banqueting is this,
And thou hast brought us here.

Now let our souls be fed
With manna from above,
And over us thy banner spread
Of everlasting love.

He brought me to the banqueting house, and his banner over me was love.
Song of Songs 2:4

In most traditions of the Christian church, the sacrament of the Lord's Supper, the Holy Communion, or the Eucharist, or the Mass, holds a central place. Whatever the celebration is called, it is held in obedience to Jesus, who commanded his disciples at their last meal together, 'Do this in remembrance of me.'

Whenever good friends gather at table together there is a sense of warm hospitality. The host has invited them to come, but they in turn open their hearts to welcome the host. So here, Christ's presence among his friends and their presence with one another together 'makes the feast'. It is in their shared relationship to him that they forge common bonds of affection.

Banquets are a time of rejoicing, of the celebration of love. The vivid imagery from the Song of Songs, where a marriage feast is being celebrated, enhances our vision of what the Eucharist can mean for us in terms of our renewed commitment to Christ, and his lifelong commitment to us.

PRAYER
Friend of sinners, your presence among us makes the feast a celebration of your love. May we who share this meal go refreshed to serve you in our neighbours and in your world. Amen.

HLS (1745) *MHB 761 [4:1 corrected as 1745] HP 614

Author of life divine,
Who hast a table spread,
Furnished with mystic wine
And everlasting bread,
Preserve the life thyself hast given,
And feed and train us up for heaven.

Our needy souls sustain
With fresh supplies of love,
Till all thy life we gain,
And all thy fullness prove,
And, strengthened by thy perfect grace,
Behold without a veil thy face.

[Jesus said] 'Those who eat my flesh and drink my blood have eternal life, and I will raise them up on the last day; for my flesh is true food, and my blood is true drink.'
John 6:54-55 (NRSV)

When the seventeenth century Dean of Lincoln, Daniel Brevint, wrote a devotional booklet entitled *The Christian Sacrament and Sacrifice* he might have been surprised to know that it would later be 'extracted' (i.e. abridged) by John Wesley, and contribute to over one hundred and sixty hymns by Charles. Brevint describes several different ways in which we can consider the Lord's Supper; here 'as it is a sign and a means of grace'.

The word 'life' appears three times in two short verses. The risen Christ, being one with God, is not only creator and 'author of life' – a phrase from Milton – but is also the preserver of life, and finally he offers that life to us, so that we are taken over by the life of God. The bread and wine are tangible reminders that God sustains our bodies every day; these elements also are 'fresh supplies of love' for our souls.

Whatever our own level of understanding of our Lord's Supper, if we just come to the table for those 'fresh supplies of love', this is all we need to ask or receive.

PRAYER
Lord Jesus Christ, present with us now . . . Breathe your spirit upon us and upon this bread and wine, that they may be heaven's food and drink for us, renewing, sustaining and making us whole, and grant that we may be your body on earth, loving and caring for the world.[1] *Iona Community*

---

*HLS (1745) HP 596

Happy the souls to Jesus joined,
And saved by grace alone;
Walking in all thy ways, we find
Our heaven on earth begun.

The church triumphant in thy love,
Their mighty joys we know;
They sing the Lamb in hymns above,
And we in hymns below.

Thee in thy glorious realm they praise,
And bow before thy throne,
We in the kingdom of thy grace –
The kingdoms are but one.

The holy to the holiest leads;
From hence our spirits rise,
And whoso in thy statutes treads
Shall meet thee in the skies.

For by grace are ye saved through faith . . . For we are his workmanship, created in Christ Jesus unto good works, which God hath before ordained that we should walk in them.

Ephesians 2:8,10

This hymn contains a skilful blending of the motifs from Scripture, depicting the church triumphant gathered around the throne, with John Wesley's teaching about the sacrament of the Lord's Supper being the place where the church on earth and the church in heaven are linked together. Pointing out that Christ had said to his disciples that he would drink no more of the fruit of the vine till he should drink it new in the kingdom of God, Wesley comments (abridging Daniel Brevint):

> In the purpose of God, his church and heaven go both together, that being the way that leads to this, as the *holy place* to the *holiest*, both of which are implied in what Christ calls the 'kingdom of God'.

This phrase is taken up into Charles Wesley's hymn, reminding us that as we walk in the way of holiness, we find that heaven begins for us even here on earth.

PRAYER
Grant, O God, that as I walk in your ways even the humdrum events of every day may be infused with glimpses of glory, and that as I come to your table I may enjoy a foretaste of the heavenly feast. So may I praise you on earth as I shall praise you in heaven. Amen.

---

*HLS (1745) [4:3 and he that] HP 816

Ah, tell us no more
The Spirit and power
Of Jesus our God
Is not to be found in this life-giving food!

Did Jesus ordain
His supper in vain,
And furnish a feast
For none but his earliest servants to taste?

In rapturous bliss
He bids us do this;
The joy it imparts
Hath witnessed his gracious design in our hearts.

With bread from above,
With comfort and love
Our Spirit he fills,
And all his unspeakable goodness reveals.

O that all now would haste
To the spiritual feast,
At Jesus's word
'Do this', and be fed with the love of our Lord!

Jesus took bread . . . and said, Take, eat: this is my body. And he took the cup . . . and he said unto them: This is my blood . . .

Mark 14:22-24

Joyous celebration has not been the hallmark of Communion in the Protestant tradition. That may explain why this hymn has never been used in a hymn book since 1761. Its dance-like rhythm, exuberant language in words like 'rapturous bliss', and its assurance of 'unspeakable goodness' as we are 'fed with the love of our Lord' emphasise the sheer joy of sharing in the feast. And this expresses Wesley's own experience of the 'comfort and love' he has known when partaking of Communion. Small wonder that he has no time for those who deny the importance of the sacrament. On the contrary – let everyone come and taste that the Lord is good.

PRAYER
Gracious God, your body brings love and your blood gives life. May I accept them both with joy and thanksgiving. Amen.

---

*HLS (1745) [5:1 O that all men would haste] PW 3, 282-3

O the depth of love divine,
Th' unfathomable grace!
Who shall say how bread and wine
God into us conveys!
How the bread his flesh imparts,
How the wine transmits his blood,
Fills his faithful people's hearts
With all the life of God!

How can heavenly spirits rise,
By earthly matter fed,
Drink herewith divine supplies,
And eat immortal bread?
Ask the Father's wisdom how;
Him that did the means ordain!
Angels round our altars bow
To search it out in vain.

Sure and real is the grace,
The manner be unknown;
Only meet us in thy ways,
And perfect us in one.
Let us taste the heavenly powers;
Lord, we ask for nothing more:
Thine to bless, 'tis only ours
To wonder and adore.

He answered and said, Whether he be a sinner or no, I know not: one thing I know, that, whereas I was blind, now I see.

John 9:25

Reading the whole of John 9 gives a clue to understanding the force behind this hymn. Its subject is the mystery of the real presence of Christ in the bread and wine of the Lord's Supper. Wesley intimates that the numerous 'how' questions in this hymn are as unanswerable by reason as those repeatedly put to the blind man by those who were calling into question his healing by Jesus. What mattered to him is that he who once was blind could now see.

PRAYER
Lord, I know not how you feed my soul;
I only bow in gratitude to receive your blessing. Amen.

---

*HLS (1745) 57 [1:4 God into man]

148 THE SACRAMENT AS A SIGN AND A MEANS OF GRACE

O thou who this mysterious bread
Didst in Emmaus break,
Return, herewith our souls to feed,
And to thy followers speak.

Unseal the volume of thy grace,
Apply the gospel word,
Open our eyes to see thy face,
Our hearts to know the Lord.

Of thee communing still, we mourn
Till thou the veil remove;
Talk with us, and our hearts shall burn
With flames of fervent love.

Enkindle now the heavenly zeal,
And make thy mercy known,
And give our pardoned souls to feel
That God and love are one.

And it came to pass, as he sat at meat with them, he took bread, and blessed it, and brake, and gave to them. And their eyes were opened, and they knew him; and he vanished out of their sight.

Luke 24:30-31

In this hymn for use at the Lord's Supper, Wesley gives us also a poem for private devotion. He takes the original story of the Emmaus resurrection experience (Luke 24:13-34) and develops many elements of it into a prayer to Christ. The first request is that Jesus come back to us to feed our souls and speak with us. The second request is that he expound the Scriptures to us. And the third request is that he stay to talk with us, so that our hearts too may burn 'with flames of fervent love'.

PRAYER

We do not presume to come to this thy Table, O merciful Lord, trusting in our own righteousness, but in thy manifold and great mercies. We are not worthy so much as to gather up the crumbs under thy Table. But thou art the same Lord, whose property is always to have mercy: Grant us therefore, gracious Lord, so to eat the flesh of thy dear Son Jesus Christ, and to drink his blood, that our sinful bodies may be made clean by his body, and our souls washed through his most precious blood, and that we may evermore dwell in him, and he in us. Amen.[1]

Methodist Service Book

HLS (1745) *HP 621 UMH 613

Victim divine, thy grace we claim,
While thus thy precious death we show;
Once offered up, a spotless Lamb,
In thy great temple here below,
Thou didst for all the world atone,
And standest now before the throne.

We need not now go up to heaven,
To bring the long-sought Saviour down;
Thou art to all already given,
Thou dost even now thy banquet crown:
To every faithful soul appear,
And show thy real presence here!

How much more shall the blood of Christ, who through the eternal Spirit offered himself without spot to God, purge your conscience from dead works to serve the living God?

Hebrews 9:14

In one sense the idea of Christ as divine victim seems to be credible only to those who live in a world of blood sacrifice. In another sense, we can understand the victim image, for we live in a world of terrible victimisation of innocent people. In this hymn Christ, himself the innocent victim, lifts all our human suffering and the sin that causes it into the presence of God, in an atoning love that makes us 'at one' with God. As we, in the Eucharist, represent that sacrifice offered once and for all, we too become conscious of Christ's real presence among us as host at the banquet. This celebration of the 'real presence' of Christ reflects the Wesleys' profoundly catholic view of the Eucharist, in which Christ is both the sacrifice and the one who offers it at the altar – both victim and priest.

PRAYER
Lord Christ, whose presence among us is made tangible in the Eucharist, help us to live in your presence throughout all our days. Amen.

HLS (1745) *RV 57 [1:5 for all mankind atone] HP 629

Come, thou everlasting Spirit,
  Bring to every thankful mind
All the Saviour's dying merit,
  All his sufferings for mankind:

True recorder of his passion,
  Now the living faith impart,
Now reveal his great salvation,
  Preach his gospel to our heart.

Come, thou witness of his dying;
  Come, Remembrancer divine,
Let us feel thy power, applying
  Christ to every soul, and mine.

But the Comforter, which is the Holy Ghost, whom the Father will send in my name, he shall teach you all things, and bring all things to your remembrance.

John 14:26

For both Jews and Christians, remembering the past and retelling the story of their deliverance has always been a central part of their worship of God. But the exact recollection of events is not easy. Details grow indistinct as time passes and people differ about their significance. Mindful that Jesus told his disciples to continue to celebrate the Last Supper 'in remembrance of me', and that he had promised in John's gospel that the Spirit would bring all things back to their memory, Charles Wesley calls in this hymn for the help of that same Spirit in recalling the suffering of Christ.

'Come Holy Spirit' is an ancient prayer of the church. In the first verse the Spirit is asked to help us to recollect the actual death on the cross. Then he asks the Spirit, who prompted the gospel writers to set down their account of the Passion, to come and interpret that gospel to our hearts. Finally, he calls on the Spirit to give us an eyewitness memory of the event itself, so that it may have power to move our hearts as it did those who were the first witnesses. Note the movement between the universal 'every soul' and the personal 'and mine'. The memory of a death that was for all must become for me a personal experience of the living presence of Christ. Interwoven through all three verses is the truth that the Spirit was there in the suffering and death of Jesus, and therefore is the 'true recorder' of the event.

MEDITATION
Though this hymn has its setting within the Communion Service, the prayer can be used in private meditation as well as in public worship. The mystical presence of the Holy Spirit can be a part of our whole life, reminding us always to be thankful.

HLS (1745) *HP 298

Come, Holy Ghost, thine influence shed,
And real make the sign;
Thy life infuse into the bread,
Thy power into the wine.

Effectual let the tokens prove
And made, by heavenly art,
Fit channels to convey thy love
To every faithful heart.

The love of God is shed abroad in our hearts by the Holy Ghost which is given unto us.

Romans 5:5

This short but complete hymn seems simple enough. The prayer that the Spirit should give power to bread and wine to make them fit channels of God's grace to us, is emphasised within the Eastern tradition of the church; in the Western tradition the moment when the priest recites the words of Christ has been the central moment of consecration.

How can one see this happening today? At a recent thanksgiving service in an inner-city mission church in Vancouver, the Communion table had on it not just the symbolic bread and wine, but great loaves of bread, bunches of grapes and a cooked salmon. Some of us had brought gifts to decorate the church, and these were to be given to others later – but here were real gifts of the presence of God given back to us. We are a very mixed lot in that church – rich and poor, people whose mother tongue is an aboriginal language or Chinese or Spanish or French; able-bodied and disabled, street people and teachers, former loggers and the unemployed, old and young and many in between. It seemed like the great banquet of the kingdom as, at the appropriate moment in the Lord's Supper, we gathered around the table all together in surprised joy to share the feast with each other. How good it was that real, familiar food was the channel to convey the love of God to every faithful heart!

PRAYER
God of surprises, help me to look through tradition and symbol to see the new ways through which you are working to show your love in the world. Grant that I too may be nourished at your table. Amen.

HLS 1745 *HP 602 [1:2 and realise]

152 CONCERNING THE SACRIFICE OF OUR PERSONS

Father, Son, and Holy Ghost,
One in Three, and Three in One,
As by the celestial host,
Let thy will on earth be done;
Praise by all to thee be given,
Glorious Lord of earth and heaven.

Take my soul and body's powers,
Take my memory, mind, and will,
All my goods, and all my hours,
All I know, and all I feel,
All I think, and speak, and do;
Take my heart, but make it new.

Now, O God, thine own I am,
Now I give thee back thy own,
Freedom, friends, and health, and fame
Consecrate to thee alone:
Thine I live, thrice happy I;
Happier still if thine I die.

Here we offer and present unto thee, O Lord, ourselves, our souls and bodies, to be a reasonable, holy, and lively sacrifice unto thee.

Book of Common Prayer, Post Communion Prayer

One of Charles Wesley's favourite words is 'all'. Often it is used to emphasise the universality of God's grace. But in this hymn it is repeated frequently to emphasise the totality of our response. There can be no half measures in our commitment to Christ. Nothing less than yielding up our whole being is a 'reasonable, holy and lively sacrifice'. Only in the undivided service of love can we find complete happiness.

PRAYER SUGGESTION

Ponder the different gifts offered in verses two and three. Does this demand a radical change of life for you, or just a change of focus? Perhaps this is a way to renew vows that you have made already.

---

*HLS (1745) RV 58 CH 418 HP 791

WALKING AND TALKING (1)

When quiet in my house I sit,
Thy Book be my companion still;
My joy thy sayings to repeat,
Talk o'er the records of thy will,
And search the oracles divine,
Till every heartfelt word be mine.

O may the gracious words divine
Subject of all my converse be!
So will the Lord his follower join,
And walk and talk himself with me;
So shall my heart his presence prove,
And burn with everlasting love.

These words, which I command thee this day, shall be in thine heart: And thou shalt teach them diligently unto thy children, and shalt talk of them when thou sittest in thine house, and when thou walkest by the way.

Deuteronomy 6:6-7

The commandments of Moses in Deuteronomy, a restatement of those of Exodus 20, contain the overriding law: 'And thou shalt love the LORD thy God with all thine heart, and with all thy soul, and with all thy might' (v5). Wesley suggests that studying the law of God is not simply a duty. It is a joy. Even sitting quietly at home with the Scriptures can be a heart-warming encounter with the living Christ, like that of the disciples at Emmaus.

The Mosaic law of love, preserved in our hearts, becomes the presence of love in the person of Christ. And we can talk and walk with him every day of our lives.

PRAYER
God of truth, as I read the record of your people and their encounter with you so long ago, may I make my own response to your word. Take away all false piety, and replace it with the strong sense of your loving presence. Amen.

SH (1762) *CH 319 MHB 310

WALKING AND TALKING (2)

Oft as I lay me down to rest,
O may the reconciling word
Sweetly compose my weary breast!
While, on the bosom of my Lord,
I sink in blissful dreams away,
And visions of eternal day.

Rising to sing my Saviour's praise,
Thee may I publish all day long;
And let thy precious word of grace
Flow from my heart, and fill my tongue;
Fill all my life with purest love,
And join me to thy Church above.

When I remember thee upon my bed, and meditate on thee in the night watches, Because thou hast been my help, therefore in the shadow of thy wings will I rejoice.
Psalm 63:6-7

These two verses focus on night and morning. Wesley – in the tradition of the Psalms – advocates the Word of God as a night-time companion. Reading the Bible before we go to sleep, as many have found, is conducive to a peaceful night. Elsewhere, he also speaks of the value of dreams:

Only tell me I am thine,
And thou wilt not quit thy right;
Answer me in dreams divine,
Dreams and visions of the night.

In Jungian psychology, dreams are one of the ways into our subconscious. In the ancient world, dreams were understood to be used as a vehicle for messages from God. Wesley draws on the biblical heritage to pray that in this most vulnerable time when we have no control of our thoughts, God will enter our lives through our dreams.

Many of us also find, with Wesley, that praise is a necessary start to a busy day, and those moments of conscious prayer stay with us even in the difficult times.

PRAYER
Gracious Spirit, guard my sleeping and dreaming.
Gracious Spirit, prompt my waking and working.
May each hour of night and day be spent in your presence,
and to you be all praise and glory. Amen.

SH (1762) *CH 319 MHB 310

Come, divine Interpreter,
  Bring me eyes thy book to read,
Ears the mystic words to hear,
  Words that did from thee proceed,
Words that endless bliss impart,
  Kept in an obedient heart.

All who read, or hear, are blest,
  If thy plain commands we do;
Of thy kingdom here possessed,
  Thee we shall in glory view–
When thou comest on earth to abide
  Reign triumphant at thy side.

Blessed is the one who reads aloud the words of the prophecy, and blessed are those who hear and who keep what is written in it.

Revelation 1:3 (NRSV)

This short hymn on a passage from Revelation is characteristic of Charles Wesley's gift for expanding original images to larger purposes. He invokes the divine help that is necessary if we are to understand the Bible. One needs reading glasses – 'bring me eyes' – and a good hearing aid – 'ears the mystic words to hear' – to find the spiritual truth in the Word of God. Having understood the Word, we are then called to do it.

More light is thrown on the expression 'divine interpreter' by the story of Joseph's dream, where Joseph asks the prison guards: 'Do not interpretations belong to God?' (Genesis 40:8). The question is relevant today when so many contradictory voices call out 'the Bible says', and the meaning of what once seemed 'plain commands' is subject to honest debate.

MEDITATION
Use this hymn as a prayer before Bible reading. As you read, try to imagine to whom the words were first addressed, and to understand its message to them. In a very different world today, what are the same words saying to us, and to you in particular? Is there something you are being invited to do?

PRAYER
We bring before you, O God, all who work to interpret your Word for our world. We ask you to bless the work of those who translate the Scriptures, those who examine the texts, those who expound the message. May your Word go forth with power and accomplish your purpose. For your name's sake. Amen.

---

*SH (1762) HP 468 [1:2 Bring us] UMH 594

THE WRITTEN WORD

The written word, entire and pure,
The word which always shall endure,
   My rule of faith and life I own;
Not reason or tradition vain,
Not the authority of man,
   Not an internal light alone.

Built, through the sacred oracles,
On Christ, the Rock that never fails,
   Religion from the fountain brought:
I find it in the heavenly book,
What Moses and the prophets spoke,
   What Christ and his apostles taught.

[Paul said to Felix:] 'I worship the God of our ancestors, believing everything laid down according to the law or written in the prophets.'

Acts 24:14 (NRSV)

In this meditation based on the words of Paul, Charles Wesley vigorously affirms the supremacy of Scripture as his rule of faith and life.

The late American scholar, Albert Outler, coined the phrase 'the Wesley quadrilateral' to describe how the Wesleys' reliance on the Bible was supported by their reference also to tradition, reason and experience as their guide to life. By their upbringing in a strict Anglican home they had learned to value tradition; by their classical education they had learned to employ reason; by their own spiritual pilgrimage they had learned to grow through experience. But in this hymn Wesley nonetheless insists that no 'internal light' (a phrase used by the Quakers) should be allowed to divert from the illumination which Scripture alone can give.

In one of his letters, John Wesley gives a good guide as to how he himself used the Scriptures:

> I apply no Scripture phrase either to myself or any other without carefully considering both the original meaning and the secondary sense, wherein (allowing for different times and circumstances) it might be applied to ordinary Christians.

PRAYER
God, grant me all the gifts of tradition, reason and experience in understanding your Word. Amen.

---

*PW 12, 411

Father of all, in whom alone
We live, and move, and breathe,
One bright celestial ray dart down,
And cheer each child beneath.

While in thy word we search for thee
(We search with trembling awe!)
Open our eyes, and let us see
The wonders of thy law.

Now let our darkness comprehend
The light that shines so clear;
Now the revealing Spirit send,
And give us ears to hear.

Before us make thy goodness pass,
Which here by faith we know;
Let us in Jesus see thy face,
And die to all below.

Yet he is not far from each one of us, for 'In him we live and move and have our being.'

Acts 17:28 (RSV)

Open thou mine eyes, that I may behold wondrous things out of thy law.

Psalm 119:18

Charles Wesley wrote many hymns about our need for enlightenment in reading the Bible. Like Paul, he believed that God is not far from any one of us, and, like the psalmist, he believed that our eyes can be opened to discern God's presence as we read the Scriptures.

Verses three and four suggest that with such illumination, we can experience the reversal of what is described in John 1:5: 'The light shineth in darkness; and the darkness comprehended it not.' With the Spirit's revealing help, we can come to comprehend the truth, in spite of our darkness. Similarly, we can experience the reversal of Exodus 33:18-20, where Moses says to God, 'Show me your glory,' and God replies, 'I shall make all my goodness pass before you. But my face you cannot see, for no mortal may see me and live.' In the incarnate Jesus we *can* see the face of God and live; our death is to our old way of life.

PRAYER
God, you who are the very foundation of my being, guide me into all truth as I read your Word, and show me your goodness. Amen.

HSP (1740) *CH 86 [1:4 cheer thy sons] MHB 304

Saviour, I still to thee apply,
Before I read or hear,
Creator of the seeing eye,
And of the hearing ear:
The understanding heart bestow,
The wisdom from above,
So shall I all thy doctrines know,
And all thy sayings love.

Because they seeing see not; and hearing they hear not, neither do they understand.
Matthew 13:13

A simple, profound prayer for use before reading the Bible or hearing a sermon. Some background to the biblical text on which it is based makes it even richer in meaning.

Matthew shows the disciples asking Jesus why he teaches in parables. Jesus replies that some people 'look without seeing, and listen without hearing or understanding' (NEB). Perhaps these parables will wake them up, and make them see in a different way, for a parable by its very nature allows the hearer to become part of the story. Perhaps when we really listen to the Word with an open mind and heart, we also will hear in a new way.

But there is an older echo too. It was Solomon, the new king, wanting to serve the Lord and be a good ruler, who had a dream that God said, 'Ask what I shall give thee.' Solomon did not choose material gifts or long life or victory against enemies, but instead said: 'Give therefore thy servant an understanding heart [a heart with skill to listen (NEB)] to judge thy people, that I may discern between good and bad . . .' (1 Kings 3:9). In asking for an understanding heart, we may well be asking for the best gift in the world.

PRAYER
Saviour, open our eyes that we may see your radiance reflected in the world around us; open our ears that we may hear your voice speaking to us through your Word; open our hearts that we may have a wise understanding of those whose lives touch ours this day. Amen.

---

*PW 10, 269

Spirit of truth, essential God,
    Who didst thine ancient saints inspire,
Shed in their hearts thy love abroad
    And touch their hallowed lips with fire;
Our God from all eternity,
World without end we worship thee!

Still we believe, almighty Lord,
    Whose presence fills both earth and heaven,
The meaning of the written word
    Is still by inspiration given;
Thou only dost thyself explain
The secret mind of God to man.

All scripture is given by inspiration of God, and is profitable for doctrine, for reproof, for correction, for instruction in righteousness.

2 Timothy 3:16

Ask any five people what they mean by 'the Word of God' and you will probably get five different answers. Scholars have gone a long way to examine the when, where, how, and even the why of the Bible and its individual books, so that we have vast resources for finding out more about it. Charles and John Wesley never ignored the scholarship of their day but still said that the final clue to our right understanding is the inspiration of God, the inner witness of the Spirit.

The same God, who in the past inspired the writers of Scripture, breathes in us today as we hear the sacred text in worship, or as we read it to ourselves, and opens for us 'the meaning of the written word', explaining the 'secret mind of God' to us now.

PRAYER
Timeless One, yet God of all time, now give me your Spirit of truth that I may read your inspired Word with an informed and understanding heart.

HT (1767) *CH 247 HP 480

COME, HOLY GHOST

Come, Holy Ghost, our hearts inspire,
    Let us thy influence prove;
Source of the old prophetic fire,
    Fountain of life and love.

Come, Holy Ghost, (for moved by thee
    The prophets wrote and spoke),
Unlock the truth, thyself the key,
    Unseal the sacred book.

Expand thy wings, prolific Dove,
    Brood o'er our nature's night;
On our disordered spirits move,
    And let there now be light.

God through himself we then shall know,
    If thou within us shine;
And sound, with all thy saints below,
    The depths of love divine.

No prophetic writing is a matter for private interpretation. It was not on any human initiative that prophecy came; rather, it was under the compulsion of the Holy Spirit that people spoke as messengers of God.

2 Peter 1:20-21 (REB)

This hymn is a prayer that the same Spirit which inspired the words of the Bible might shine in our hearts to make us understand what they really mean. In every generation the work of scholars and interpreters brings fresh insight into the meaning of the Bible. There are also times, though, when something strikes a reader anew, when a word becomes clear, or a life experience illuminates and confirms something in the Bible we could not see before. The Spirit has inspired us.

When John Milton set out to serve God by writing his great poem, *Paradise Lost,* he prayed not only for the power of the poetic muse, but also for the illumination of the Holy Spirit:

> Instruct me, for thou know'st thou from the first
> Wast present, and with mighty wings outspread
> Dovelike sat'st brooding on the vast abyss
> And mad'st it pregnant: what in me is dark
> Illumine . . . (*PL* 1:19-24)

Wesley takes these words and makes them his own in the third verse of this hymn.

MEDITATION
Rewrite parts of this hymn to make it personal, and use it before reading the Bible.

---

*HSP (1740) CH 85 [3:1 celestial dove] HP 469 UMH 603

Lord, we believe to us and ours
The apostolic promise given;
We wait the pentecostal powers,
The Holy Ghost sent down from heaven.

If everyone that asks may find,
If still thou dost on sinners fall,
Come as a mighty rushing wind;
Great grace be now upon us all.

Wisdom and strength to thee belongs,
Sweetly within our bosoms move,
Now let us speak with other tongues
The new strange language of thy love.

To testify the grace of God,
Today as yesterday the same,
And spread through all the earth abroad,
The wonders wrought by Jesus' name.

And when the day of Pentecost was fully come, they were all with one accord in one place. And suddenly there came a sound from heaven as of a rushing mighty wind, and it filled all the house where they were sitting. And there appeared unto them cloven tongues like as of fire . . . and they were all filled with the Holy Ghost, and began to speak with other tongues.

Acts 2:1-4

This hymn has little of the exuberance of many of Wesley's other Pentecost hymns. One can imagine it being sung reverently and quietly as a congregational invitation to the Spirit. It is unfortunate that the later verses are rarely sung today, for they move it away from contemplative meditation into a world where people recognise little of the love of God. It becomes a challenge to us to witness to the faith by the gifts of God's Spirit. In a lovely allusion to Paul's hymn to love (1 Corinthians 13), we are encouraged to seek the gift of a language of love, for a world where God's love is too often a stranger.

PRAYER

As the invisible wind shakes the branches, as they bow before its power, so may your Spirit shake our lives into a yielding love and obedience to your will, through Jesus Christ our Lord. Amen.

HSP (1742) [1:3 to taste the heavenly powers 2:1 If thou art still to sinners given] *HP 307

PROMISE OF THE COMFORTER

Jesus, we on the word depend
  Spoken by thee while present here:
'The Father in my name shall send
  The Holy Ghost, the Comforter.'

That heavenly Teacher of mankind,
  That Guide infallible impart,
To bring thy sayings to our mind,
  And write them on our faithful heart.

He only can the words apply
  Through which we endless life possess;
And deal to each our legacy,
  Our Lord's unutterable peace.

That peace of God, that peace of thine,
  O might he now to us bring in,
And fill our souls with power divine,
  And make an end of fear and sin.

The Comforter, which is the Holy Ghost, whom the Father will send in my name, he shall teach you all things, and bring all things to your remembrance, whatsoever I have said unto you. Peace I leave with you, my peace I give unto you: not as the world giveth, give I unto you. Let not your heart be troubled, neither let it be afraid.
John 14:26-27

The hymn starts in a conversational tone. As a child might speak to her father – 'You promised – don't forget' – so Wesley, on behalf of all of us, tells Jesus that we are depending on his word; he promised that though he had to go away, he would send the Comforter.

As the hymn progresses, it stays close to the teaching of Jesus in the Gospel of John but, as might be expected, builds on it. The Comforter will not just be a Teacher, but an infallible inner, heart-directing Guide; the 'writing' allusion is to the new covenant described in Jeremiah 31:31-34. Christ's peace is for Wesley 'unutterable'; to it is added the power of the Spirit, promised by Jesus to the disciples in words recorded in Acts 1:8: 'Ye shall receive power after that the Holy Spirit is come upon you.'

PRAYER
May the peace of God, which passes all understanding, keep our hearts and minds in the knowledge and love of God and of his Son, Jesus Christ. Amen.

HPT (1746) PW 4, 179 *MHB 275 [3:4-5 And deal to each his/His Lord's]

O come and dwell in me,
Spirit of power within,
And bring the glorious liberty
From sorrow, fear, and sin.

Hasten the joyful day
Which shall my sins consume,
When old things shall be passed away,
And all things new become.

I want the witness, Lord,
That all I do is right,
According to thy mind and word,
Well-pleasing in thy sight.

I ask no higher state;
Indulge me but in this,
And soon or later then translate
To thine eternal bliss.

Where the Spirit of the Lord is, there is liberty.

2 Corinthians 3:17

This is a simple but urgent prayer of petition. Maria, a seventy year old member of Alcoholics Anonymous, is similarly definite about the way God can meet her needs. She has spent a lifetime battling against alcohol and drug addiction caused initially by a destructive childhood. She often feels deep distress because her schizophrenic daughter defies medical treatment, and Maria feels helpless. Her own health is desperately precarious. In spite of, or perhaps because of all this, she is a comfort and an inspiration to others in their times of distress. When she cannot help being swamped by circumstances, she tells of how God alone can save her from fear and turn her sorrow to joy, as he has done so often in the past. This is the power of God within her which brings glorious victory, her 'higher power'. This is the power Wesley seeks here, the power available to us.

PRAYER
God, grant me the inner assurance of your power, that can set me free from whatever holds me captive and can prepare me for that perfection which is your will for my life now and in eternity. Amen.

SH (1762) *CH 356 [3:3 will and word 4:4 To my; Thine = 1762] HP 293 UMH 388

164 THE COMFORTER COMES

Granted is the Saviour's prayer,
Sent the gracious Comforter;
Promise of our parting Lord,
Jesus to his heaven restored:

Christ who, now gone up on high,
Captive leads captivity;
While his foes from him receive
Grace that God with them may live.

God, the everlasting God,
Makes with mortals his abode;
Whom the heavens cannot contain,
He vouchsafes to dwell in man.

Never will he thence depart,
Inmate of a humble heart;
Carrying on his work within,
Striving till he casts out sin.

I will pray the Father, and he shall give you another Comforter, that he may abide with you for ever.

John 14:16

It is said, 'When he ascended on high he made captivity itself a captive; he gave gifts to his people.'

Ephesians 4:8 (NRSV)

Today's selection is part of a longer, ten-verse hymn, some of which will be continued tomorrow. The opening verses are, for Charles, unusual in tone. Without any reference to his personal experience, he simply declares that the words of Scripture have been fulfilled, the promised Comforter (strengthener) has come and is now available to all who will humbly receive him. The condensed lines of the second verse echo Paul's words in Ephesians, which are themselves a striking reversal of the imagery in Psalm 68:18, on which they are based. There the king demands gifts of his captives; here the ascended Christ gives gifts to those who were formerly his enemies.

Verse three echoes the words of King Solomon who said, 'Will God indeed dwell on the earth? behold the heaven and heaven of heavens cannot contain thee' (1 Kings 8:27). Now Charles, in the light of the fulfilled promise of Jesus, (John 14:23) knows that God has come to abide among us.

PRAYER
Spirit of God, come into my life as you came at the first Pentecost, bringing your gifts of grace and casting out my sin. Amen.

HSP (1739) PW 1, 188 *HP 287 [2:4 with man]

COME, DIVINE GUEST

Come, divine and peaceful Guest,
Enter our devoted breast;
Holy Ghost, our hearts inspire,
Kindle there the Gospel-fire.

Now descend, and shake the earth;
Wake us into second birth;
Now thy quickening influence give,
Blow – and these dry bones shall live!

Pain and sin and sorrow cease,
Thee we taste, and all is peace;
Joy divine in thee we prove,
Light of truth and fire of love.

Suddenly there came a sound from heaven as of a rushing mighty wind, and it filled all the house where they were sitting. And there appeared unto them cloven tongues like as of fire, and it sat upon each of them. And they were all filled with the Holy Ghost.
Acts 2:2-4

At this point, the hymn of declaration we looked at yesterday turns into a personal and corporate prayer to the Spirit: 'Come!' As the group of disciples waited before the first Pentecost, so the congregation of people waits for corporate inspiration – literally a 'breathing into' ourselves of the life of God.

Jesus had told Nicodemus that unless he was born again of water and spirit he could not see the kingdom of God (John 3:3,5). So Wesley asks for us a most dramatic rebirth. It may take the shaking of the earth itself to wake us up. His source comes from the prophecy of Haggai, familiar to many through the music of Handel's *Messiah*: 'My Spirit remaineth among you . . . I will shake the heavens, and the earth, and the sea, and the dry land . . . and the desire of all nations shall come (Haggai 2:5-7).

Take time to savour the last four short lines of the hymn! We 'taste' and 'prove' the end of sin and sorrow, and we receive the gifts of peace and joy and not just love, but the burning 'fire of love'.

PRAYER
Come, Holy Spirit, shake the earth and awaken us to the power of your light and love. Amen.

---

*HSP (1739) PW 1, 189 *HP 287

166 HYMN TO THE HOLY GHOST (1)

Come, Holy Ghost, all-quickening fire,
  Come, and in me delight to rest;
Drawn by the lure of strong desire,
  O come and consecrate my breast!
The temple of my soul prepare,
And fix thy sacred presence there!

If now thy influence I feel,
  If now in thee begin to live,
Still to my heart thyself reveal;
  Give me thyself, for ever give:
A point my good, a drop my store,
Eager I ask, and pant for more.

Eager for thee I ask and pant:
  So strong, the principle divine
Carries me out with sweet constraint
  Till all my hallowed soul be thine,
Plunged in the Godhead's deepest sea,
And lost in thy immensity.

Know ye not that ye are the temple of God, and that the Spirit of God dwelleth in you?
1 Corinthians 3:16

As the hart panteth after the water brooks, so panteth my soul after thee, O God.
Psalm 42:1

This is a hymn in six verses, three of which will be considered tomorrow. It burns with the fire of Charles' own recent conversion experience, on Pentecost Sunday 1738. Into it he pours all his skill as a poet. No hymn book today prints all six verses, so we miss the great rising and falling movement of the poem which starts and ends with the same verse – the invocation of the Spirit, 'Come!' The centre of the poem, expressed in the two middle verses (verse three above, and verse one in tomorrow's text) is the assured confidence of bliss in union with God that will be brought about when prayer is answered and the Spirit *does* come.

Jesus had promised to send the Comforter (John 15:16); Charles, knowing the power given at Pentecost to the earliest disciples, claims this for himself. Note the words of passion: 'delight'; the 'lure of strong desire'; 'I ask and pant for more'; the 'sweet constraint' of being possessed by God, and finally, the powerful elemental image of being lost in the 'Godhead's deepest sea'.

PRAYER
Come, Holy Spirit and prepare a place in my heart, that I too may be lost in the immensity of your love. Amen.

HSP (1739) *CH 363 HP 282

My peace, my life, my comfort thou,
  My treasure and my all thou art;
True witness of adoption, thou
  Engraving pardon on my heart,
Seal of my sins in Christ forgiven,
Earnest of love, and pledge of heaven.

Come then, my God, mark out thine heir,
  Of heaven a larger earnest give!
With clearer light thy witness bear;
  More sensibly within me live:
Let all my powers thine entrance feel,
And deeper stamp thyself the seal!

Come, Holy Ghost, all-quickening fire,
  Come, and in me delight to rest;
Drawn by the lure of strong desire,
  O come and consecrate my breast!
The temple of my soul prepare,
And fix thy sacred presence there!

In whom ye also trusted, after that ye heard the word of truth, the gospel of your salvation: in whom also after that ye believed, ye were sealed with that holy Spirit of promise, which is the earnest of our inheritance until the redemption of the purchased possession, unto the praise of his glory.

Ephesians 1:13-14

Someone once said that only those who had already received mercy could ask for it with assurance; so it is with the coming of the Spirit. The passion expressed by Wesley in the first part of this hymn continues in this latter half, because he wants more of what he has already received. The first verse says what the Spirit gives already: peace, life, comfort, treasure, witness to the family relationship with God, pledge of forgiveness, love and life in God. What more could one want?

Everything! The second verse is full of 'more' words: 'larger', 'clearer', 'more sensibly' (i.e. perceptibly), 'deeper' and, finally, not just the stamp of forgiveness but the deeper imprint of the presence of the Holy Spirit. The final verse repeats the first verse of the hymn, marking the spiral of life in the Spirit.

PRAYER
Come again, O Holy Spirit. As you have already come to my life, come again and find in me your welcome home. Amen.

HSP (1739) [1:3 witness of my sonship 2:1,5 thy] *CH 363 HP 282

I want the Spirit of power within,
Of love, and of a healthful mind:
Of power, to conquer inbred sin;
Of love, to thee and all mankind;
Of health, that pain and death defies,
Most vigorous when the body dies.

O that the Comforter would come,
Nor visit as a transient guest,
But fix in me his constant home,
And take possession of my breast,
And fix in me his loved abode,
The temple of indwelling God!

Where the indubitable seal
That ascertains the kingdom mine,
The powerful stamp I long to feel,
The signature of love divine?
O shed it in my heart abroad –
Fullness of love, of heaven, of God!

For God hath not given us the spirit of fear; but of power, and of love, and of a sound mind.

2 Timothy 1:7

The first verse of the poem echoes Paul's encouraging words to his young friend and helper Timothy, who had been brought up in the faith of God by his mother Eunice, and his grandmother Lois. The poet's first line shows that he feels he needs these gifts of the Spirit as much as Timothy did. What he calls 'inbred sin', what we might translate as an urge to do wrong, haunts him. Note how lines two-six describe more fully the gifts of the Spirit, ending with the paradoxical image of spiritual health and death.

The second verse is set in John's gospel (14:16). Jesus tells his friends that although he has to leave them, he will ask God to send another Comforter who will 'be with you for ever'. Wesley's phrase 'fix in me' demands that the Holy Spirit make a permanent home in us. Paul's words to the Corinthians, 'Do you not know that you are God's temple and that God's Spirit dwells in you?' (1 Corinthians 3:16 NRSV), are the source of the last line.

Handcraft often carries the signature or distinguishing stamp of its maker. Wesley yearns for a similar seal of unquestioned authenticity – the imprint of divine love permeating his whole being (see Ephesians 1:13).

MEDITATION
Look up the Bible references in this passage and read them in context. Now read the hymn again, making into your own prayer the parts that ring true for you.

HSP (1740) [2:3 and make my soul] *CH 365 HP 291

O that the world might know
The all-atoning Lamb!
Spirit of faith, descend, and show
The virtue of his name;
The grace which all may find,
The saving power, impart,
And testify to all the world,
And speak in every heart.

Inspire the living faith
(Which whosoe'er receive,
The witness in themselves they have,
And consciously believe),
The faith that conquers all,
And doth the mountain move,
And saves whoe'er on Jesus call,
And perfects them in love.

Whatever is born of God conquers the world. And this is the victory that conquers the world, our faith . . . Those who believe in the Son of God have the testimony in their hearts.

1 John 5:4,10 (NRSV)

'Spirit of faith come down/Reveal the things of God' is the first line of this hymn and, though not used here, is its underlying theme. These last two verses stress the power of faith to change lives, to move the mountains of ingrained habit and despair.

Inner certainty of faith (or the 'inner witness') is something only recognised after one receives it. Sometimes this is described as a conversion experience, and there have been those – John Wesley among them – who seek to define and categorise components of this experience.[1] Charles happily uses the language of grace, faith, assurance and perfect love with little or no distinction, because at a deep level he understands the experience of God's love for us to be all one.

Martin Luther, in his *Preface to Romans* in the 1522 German New Testament, describes faith as 'a lively, reckless confidence in the grace of God, so sure of itself that the believer could die a thousand times for it . . . [it makes a person] bold hearted, joyful toward God and all creation.' It is a gift well worth asking for.

PRAYER
God of all trust, may we who confess your faith prove it in our lives, with abundant joy, outrageous hope, and dependence on nothing but your word alone, through Jesus Christ. Amen.[2] *Janet Morley*

HPT (1746) *CH 83 [1:7 all mankind 2:2-4 receives/in himself he hath/ . . . believes] HP 325

170 SPIRIT OF LIFE AND POWER AND LOVE

Father of everlasting grace,
Thy goodness and thy truth we praise,
  Thy goodness and thy truth we prove;
Thou hast, in honour of thy Son,
The gift unspeakable sent down,
  The Spirit of life, and power, and love.

Send us the Spirit of thy Son,
To make the depths of Godhead known,
  To make us share the life divine;
Send him the sprinkled blood to apply,
Send him our souls to sanctify,
  And show and seal us ever thine.

So shall we pray, and never cease,
So shall we thankfully confess
  Thy wisdom, truth, and power, and love,
With joy unspeakable adore,
And bless and praise thee evermore,
  And serve thee as thy hosts above.

Thanks be unto God for his unspeakable gift.

2 Corinthians 9:15

Originally the first hymn in a tract called 'Hymns for Whit-Sunday', this selection shows exuberant, confident joy in the 'goodness and truth' of the Holy Spirit. This is a corporate vision: the whole community of faith rejoices in the gift of the Spirit who comes to all of us with 'life, and power, and love'. All those qualities of God, seen in Christ, can now be ours because we have received this gift.

Notice how our response to 'the gift unspeakable' (indescribable) in verse one is to adore 'with joy unspeakable' (inexpressible) in verse three. This suggests a reciprocal relationship – a friendship with God that takes the gift of the Spirit and responds with a joy that surpasses description. This is more than a God-me relationship. It implies that we are caught up into communion with all the saints who have gone before us, and will come after us, in one continuous song of praise, and life of service.

PRAYER
Parent God, in whom we with all things live and move and have our being, may we feel and prove the life, power and love of your Spirit, that all our days may be joyful in your praise and your service. Amen.

Hymns of Petition and Thanksgiving (1746) *CH 366 HP 300

Sinners, lift up your hearts
  The promise to receive!
Jesus himself imparts,
  He comes in us to live:
The Holy Ghost to us is given;
Rejoice in God sent down from heaven.

Jesus is glorified,
  And gives the Comforter,
His Spirit, to reside
  In all his members here:
The Holy Ghost to us is given;
Rejoice in God sent down from heaven.

To make an end of sin,
  And Satan's works destroy,
He brings his kingdom in,
  Peace, righteousness and joy:
The Holy Ghost to us is given;
Rejoice in God sent down from heaven.

And it shall come to pass in the last days, saith God, I will pour out of my Spirit upon all flesh, and your sons and your daughters shall prophesy, and your young men shall see visions, and your old men shall dream dreams.

Acts 2:17

The scene is Peter's declaration to the crowd on the day of Pentecost that Christ's promise had been fulfilled. The Holy Spirit has come to dwell among God's people, giving them the power to prophesy and to proclaim the coming of the kingdom. That power has been poured out, as the prophet Joel had foretold, on young and old, on women and men alike (2:28).

The hymn asserts that it is also a gift available to all of us, an occasion for great celebration and repeated acclamations of joy. God has come down to earth, to show us the life of heaven.

PRAYER
Spirit of truth, whom the world can never grasp, touch our hearts with the shock of your coming; fill us with desire for your disturbing peace; and fire us with longing to speak your uncontainable word, through Jesus Christ. Amen.[1] *Janet Morley*

---

*UPCW 2, 287 [1:4-5 in man/to man (and so in vv 2 & 3)]

Praise be to the Father given;
Christ he gave
Us to save
Now the heirs of heaven.

Pay we equal adoration
To the Son;
He alone
Wrought out our salvation.

Glory to the eternal Spirit!
Us he seals,
Christ reveals,
And applies his merit.

Worship, honour, thanks and blessing,
One and Three,
Give we thee,
Never, never ceasing.

Glory be to the Father, and to the Son, and to the Holy Ghost, as it was in the beginning, is now and ever shall be: world without end. Amen.

A fourth century doxology

First published as early as 1740, this hymn was later included in *Hymns to the Trinity* (1746). Its unusual rhythm and delightful rhyme show the influence of John Cennick, whose ' 'Ere I sleep for every favour' had been corrected for the press by Wesley in 1739.

The classic doctrine of the Trinity was the language chosen by the church in the fourth century to name the reality of the God they knew in Jesus Christ, through the presence of the Holy Spirit. This little poem may seem simple, but its skilled interweaving of ideas is almost Celtic in pattern. We are included from the very first verse with its play on the verb 'give'; that is, we give praise to God, and God gives Christ to us. The second verse explains the work of Christ, then in the third verse, the Spirit refers us back to Christ again. In the last verse, the focus returns to our giving once more – this time our worship to the Trinity.

PRAYER

Be the eye of God welling with you, the foot of Christ in guidance with you, the shower of the Spirit pouring on you, richly and generously.[1]

---

*HSP (1740) RV 116

HOLY, HOLY, HOLY

Hail! holy, holy, holy Lord!
Whom One in Three we know;
By all thy heavenly host adored,
By all thy Church below.

One undivided Trinity
With triumph we proclaim;
The universe is full of thee,
And speaks thy glorious name.

Thee, holy Father, we confess,
Thee, holy Son, adore,
Thee, Spirit of true holiness,
We worship evermore.

Thine incommunicable right,
Almighty God, receive,
Which angel choirs, and saints in light,
And saints embodied give.

And one cried unto another, and said, Holy, holy, holy, is the LORD of hosts: the whole earth is full of his glory.

Isaiah 6:3

In this meditation on Isaiah's vision in the temple, the three times 'holy' of the angelic cry to God is turned into a prayer of praise to the three persons of God: Father, Son, and Spirit – the 'undivided Trinity'.

It is not just mortals and angels who sing this praise, but a third voice joins in. The whole universe is full of God, the three-in-one, and 'speaks' the praise of God. The Hebrew people, like many aboriginal people today, understood that nature 'spoke'; thus they listened to the voice of creation. Then in verse four another group of three : the angels, the saints above, and we ourselves (the 'saints embodied') paradoxically give back this 'right' to God, to be worshipped by the whole of creation.

PRAYER
Glory to God, glory to Jesus, glory to the Spirit,
Alleluia, amen. Alleluia, amen. Alleluia, amen.

---

*HT (1767) CH 251 MHB 37

TO THE TRINITY

Holy, holy, holy Lord,
God the Father and the Word,
God the Comforter, receive
Blessing more than we can give!

Thee while dust and ashes sings,
Angels shrink within their wings;
Prostrate Seraphim above
Breathe unutterable love.

Happy they who never rest,
With thy heavenly presence blest;
They the heights of glory see,
Sound the depths of Deity!

Fain with them our souls would vie,
Sink as low, and mount as high:
Fall, o'erwhelmed with love, or soar,
Shout, or silently adore.

Abraham said, 'May I make so bold as to speak to the Lord, I who am nothing but dust and ashes.'

Genesis 18:27(REB)

The four beasts . . . rest not day and night saying, Holy, holy, holy, Lord God Almighty, which was, and is, and is to come.

Revelation 4:8

The visionary language of the Bible, the early church and classical poets such as Milton, assumes a universe where heaven is alive with marvellous creatures, among them a host of different forms of angels. This is all in the consciousness of Charles Wesley as he tries to capture the incomprehensible nature of the Trinity. In this poem, the whole creation gives praise: we sing it, while the angels, in a delightful turn of phrase, 'shrink within their wings', amazed by the songs of redeemed humanity. The seraphim reach heights of adoration simply by breathing the love too deep for words.

In the last two verses, we humans join the heavenly company to experience the dimensional contrasts of height and depth, sinking and rising, falling and soaring. Finally we move to contrasts of verbal praise – a shout, or, like the seraphim, the breath of silence.

PRAYER
Triune God, help me to adore the mystery of your being in silent praise. Amen.

HT (1767) *CH 252

AARON'S BLESSING

Come, Father, Son and Holy Ghost,
  One God in Persons three!
Bring back the heavenly blessing, lost
  By all the world, and me.
Thy favour, and thy nature too,
  To me, to all restore!
Forgive and after God renew
  And keep us evermore.

Eternal Sun of Righteousness,
  Display thy beams divine,
And cause the glory of thy face
  Upon my heart to shine.
Light in thy light O may I see,
  Thy grace and mercy prove,
Revived and cheered and blessed by thee,
  The God of pardoning love.

Lift up thy countenance serene,
  And let thy happy child
Behold, without a cloud between,
  The Godhead reconciled;
That all-comprising peace bestow
  On me, through grace forgiven;
The joys of holiness below,
  And then the joys of heaven.

The LORD bless thee, and keep thee: The LORD make his face shine upon thee, and be gracious unto thee: The LORD lift up his countenance upon thee, and give thee peace.
Numbers 6:24-26

The three parts of what is now known as the 'Aaronic blessing' are reflected in these three verses. God's instruction to Moses that he should tell Aaron and his sons this proper form of blessing for the people of Israel becomes an opportunity for Wesley to explore particular Christian implications of these beautiful words. For the Christian it is the revelation of God in the face of Christ that brings renewal, cheer and blessing. This sun illuminates our lives with 'pardoning love', giving us joy in this life, and leading us on to the joys of the next.

PRAYER
O God, give me the peace of a life lived in the light of your smile this day. Amen.

SH (1762) [1:4 all mankind] *CH 243

COME AND FIND HIM

Come ye that seek the Lord,
Him that was crucified,
Come listen to the Gospel-word,
And feel it now applied.

The Lord is risen indeed,
And did to us appear,
He hath been seen, our living Head,
By many a Peter here.

Raised from the dead we are
The members with their Lord,
And boldly in his name declare
The soul-reviving Word.

He lives, who spilt his blood:
Believe our record true,
The arm, the power, the Son of God
Shall be revealed in you.

Peter, standing with the eleven, raised his voice and addressed them: 'Listen to what I say . . . This Jesus God raised up, and of that all of us are witnesses.'
Acts 2:14,32 (NRSV)

A hymn based on Peter's bold sermon on the day of Pentecost. Peter was the one who had most blatantly denied he knew Jesus after his arrest; now, by the gift of the Spirit, he courageously and eloquently interprets Scripture, quoting the words of king David and the prophet Joel, but above all speaking for himself as an eyewitness of the resurrection of Jesus.

The hymn captures the enthusiasm and urgency of Peter's speech. It emphasises that Peter's experience is one that can be shared by all who believe in Christ.

PRAYER
Lord, though our eyes have not seen you, our hearts can know you in all your risen presence. Help us to proclaim to others the glorious message of your resurrection, through the power of your Spirit. Amen.

HLR (1746) *PW 4, 143-4

Abundant grace indeed
On the first saints bestowed!
From every selfish temper freed
Their hearts with love o'erflowed;
Who suffered none to lack,
Their fruits of grace were shown,
Their mutual love for Jesus' sake
Declared they all were one.

By the same strength of grace
And cordial charity,
Produced in every age and place
The same effects must be.
And thus, ye heirs of light,
Thus only can ye prove
The length and breadth and depth and height
Of truly perfect love.

And with great power gave the apostles witness of the resurrection of the Lord Jesus: and great grace was upon them all.

Acts 4:33

In the power of the Pentecost experience, the whole body of believers in the early church shared with each other everything they had, and claimed nothing as their own. Wesley makes it quite clear that God's gift of 'abundant grace' was the force behind this life of mutual love in action, for they had been liberated from all selfish instincts.

But this is not just an historic tale. In the second verse of this short meditation we are reminded that this same grace is available for 'every age and place' and produces the same effects. The last four lines address us personally. Only in the practice of mutual giving can we 'prove' (demonstrate) the dimensions of God's love, and live by that grace in unity with one another.

PRAYER
God of all, you call us to many different ways of living; inspire us with your vision of mutual love so that we may learn to share our possessions and our lives in ways we have never before imagined. Bestow on us your grace, that we may have the power to live out what we believe, for it is in giving that we receive . . . it is in dying that we are born to eternal life. Amen.

---

*UPCW 2, 297 [2:5 sons of light]

Peter with himself compare!
Lately he his Lord forswore;
Now at man's unrighteous bar
Stands th'undaunted confessor,
Bold in presence of his foes,
Peter out of weakness strong,
Filled with faith's assurance, shows
Power doth all to God belong!

They inquired, 'By what power, or by what name did you do this?' Then Peter, filled with the Holy Spirit, said to them . . . 'By the name of Jesus Christ of Nazareth, whom you crucified, whom God raised from the dead.'

Acts 4:7,8,10 (NRSV)

This enquiry takes place because Peter and John, in the name of Jesus and the power of the Spirit given to them at Pentecost, had healed a lame man who was begging at the Temple gate. The crowd, recognising what had happened, 'were filled with wonder and amazement' and listened as the healers told the story of Jesus' death and resurrection, and preached the need for repentance. The religious authorities arrested them on the grounds of false teaching.

This short meditation on Acts 4:8 pinpoints Peter's transformation. From being a person who, when confronted by servants after Christ's arrest, denied that he knew him, Peter has now become this 'undaunted confessor' of his Lord.

In gospel accounts, Peter's impetuosity, warmth and enthusiasm make him one of the closest friends of Jesus. Peter loves him more dramatically, hurts him more profoundly, and needs forgiveness more urgently than the others. Luke's account of Peter in the Acts of the Apostles shows him infused with a new steadfastness. Wesley reminds us that this transformation from weakness to strength demonstrates the power of God to enable us to overcome our fears and inner timidity and live boldly in the gospel.

PRAYER
Gracious God, infuse me with your power that my life may be transformed in the pattern of Christ and that I may live confidently in the power of your Spirit. Amen.

---

*UPCW 2, 293

Which of the Christians now
Would their possessions sell?
The fact ye scarce allow,
The truth incredible,
That those of old so weak should prove,
And as themselves their neighbour love.

Of your redundant store
Ye may a few relieve,
But all to feed the poor
Ye cannot, cannot give,
Houses and lands for Christ forgo,
Or live as Jesus lived below.

Jesus, thy church inspire
With apostolic love,
Infuse the one desire
To insure our wealth above,
Freely with earthly goods to part,
And joyfully sell all in heart.

There was not a needy person among them, for as many as were possessors of lands or houses sold them, and brought the proceeds of what was sold and laid it at the apostles' feet; and distribution was made to each as any had need.

Acts 4:34-35 (RSV)

The irony in the last two lines of the first verse expresses what the world would think. It would be foolish to love your neighbour to the extent that those first, post-Pentecost believers did. It is good enough to aid a few people from the surplus of your wealth, but quite impossible to give up all you possess.

In the last verse Charles Wesley aspires to the impossible. He prays for that 'one desire' which alone can inspire to give all we have for the sake of others. We are taken back to the words of Jesus to the rich young ruler, who was wanting to inherit eternal life. Though he was a law-abiding young man, Jesus said to him, 'One thing you lack. Sell all that you have and give to the poor, and you will have treasure in heaven, and come, follow me.' That one thing means everything.

PRAYER

Empowering God, I thank you for all the saints in every age who have followed your call to live the life of the poor man, Jesus: those who live in community so they can share their goods, those who buy houses to shelter the homeless, those who provide food for the hungry, and those who care for the sick and dying. Grant me the grace to hear your voice, and like them, to do your will. Amen.

---

*UPCW 2 297-8 [1:2 Would his 1:5 That men]

Joined to a sinful multitude,
The one who singularly good
Defends the poor oppressed,
Who speaks unmoved, unterrified,
May often to the righteous side
Bring over all the rest.

Superior though we stand alone,
Our duty is the truth to own
Of virtue in distress;
Our counsel to the crowd we give,
Our testimony bold, and leave
With God the whole success.

They were convinced by him.

Acts 5:39 (NRSV)

The scene is the confrontation between the apostles in their new-found Pentecostal power, and the council in Jerusalem, which was enraged by their preaching the resurrection of Jesus and proclaiming him as Messiah. But Gamaliel, a leader of the Pharisees known for his wisdom and tolerance, persuaded the Council to leave the apostles alone, arguing that if the undertaking were simply of human origin, it would fail, but if it were truly of God, then they would not be able to overthrow it. In that case, they might even be found to be fighting against God.

Wesley's poem is an invitation to us to learn from the wisdom and courage of Gamaliel. It is an encouragement to all who dare to speak out against the tide of popular opinion. The social consequences of defending the poor or oppressed can be grim, but those who remain 'unmoved' and 'unterrified' by such opposition may win others to their point of view, and finally be proved right. Even if their voices are not heeded immediately, they can be sure that God hears them, and that the truth will eventually be vindicated.

PRAYER
O God, in times when defence of the poor, the stranger, the homeless and the weak is not popular, grant me the wisdom to know what to say, and the courage to say it, for the sake of Jesus Christ our Lord. Amen.

---

*UPCW 2, 304 [1:2 The man 2:1-2 He stands . . . /His duty 2:4-5 His counsel . . . he gives/His testimony . . . leaves]

Still at the stated hours of prayer
We hold communion with our God,
Who then doth his designs declare,
And sheds his richest love abroad.
Detached, upborne from things below
We comprehend our Saviour's mind,
And feel, when him we fully know,
Our hearts enlarged to all mankind.

Peter went up upon the housetop to pray about the sixth hour.

Acts 10:9

From his childhood, Charles Wesley must have learned the rule of regular discipline in daily prayer. His mother Susanna made it her practice to set aside one hour each morning and evening for her own devotions, and in addition to spend an hour each day with one of her many children in turn, to teach them the habit of prayer. John and Charles kept up this practice of daily prayer times, first as students in the 'Holy Club' at Oxford, and then throughout their adult lives. One of the most cherished shrines of Methodism is the bare, simple prayer room opening out from John's bedroom in his house at Wesley's Chapel in London. Such a habit of prayer encourages both a detachment from our own immediate pressing concerns, and a commitment to a continuing compassion for all humanity.

PRAYER
Enable me, O God, to collect and compose my thoughts before an immediate approach to you in prayer . . . Help me to entertain an habitual sense of your perfections, as an admirable help against cold and formal performances. Save me from engaging in rash and precipitate prayers and from breaking away to follow business or pleasure as though I had never prayed. *Susanna Wesley*

*UPCW 2, 236

Lord, if at thy command
The word of life we sow,
Watered by thy almighty hand,
The seed shall surely grow;
The virtue of thy grace
A large increase shall give,
And multiply the faithful race
Who to thy glory live.

Now then the ceaseless shower
Of gospel blessings send,
And let the soul-converting power
Thy ministers attend.
On multitudes confer
The heart-renewing love,
And by the joy of grace prepare
For fuller joys above.

And the hand of the Lord was with them: and a great number believed, and turned unto the Lord.

Acts 11:21 (read also Mark 4:1-20)

This little poem gets to the heart of what mission means – co-operation between ourselves and God.

Our share of the work is found in the first two lines of the poem; we sow the seed of the 'word of life' (John 6:68); God does the rest. Taking images from the parable of the sower and adding a few of his own, Wesley speaks of God's work which is really beyond our control. Ministers, whether clergy or lay, who speak and exemplify the word, want God's 'soul-converting power': all want 'heart-renewing love' – two phrases which are nicely balanced. The words 'watered' and 'ceaseless shower' speak of welcome fertility in a dry land. And all this leads to joy (Ezekiel 34:26).

The question of whether Jesus came only to his own Jewish people (the 'faithful race') or for everyone (Gentiles as well) was a major issue in the early church. See how, in the last two lines of verse one, Wesley simply includes all 'the faithful race/Who to thy glory live'. The word of life is for all.

PRAYER
O God of all, help me to break down barriers and reject all labels that limit my vision of wholeness for all your people. Help me to listen with understanding and to act with compassion. Through Jesus Christ our Lord. Amen.

Acts (MS) *HP 771

To me, almighty Saviour, give
Thy servant's sayings to receive,
The true simplicity impart,
The nobleness of Lydia's heart.
Of every heart thou hast the key,
Command that mine may yield to thee,
May hear the whisper in thy word,
And opening now admit its Lord.

And a certain woman named Lydia, a seller of purple, of the city of Thyatira, which worshipped God, heard us: whose heart the Lord opened, that she attended unto the things which were spoken of Paul.

Acts 16:14

There are not many women commemorated by name in the New Testament. This is surprising, since women played a great role in the history of the first century church. But there are a few Wesley hymns, particularly those written for the funeral services of women helpers, which do pay a great tribute to the women partners in the gospel.

In Acts, Lydia's name is honoured as the founder and patroness of the church in Philippi. It was to that church that Paul wrote his most joyful letter. He speaks of how he thanks God for every memory of those who have been his partners in the gospel 'from the first day until now'.

Lydia was clearly one of those most valued partners. She held the key that opened the door to the gospel in that city. Keys are small but essential objects. They give to their owners the power to receive or reject any who would enter the house. To give up that key to someone else is to surrender power to that person. So in this verse we are bidden, like Lydia, to open up the door of our heart, our home, our city to the Lord and to hand over to him the key to our lives.

PRAYER
God, I hold many keys in my hand, each of them opening up doors into my world. I want you to come in and share that world with me. Show me how to open up doors for others too, so that together we may walk in new ways of partnership in your gospel and fellowship in your church. Through Jesus Christ our Lord. Amen.

*SH (1796)

IN WHOM WE LIVE AND MOVE

Father, in whom we live,
In whom we are, and move,
The glory, power and praise receive
Of thy creating love.
Let all the angel throng
Give thanks to God on high;
While earth repeats the joyful song,
And echoes to the sky.

Incarnate Deity,
Let all the ransomed race
Render in thanks their lives to thee,
For thy redeeming grace.
The grace to sinners showed
Ye heavenly choirs proclaim,
And cry: 'Salvation to our God,
Salvation to the Lamb!'

Spirit of holiness,
Let all thy saints adore
Thy sacred energy, and bless
Thy heart-renewing power.
Not angel tongues can tell
Thy love's ecstatic height,
The glorious joy unspeakable,
The beatific sight.

For in him we live, and move, and have our being; as certain also of your own poets have said, For we are also his offspring.

Acts 17:28

Though some seventeen biblical allusions have been found in this hymn of praise to the Trinity, it seems appropriate to think of it in the 'inter-faith' setting of its first two lines. Paul, speaking in Athens to Greeks whose pantheon of gods allowed for one unknown, told them this was the God their own writers – Epimenides and Aratus – had hinted at. This was the God 'who made the world and everything in it, being Lord of heaven and earth' (Acts 17:24 RSV).

Each of the first three verses of this exuberant hymn addresses one of the three persons of the Trinity; while the last one, not given here, brings the whole together, returning us to the sense of mission reflected in Paul's message to the Athenians.

MEDITATION

In today's world of many faiths living side by side, how can I find common ground between my beliefs and those of God's other children, my sisters and brothers? Are our differences enough to divide us?

RH (1747) *HP 4 UMH 88 VU 321 [UMH, VU 1:1 Maker in whom . . .]

Far off we need not rove
To find the God of love;
In his providential care,
Ever intimately near,
All his various works declare
God, the bounteous God, is here.

We live, and move, and are,
Through his preserving care;
He doth still in life maintain
Every soul that moves and lives;
Gives us back our breath again,
Being every moment gives.

Who live, O God, in thee,
Entirely thine should be:
Thine we are, a heaven-born race,
Only to thy glory move,
Thee with all our powers we praise,
Thee with all our being love.

[Paul spoke to the Athenians:] That [all peoples of the earth] should seek the Lord, if haply they might feel after him, and find him, though he be not far from every one of us.

Acts 17:27-28

Thinking of God as the creator-parent has always been a part of the Christian tradition, and for many people nowadays is a more accessible image than that of king or ruler. The God who is intimately near cares for us as a mother cares for her child, a mother who has a strong sense of justice that things should be distributed fairly within the family.

Wesley's hymn stresses the care and closeness of God within the 'various works' of creation and, what is equally important, God's ongoing acts of creation, for every moment God 'gives us back our breath again'. Our response is love.

PRAYER
Strong, compassionate God, you care for all your created world. Enlarge my heart with love, that I may preserve and nourish all living things and so be a co-creator with you. Amen.

MSS Acts *PW 12, 342 MHB 440

Your duty let the Apostle show:
Ye ought, ye ought to labour so,
In Jesus' cause employed;
Your calling's works at times pursue,
And keep the tent-maker in view,
And use your hands for God.

Work for the weak, and sick, and poor,
Raiment and food for them procure,
And, mindful of his word,
Enjoy the blessedness to give,
Lay out your gettings, to relieve
The members of your Lord.

Your labour which proceeds from love,
Jesus shall graciously approve,
With full felicity;
With brightest crowns your loan repay
And tell you in that joyful day
'Ye did it unto me.'

I have showed you all things, how that so labouring ye ought to support the weak, and to remember the words of the Lord Jesus, how he said, 'It is more blessed to give than to receive.'

Acts 20:35

The apostle Paul, while on his missionary journeys, continued to support himself by plying his trade as a tent-maker. But he had also to rely on the gifts of others to supply all the needs of the people to whom he ministered.

Charles Wesley, like his brother John, commends the use of money as both the reward for work well done, and the means of providing practical help to those who are in need. 'Gain all you can, save all you can, give all you can,' preached John. In this hymn, Charles reminds us that thus we not only fulfil our own vocation; in giving to others we are also giving to Christ.

PRAYER
Lord, grant me the capacity to provide for my own needs, and the generosity to provide for the needs of others. May both my earning and my giving be done for your glory. Amen.

---

*UPCW 2, 403-4

Jesus wept! and never chid
  Tears of social tenderness;
Saints are not by him forbid
  Thus their frailty to confess,
Thus by passion pure to prove
Saints can feel both grief and love.

When he had finished speaking, he knelt down with them all and prayed. There was much weeping among them all; they embraced Paul and kissed him, grieving especially because of what he had said, that they would not see him again. Then they brought him to the ship.

Acts 20:36-38 (NRSV)

Paul, travelling hurriedly to Jerusalem to be there for the feast of Pentecost, stops at the sea port of Miletus, and rather than travel inland to Ephesus, he asks the men and women who are elders of the church there to come and meet him. This is his last missionary journey and as a farewell it is full of emotion. By all accounts they have loved each other in word and deed. Among other words of comfort, Paul tells them that by continuing in Christian love they are helping the weak and are remembering the words of Jesus, 'It is more blessed to give than to receive.'

Tears are nothing to be ashamed of. Jesus himself wept at the tomb of his dear friend Lazarus. He comforted those who wept at his own tomb. He understood the sorrow that wells up from the heart and waters the eyes in a way that can relieve the stress of grief. This is no giving in to frailty, but rather proving the sincerity of love.

PRAYER
Creator God, who has mysteriously and wonderfully made me body, mind and spirit, give me the courage to face my fears . . . my grief . . . my loss with the truth that will make me free. In my joy be my spirit of joy, in my tears my vision of a larger life. Amen.

---

*PW 12, 380 [1:6 are men of grief and love]

LOVE TO ALL

Father, whose everlasting love
  Thy only Son for sinners gave,
Whose grace to all did freely move,
  And sent him down the world to save:

Help us thy mercy to extol,
  Immense, unfathomed, unconfined;
To praise the Lamb who died for all,
  The general Saviour of our kind.

Thy undistinguishing regard
  Was cast on Adam's fallen race;
For all thou hast in Christ prepared
  Sufficient, sovereign, saving grace.

The world he suffered to redeem;
  For all he has the atonement made;
For those that will not come to him
  The ransom of his life was paid.

Arise, O God, maintain thy cause!
  The fullness of the nations call;
Lift up the standard of thy cross,
  And all shall own thou diedst for all.

God commendeth his love toward us, in that, while we were yet sinners, Christ died for us.

Romans 5:8

What seems to be a general hymn on the love of God is actually part of a seventeen-verse poem written by Wesley to attack the view – held by some of his fellow evangelists – that restricted God's saving grace to an elect minority of the human race. In contrast to all religious or social élitism, both Wesley brothers emphasised the universal intention of God's redeeming work in Christ.

Note the words Charles uses: 'world', 'general', 'undistinguishing', 'freely', 'immense', 'unfathomed', 'unconfined'. All express the unconditional, limitless love of God for the world. No group, however defined, has a premium on God's love.

PRAYER
Forgive me, O God, for the times I am tempted to limit your grace to persons who I think deserve it, to those who belong to my own church, race, or nationality. Help me to experience your unconditional love for me and for all the world. Amen.

HGEL (1741) *HP 520 [2:4 mankind]

Where shall my wondering soul begin?
    How shall I all to heaven aspire?
A slave redeemed from death and sin,
    A brand plucked from eternal fire,
How shall I equal triumphs raise,
And sing my great deliverer's praise?

O how shall I the goodness tell,
    Father, which thou to me hast showed?
That I, a child of wrath and hell,
    I should be called a child of God!
Should know, should feel my sins forgiven,
Blest with this antepast of heaven!

And shall I slight my Father's love,
    Or basely fear his gifts to own?
Unmindful of his favours prove?
    Shall I, the hallowed cross to shun,
Refuse his righteousness to impart
By hiding it within my heart?

The law of the Spirit of life in Christ Jesus hath made me free from the law of sin and death.

Romans 8:2

Two days after a transforming experience on Whitsunday, 21st May 1738, Charles recorded in his journal words which probably refer to this hymn:

> At nine I began an hymn upon my conversion, but was persuaded to break off, for fear of pride. Mr Bray [his host] coming, encouraged me to proceed in spite of Satan. I prayed Christ to stand by me, and finished the hymn . . . In his name therefore and through his strength I will perform my vows unto the Lord, of not hiding his righteousness within my heart.

The next evening brother John came to his house having felt his heart 'strangely warmed' at a Moravian meeting. Charles wrote again:

> Towards ten, my brother was brought in triumph by a troop of our friends, and declared, 'I believe.' We sang the hymn with great joy, and parted with prayer.

PRAYER

God, help me to know with such certainty that my sins are forgiven that I cannot hide my joy, but must tell others of your goodness. Amen.

---

*HSP (1739) RV 1 CH 29 HP 706 UMH 342

No – though the ancient dragon rage
  And call forth all his hosts to war;
Though earth's self-righteous ones engage,
  Them, and their god alike I dare:
Jesus the sinner's friend proclaim,
Jesus, to sinners still the same.

Outcasts of earth, to you I call,
  Harlots, and publicans, and thieves!
He spreads his arms to embrace you all;
  Sinners alone his grace receives:
No need of him the righteous have,
He came the lost to seek and save.

Jesus said to them [the chief priests and elders of the people], 'Truly I tell you, the publicans and the prostitutes are going into the kingdom of God ahead of you.'
Matthew 21:31 (NRSV)

The first part of this hymn ended with the question: 'Shall I . . . /Refuse his righteousness to impart/By hiding it within my heart?' Today's answer is 'no', and the reasons are clear. There are two opponents: one is Satan (the ancient dragon mentioned in Revelation 20:2) and the second, the self-righteousness of religious people. Charles, knowing too well his own faults, claims as his companions those who Jesus said would receive the kingdom first: the tax collectors and prostitutes. The Jesus who 'spreads his arms to embrace you all' is the Jesus who hung, open-armed on the cross.

Self-righteousness is not one of the primary sins of prostitutes. How can it be when the whole world looks down on them? Wendy and Chris are street-women in Vancouver who use an ecumenical drop-in centre which provides coffee and a place of refuge from the streets. On Sunday mornings they often slip into a back pew in church. One Sunday they heard for the first time the story of the Pharisee and the publican; their faces beamed with joy. 'Right on!' said Wendy, 'This man Jesus is really neat,' and then with a grin, 'Why doesn't that story get told more often?'

THE JESUS PRAYER
Lord Jesus Christ, Son of God, have mercy on me, a sinner.

---

*HSP (1739) [1:3 self-righteous sons 2:1 of men] RV 1 CH 29 HP 706 UMH 342

Holy, and true, and righteous Lord,
  I wait to prove thy perfect will;
Be mindful of thy gracious word,
  And stamp me with thy Spirit's seal.

Open my faith's interior eye,
  Display thy glory from above;
And all I am shall sink and die,
  Lost in astonishment and love!

Now let me gain perfection's height;
  Now let me into nothing fall,
As less than nothing in thy sight,
  And feel that Christ is all in all!

And be not conformed to this world: but be ye transformed by the renewing of your mind, that ye may prove what is that good, and acceptable, and perfect, will of God.
Romans 12:2

'Christian perfection' is a phrase much misunderstood. It carries all the baggage of earnestly trying to do better, of misplaced zeal and strenuous virtue. But that was not how Wesley understood it. All the paradoxes of this third verse get to the heart of the matter: the height of Christian perfection is to lose oneself in God – a blending of oneness so that the 'I' loses itself in 'astonishment and love'.

Here we have entered a world beyond words. This is a mystical experience of pure joy, a spiritual weightlessness, a falling into nothingness to find 'that Christ is all in all'.

PRAYER
O thou beloved: Love eternal, my whole good, happiness which hath no bounds, I desire to appropriate thee with the most vehement desire, and the most worthy reverence . . . Make clean, make glad, make bright and make alive my spirit, with all the powers thereof, that I may cleave unto thee in ecstasies of joy.
Thomas à Kempis

HSP (1742) *CH 381 HP 726

DEDICATION (1)

Lord, in the strength of grace,
With a glad heart and free,
Myself, my residue of days,
I consecrate to thee.

Thy ransomed servant, I
Restore to thee thine own;
And from this moment, live or die
To serve my God alone.

Who then will offer willingly, consecrating themselves today to the LORD?
1 Chronicles 29:5 (NRSV)

Whether we live therefore, or die, we are the Lord's.
Romans 14:8

In the book of Chronicles is a long list of material gifts which David and others gave for the building of the temple. We are told that 'the people rejoiced because they had given willingly'. Wesley takes this idea and transforms it into a dedication of himself; still in the spirit of rejoicing, no mournful giving up of life, rather an entry into a larger space.

In many Methodist traditions, people still take part in an annual Covenant Service of rededication to God. The vows have been considered by some to be a commitment no less demanding than that of a monastic order. It is an entrusting of our whole life into the hands of God:

I am no longer my own, but yours
Put me to what you will
Rank me with whom you will
Put me to doing, put me to suffering
Let me be employed for you
Or laid aside for you
Exalted for you
Or brought low for you
Let me be full
Let me be empty
Let me have all things
Let me have nothing
I freely and wholeheartedly yield all things to your pleasure and disposal.[1]

PRAYER
God of truth, such commitment demands great faith, yet I know that the joy of perfect freedom comes as a reward for serving you with my whole heart. Save me from half-heartedness; show me the right path and give me strength to follow it. Amen.

---

*SH (1762) CH 414 HP 800

Let him to whom we now belong
His sovereign right assert,
And take up every thankful song
And every loving heart.

He justly claims us for his own,
Who bought us with a price;
The Christian lives to Christ alone,
To Christ alone he dies.

Jesus, thine own at last receive,
Fulfil our hearts' desire,
And let us to thy glory live,
And in thy cause expire.

Our souls and bodies we resign;
With joy we render thee
Our all, no longer ours, but thine,
Through all eternity.

For whether we live, we live unto the Lord; and whether we die, we die unto the Lord; whether we live therefore, or die, we are the Lord's.

Romans 14:8

There is in this hymn an air of joyful abandonment to God. Perhaps that is best understood by those who have made that commitment and whose 'heart's desire' has its home in the will of God. It is splendidly matched to the eighteenth century tune 'Byzantium' (also known as 'Jackson') sung to these words by many Methodists for the last hundred years. Paul's words to the Romans carry the same buoyant, carefree tone.

Two American friends, Jim and Shelley Douglass, years ago decided to give up all and live by the teaching of Jesus in the Sermon on the Mount, devoting their lives in particular to non-violent protest against war. With others, they lived for some years in a base community called Ground Zero, as close as possible to a military installation armed with nuclear warheads. There are many such people, who in dramatic or humdrum ways decide to 'live to Christ alone', and find deep peace and satisfaction in doing so.

POINT TO PONDER
What would I have to give up to live wholly like this? What am I called to be and do?

*HSP (1745) CH 416 HP 698

THE COLLIERS' HYMN

Teacher, Friend of foolish sinners,
Take the praise of thy grace
From us young beginners;
Struck with loving admiration
Hear us tell of thy zeal
For our souls' salvation.

Thou hast in the weak and feeble
Power displayed, called and made
Us thy favourite people;
Us the vulgar, and obscure
Thou dost own, as unknown,
Ignorant and poor.

Simple folk and undiscerning,
Nothing we know but thee,
Love is all our learning;
Here is knowledge rare, and hidden
From the wise, who despise
All our inward Eden.

Consider your own call, brothers and sisters: not many of you were wise by human standards, not many were powerful, not many were of noble birth. But God chose what is foolish in the world . . . what is weak . . . what is low and despised.
1 Corinthians 1:26-28 (NRSV)

Across the centuries, Christian laymen and women have found in these verses of Scripture warrant for their reading and preaching of Scripture, even when they were opposed by the authorities of their church. Charles Wesley places his version of these words on the lips of the colliers who had responded with enthusiasm to the ministry of the early Methodists. Coal miners were indeed amongst the social outcasts of eighteenth-century Britain. But in the gospel message of God's redeeming love for all without exception, they learned their own worth as children of God. When some became lay preachers and were mocked as 'illiterate mechanics' (Laurence Sterne) they could, as Wesley reminds them, rejoice in knowing Christ, in having 'love as all their learning'.

PRAYER
God, grant me your grace, that my knowledge may always be directed by love for you and for all your world, in the name of Jesus, friend of the poor. Amen.

---

*FH (1767) RV 110

All praise to our redeeming Lord,
Who joins us by his grace,
And bids us, each to each restored,
Together seek his face.

He bids us build each other up;
And, gathered into one,
To our high calling's glorious hope
We hand in hand go on.

The gift which he on one bestows,
We all delight to prove;
The grace through every vessel flows
In purest streams of love.

And if our fellowship below
In Jesus be so sweet,
What height of rapture shall we know,
When round his throne we meet!

The members should have the same care one for another. And whether one member suffer, all the members suffer with it; or one member be honoured, all the members rejoice with it. Now ye are the body of Christ, and members in particular.
1 Corinthians 12:25-27

This has been a favourite hymn among Methodists, for whom fellowship is so important. Written in 1747 in the early days of the movement, it reflects the experience of many men and women who met weekly in bands and classes. They could now talk to each other of the religious experiences of their lives in ways that had never been possible before. For travelling preachers, meeting each other again after various hardships on their journeys, there would be special joy when they were 'restored' to each other again.

Charles writes of the shared gift of the Spirit, and 'perfect harmony'. This buoyant hymn, with its stress on praise, 'glorious hope', grace in 'purest streams of love', 'joy unspeakable' and 'common peace', is a vision of the very special experience which comes to those working together to seek the face of Jesus Christ.

PRAYER
Praise be to you, O God, for the great gift of friends who build each other up through the service of your Son, Jesus. Amen.

---

*RH (1747) RV 71 HP 753 UMH 554

Jesus, thou soul of all our joys,
For whom we now lift up our voice,
And all our strength exert,
Vouchsafe the grace we humbly claim,
Compose into a thankful frame,
And tune thy people's heart.

Then let us praise our common Lord,
And sweetly join with one accord
Thy goodness to proclaim;
Jesus, thyself in us reveal,
And all our faculties shall feel
Thy harmonising name.

With calmly reverential joy,
We then shall all our lives employ
In setting forth thy love;
And raise in death our triumph higher,
And sing with all the heavenly choir
That endless song above.

I will sing with the spirit . . . and I will sing with the understanding also.
1 Corinthians 14:15

Both the Wesley brothers were much concerned about the proper use of music in worship. In the early days of Methodism, when most of the singing was unaccompanied, John Wesley particularly warned people to pay attention to the way they sang and to aim at pleasing God rather than themselves. When it became more common to have an orchestra to accompany the singing, Charles became anxious about what he called 'the power of sound'. In the original version of this hymn there was a verse warning against musical charms that 'bewitch and steal' the heart away from God.

The verses included here express Wesley's confidence in the enriching benefits of music. Almost all the metaphors in the hymn are musical ones, including the final vision of God's people as a heavenly choir engaged in the endless praise of God.

PRAYER
Eternal God, source of all beauty and harmony, we praise you for the gift of music; for the inspiration of those who compose it, the skill of those who perform it and the faculties which enable us to enjoy it. May it enrich our worship and keep us in tune with you. Amen.

HSP (1749) *CH 196 HP 761

DOING ALL WITH LOVE 197

All our best performances
Without love can never please;
All our pains are misemployed,
Worthless in the sight of God;
But the touch of love divine,
Makes our meanest actions shine,
Casts us in a finer mould,
Turns our nature's dross to gold.

Gracious Lord, implant in me
That celestial charity,
Let my every word and deed
From a loving heart proceed,
Hence may all my tempers rise,
Then accept my sacrifice,
Then in all my nature own
The pure Spirit of thy Son.

Let all that you do be done with love.

1 Corinthians 16:14 (NRSV)

It is tempting to add twentieth-century significance to the word 'performance'. We might think of a piano recital, a 'performance review' of personnel management, or a person 'making a performance' of a simple act. In this verse it probably means only 'work well done'. Usually this is very satisfying, but Wesley reminds us in the first two lines that it must be done with love, or it is all wasted.

The first verse echoes the words of George Herbert's poem, 'This is the famous stone/That turneth all to gold'; the second verse becomes a prayer that I may have a loving heart in all that I do. Without love as the motivating energy, our good deeds are hollow; we may even hurt others by our earnest determination to do good.

PRAYER
Teach me, my God and King,
In all things thee to see,
And what I do in anything
To do it as for thee.
George Herbert

---

*SH (1796)

Since the Son hath made me free,
Let me taste my liberty;
Thee behold with open face,
Triumph in thy saving grace,
Thy great will delight to prove,
Glory in thy perfect love.

Heavenly Saviour, Life divine,
Change my nature into thine;
Move and spread throughout my soul,
Actuate and fill the whole;
Be it I no longer now
Living in the flesh, but thou.

Holy Ghost, no more delay;
Come, and in thy temple stay;
Now thine inward witness bear,
Strong, and permanent, and clear;
Spring of life, thyself impart,
Rise eternal in my heart.

Where the Spirit of the Lord is, there is liberty. But we all, with open face beholding as in a glass the glory of the Lord, are changed into the same image.
2 Corinthians 3:17-18

Paul's view of our new relationship with God through Christ is of one that both sets us free and at the same time keeps us safe. But it also includes the mystical element of one personality being taken over by another. When Christ lives within us, we become as Christ.

'Liberty' is the key word, what Paul calls 'the glorious liberty of the children of God' (Romans 8:21). This is not just generalised freedom; rather Wesley calls it '*my* liberty'. But liberty from and for what, is a question which we each will answer in different ways. Note that Wesley expresses the experience in tangible images. Tasting God's love is like drinking from a spring of life rising in the heart.

PRAYER
Grace my relations with others this day, O God, with the generous freedom of spirit that you give to your children. Amen.

---

*HSP (1739) [2:1 Heavenly Adam] PW 1, 192-4 MHB 568

Riches unsearchable
In Jesus' love we know;
And pleasures from the well
Of life, our souls o'erflow:
From him the Spirit we receive
Of wisdom, grace and power:
And always sorrowful, we live
Rejoicing evermore.

Angels our servants are,
And keep in all our ways,
And in their hands, they bear
The sacred heirs of grace;
Our guardians to that heavenly bliss
They all our steps attend,
And God himself our Father is,
And Jesus is our friend.

As sorrowful, yet alway rejoicing; as poor, yet making many rich; as having nothing, yet possessing all things.

2 Corinthians 6:10

For he shall give his angels charge over thee, to keep thee in all thy ways. They shall bear thee up in their hands, lest thou dash thy foot against a stone.

Psalm 91:11-12

'Pleasure' is not a word many people associate with religion. But for Charles Wesley, as for Paul, following Christ was a joyful way of life. Even amid poverty and sorrow, the cheerfulness of faith could break through, bringing a sense of carefree confidence in God's protecting love. That confidence could even become a source of temptation, as it was for Jesus when the devil quoted to him the words of the psalm that is the theme of the second verse of this hymn. But we do not, as Jesus realised, require sensational proofs and spectacular displays of that love. Daily our lives are grounded in the richness of relationship with our divine parent and friend.

PRAYER
Forgive me, O God, for those times I fail to live in trust of your loving care. Give me a continuing sense of what it means to be your child, and to know the friendship of Jesus. Amen.

---

*RH (1747) CH 21 [2:4 sacred sons] MHB 441 (different metre)

CHEERFUL GIVING

The Lord a cheerful giver loves;
A cheerful giver loves the Lord,
And while by works his faith he proves,
Receives an hundredfold reward,
With joy restores what God had given,
Blest with anticipated heaven.

The people rejoiced, for that they offered willingly, because with perfect heart they offered willingly to the LORD: and David the king also rejoiced with great joy.
1 Chronicles 29:9

Wesley, writing one short verse on this incident in the story of the building of the temple in Jerusalem, links the joy in giving experienced by the Israelites with Paul's words to the Corinthians:

> The one who sows sparingly will also reap sparingly, and the one who sows bountifully will also reap bountifully. Each of you must give as you have made up your mind, not reluctantly or under compulsion, for God loves a cheerful giver.
> (2 Corinthians 9:6-7 NRSV)

This reciprocal love between God and the cheerful giver creates growth in generosity; the 'hundredfold reward' is an allusion to Jesus' promise to those disciples who sacrifice material success for the sake of following the gospel way (Matthew 19:29). Such images of growth imply a healthy, productive fruit of good works, arising from a sense of being loved by God.

John Wesley's sermon on 'The Use of Money' is a most practical, ethical response to our personal and social obligations. Living in a society in transition, he speaks clearly to our own predicament about money:

> *Gain all you can,* without hurting either yourself or your neighbour, in soul or body, by applying hereto with unintermitted diligence and with all the understanding which God has given you. *Save all you can,* by cutting off every expense which serves only to indulge foolish desire, to gratify either the desire of the flesh, the desire of the eye or the pride of life. Waste nothing . . . for yourself or your children. And then *give all you can;* or in other words give all you have to God.

PRAYER
Generous God, you have given me all things; help me to be generous in giving to others. Amen.

---

*SH (1762)

FREE GRACE (1)

And can it be that I should gain
 An interest in the Saviour's blood!
Died he for me, who caused his pain?
 For me, who him to death pursued?
Amazing love! How can it be
That thou, my God, should'st die for me!

I am crucified with Christ: nevertheless I live; yet not I, but Christ liveth in me: and the life which I now live in the flesh I live by the faith of the Son of God, who loved me, and gave himself for me.

Galatians 2:20

There is quite a story behind this hymn. Charles Wesley felt himself a failure in his missionary efforts in Georgia and in December 1736 he returned, despondent, to London. A rigorously ordered life of piety and good works brought him no peace of mind. This frustration was complicated by a severe illness, creating a state of emotional pressure that had to be relieved.

In mid-May 1738, while lying sick at the house of a friend, Wesley came upon Martin Luther's commentary on the above passage from Galatians. The words of Luther struck home: 'Read with great vehemency, *me* and *for me* . . . and apply it to thyself.' Charles did apply it to himself, figuratively shaking Luther by the shoulders and demanding 'And can it be . . . for *me*?' Over the next week he found peace and joy in the assurance of personal acceptance by God, something no amount of hard work had provided.

Few of us can go through life without times of profound regret, a sense of disappointment and failure and an earnest desire to work harder and do better. Like Charles, we could well learn that nothing we have done or not done can separate us from the love of God in Christ Jesus. That love is amazing; that gift is free.

PRAYER
Bountiful God, comforter of the afflicted and healer of the broken-hearted, you give me life and hope. Teach me to trust in your gift of forgiveness, that I may live without fear. Through Christ our Lord. Amen.

---

*HSP (1739) RV 5 CH 193 HP 216 UMH 363

FREE GRACE (2)

'Tis mystery all: The Immortal dies!
  Who can explore his strange design?
In vain the first-born seraph tries
  To sound the depths of love divine.
'Tis mercy all! Let earth adore,
  Let angel minds enquire no more.

He left his Father's throne above–
  So free, so infinite his grace–
Emptied himself of all but love,
  And bled for Adam's helpless race.
'Tis mercy all, immense and free;
  For, O my God, it found out me!

[Christ Jesus] though he was in the form of God, did not regard equality with God as something to be exploited, but emptied himself, taking the form of a slave, being born in human likeness. And being formed in human form, he humbled himself and became obedient to the point of death – even death on a cross.

Philippians 2:6-8 (NRSV)

Yesterday's tone was introspectively personal. Today we are invited to consider the paradox of the immortal God dying upon a cross. This is a mystery so great that even the angels cannot 'sound the depths' of such a gift of love, a theme which recurs many times in Wesley's hymns.

Here is the riddle of the 'strange design' by which Christ 'emptied himself of all but love', surely one of Wesley's most powerful lines! In six words Wesley sums up the doctrine of 'kenosis' (emptying) expressed in this passage from Philippians, making his own translation of the original Greek of Paul.

As followers of Christ we recognise that true love is willing to spend its lifeblood on behalf of others, if need be. As one friend was overheard saying to another who was loving under trying circumstances: 'The trouble with you is that you're a Christian – look what happened to Christ!'

PRAYER
Dear God, I pray for all those who in their daily lives care for others with cheerful, sacrificial love. Grant them patience, support and a sense of deep peace in doing your will. Through Jesus Christ our Lord, who lived and died among us and lives again. Amen.

---

*HSP (1739) RV 5 CH 193 HP 216 UMH 363

Long my imprisoned spirit lay
Fast bound in sin and nature's night;
Thine eye diffused a quickening ray–
I woke, the dungeon flamed with light,
My chains fell off, my heart was free,
I rose, went forth, and followed thee.

No condemnation now I dread;
Jesus, and all in him, is mine!
Alive in him, my living Head,
And clothed in righteousness divine,
Bold I approach the eternal throne,
And claim the crown, through Christ, my own.

Peter was sleeping between two soldiers, bound with two chains: and the keepers before the door kept the prison. And, behold, the angel of the Lord came upon him, and a light shined in the prison: and he smote Peter on the side, and raised him up, saying, Arise up quickly. And his chains fell off from his hands.

Acts 12:6-7

When Herod had killed James the brother of John, he put Peter in prison. The young church prayed continually for him. The incident in this passage happened the night before Peter was due to be tried and the whole story is told in Acts 12:1-19.

In this part of the hymn, Wesley brilliantly uses Peter's situation as a metaphor for his own. His recent release from the bondage of guilt helped him to imagine the freedom which Peter must have felt on his miraculous escape from prison. Charles is not only free; he too moves out – to encounter the real person of Christ. Rejoicing in Paul's words that 'There is therefore now no condemnation to them which are in Christ Jesus' (Romans 8:1), his previous dread of an angry God is gone. Now he is incorporated within the body of Christ, wearing (like clothes) Christ's righteousness, rather than relying on his own. A mystery, certainly, but the miraculous good news of the liberating and renewing forgiveness of God.

PRAYER
Loving God, I pray for all those who feel imprisoned by their past, and see little hope for the future. Help me to be for those I encounter this day a channel of your liberating grace. Amen.

---

*HSP (1739) RV 5 CH 193 HP 216 UMH 363

FOR A FAMILY

Jesus, Lord, we look to thee,
Let us in thy name agree;
Show thyself the Prince of Peace;
Bid our jarring conflicts cease.

By thy reconciling love,
Every stumbling-block remove;
Each to each unite, endear;
Come, and spread thy banner here.

Let us each for other care,
Each the other's burden bear;
To thy church the pattern give,
Show how true believers live.

Free from anger and from pride,
Let us thus in God abide;
All the depth of love express,
All the height of holiness.

Bear ye one another's burdens, and so fulfil the law of Christ.

Galatians 6:2

Setting is important here. If we sing this as a hymn in a church, it becomes a plea for unity within the congregation. If we place it in the home, in the setting of family life for which Charles wrote it, then we have to look at it in that context.

'Jarring conflicts' happen in all families. Sadly, we hear in the Western world that the greatest violence comes from family life – physical and mental abuse and even murder. Even smaller injustices, impatience and misunderstandings can impair the peace of the home.

Wesley gives us the true pattern for family life, an environment of mutual consideration, courtesy and love: the pattern of Christ's relationships. The record of Charles' own family life shows that for him this prayer was answered.

PRAYER
God, whenever I am moved to impatience and irritability with those who are nearest to me, strengthen in me an understanding and generous spirit, that our mutual love may be worthy of your name, the parent of us all. Amen.

HSP (1749) CH 495 *HP 759 UMH 562

'Tis finished! The Messiah dies,
   Cut off for sins, but not his own;
Accomplished is the sacrifice,
   The great redeeming work is done.

The veil is rent; in Christ alone
   The living way to heaven is seen;
The middle wall is broken down,
   And all the world may enter in.

The reign of sin and death is o'er,
   And all may live from sin set free,
Satan hath lost his mortal power;
   'Tis swallowed up in victory.

But now in Christ Jesus ye who sometimes were afar off are made nigh by the blood of Christ. For he is our peace, who hath made both one, and hath broken down the middle wall of partition between us.

Ephesians 2:13-14 (read verses 11-22)

When the author of Ephesians writes of the breaching of the former middle-wall of partition between Gentiles and Jews, he is using a metaphor based on the actual wall in the Temple, beyond which Gentiles could not go. Other translations have it as 'a dividing wall of hostility' (RSV), or 'the barrier of enmity which separated them' (REB).

This poem builds on that vision. The theme is the triumph of Christ who finished what he set out to do – to break down barriers and free all the world from sin by love that would not give up, even in death itself. In three of the gospels, the Temple veil that separated the inner sanctuary from all but the priests, was torn open at the moment of Jesus' death. This represents for Wesley the uniting of all people when they enter into the life of Christ.

PRAYER
Dear God, we thank you for all people in all ages who, following the example of Christ, have shown divine love in risking their lives to free others from the chains of hostility. Give us the grace to follow their good example, through Christ Jesus our Lord. Amen.

1762 *PW 12, 99-100 [2:4 all mankind] UPCW 2, 277-9 UMH 282

What shall I do my God to love,
  My loving God to praise?
The length, and breadth, and height to prove,
  And depth of sovereign grace?

Throughout the world its breadth is known,
  Wide as infinity;
So wide it never passed by one,
  Or it had passed by me.

My trespass was grown up to heaven;
  But, far above the skies,
In Christ abundantly forgiven,
  I see thy mercies rise.

The depth of all-redeeming love
  What angel tongue can tell?
O may I to the utmost prove
  The gift unspeakable!

Assert thy claim, maintain thy right,
  Come quickly from above,
And sink me to perfection's height,
  The depth of humble love.

That ye, being rooted and grounded in love, may be able to comprehend with all saints what is the breadth, and length, and depth, and height; and to know the love of Christ which passeth knowledge.

Ephesians 3:17-19

A superb meditation on the Ephesians text, this hymn was originally entitled 'After a Recovery'. Charles Wesley, convinced of his errors, had once more come back to a loving God and felt himself forgiven.

So the opening question is not rhetorical. It has all the energy of a person who feels 'abundantly forgiven', who genuinely wonders what response can be given to so generous a love. His imagination is caught by these words of Paul about the dimensions of God's love (verse one); he reflects on each dimension in turn in the light of his own experience. The last two lines of the hymn link height and depth in the apparent contradiction of a love which 'passeth knowledge'.

PRAYER
Lord, in the heights of my happiness, you are present, and in the depths of my despair, you are there. So may I never doubt that your love is sufficient for all my needs. Help me to realise, too, how your love reaches out to embrace the whole world now and for all time. Amen.

HSP (1749) [5:1 receive thy right] *CH 207 HP 46

What shall I do my God to love,
My Saviour, and the world's, to praise?
Whose tenderest compassions move
To me and all the fallen race,
Whose mercy is divinely free
To all the fallen race, and me!

I long to know, and to make known,
The heights and depths of love divine,
The kindness thou to me hast shown,
Whose every sin was counted thine:
My God for me resigned his breath;
He died to save my soul from death.

How shall I thank thee for the grace
On me and all the world bestowed?
O that my every breath were praise!
O that my heart were filled with God!
My heart would then with love o'erflow,
And all my life thy glory show.

[That ye] may be able to comprehend with all saints what is the breadth, and length, and depth, and height; and to know the love of Christ, which passeth knowledge, that ye might be filled with all the fullness of God.

Ephesians 3:18, 19

Charles Wesley was particularly fond of this passage from Ephesians; it expressed the foundation of his life, and the most constant message of his hymns – the universal, free, unbounded love of God. One of his favourite words was 'all'. Notice how often it occurs in this hymn.

In fact, the hymn keeps moving between the universal (all the world) and the particular (me), mentioned together in the first and last verses, and separately in verse two. That the God who loves all actually loves me is more than a statement of doctrine; it is a life-changing discovery. If only I could comprehend this, I would be so full of love and gratitude that it would flow over to all the world.

PRAYER
God of unlimited love, let me feel that you love me, and help me to love others in the same way. Amen.

HSP (1742) [2:2 height and depth] CH 367 *HP 47 [3:2 all mankind]

Christ, from whom all blessings flow,
Perfecting the saints below,
Hear us, who thy nature share,
Who thy mystic body are.

Join us, in one Spirit join,
Let us still receive of thine;
Still for more on thee we call,
Thee, who fillest all in all.

Closer knit to thee, our Head,
Nourish us, O Christ, and feed,
Let us daily growth receive,
More and more in Jesus live.

Jesu! we thy members are,
Cherish us with kindest care,
Of thy flesh, and of thy bone:
Love, forever love thine own.

There is one body, and one Spirit, even as ye are called in one hope of your calling; One Lord, one faith, one baptism . . . [that ye] speaking the truth in love, may grow up into him in all things, which is the head, even Christ.

Ephesians 4:4-5,15 (read Ephesians 4:1-16)

Saints are not necessarily special people. Despite the extra meaning that the word has come to acquire within some branches of the church, in Paul's understanding it refers to all believers, people like you and me. The letter from which the above quotation is taken starts with the words 'To the saints who are in Ephesus, and to the faithful in Christ Jesus' (Ephesians 1:1).

The first verses of this hymn are a prayer to Christ to take action (Hear/join us/let us/receive/nourish us/cherish us) for we, the saints here, are part of his body. Paul's metaphor of 'members', which he expounds in detail in 1 Corinthians 12, carries two meanings: 'bodily member' as part of a real body (like an arm or a leg), and membership – belonging to a community.

By using all the physical, nourishing words and the 'flesh and bone' image from the story of Adam and Eve (Genesis 2:23), Wesley enlarges our vision of what this union might mean. He rejoices in the unity he experiences, but wants 'more and more', a unity of individuals in community that shares in the life of the God who fills all-in-all.

PRAYER
O Christ, increase my awareness of the life-giving energy that unites me to you and to all members of your body. Amen.

---

*HSP 1740 RV 19 CH 504 HP 764 UMH 550

Move, and actuate, and guide,
Diverse gifts to each divide;
Placed according to thy will,
Let us all our work fulfil.

Sweetly now we all agree,
Touched with softest sympathy,
Kindly for each other care:
Every member feels its share.

Wounded by the grief of one,
All the suffering members groan;
Honoured if one member is
All partake the common bliss.

Many are we now, and one,
We who Jesus have put on:
There is neither bond nor free,
Male nor female, Lord, in thee.

Love, like death, hath all destroyed,
Rendered all distinctions void;
Names and sects and parties fall:
Thou, O Christ, art all in all.

And whether one member suffer, all the members suffer with it; or one member be honoured, all the members rejoice with it. Now ye are the body of Christ . . .
1 Corinthians 12:26-27

Here is the image of the ideal community. It continues yesterday's meditation on the image of the body to which Christ has given many gifts. In the first verse, the hymn reminds us that the gifts, and the energy to use them, come from the head; but it also stresses our responsibility in using these gifts. In the early Methodist societies class leaders were told, 'Find something for your members to do'; mere thought is not enough. The community requires a sense of directed vocation, of working hard as part of a team. It also requires sensitivity and compassion, and a willingness to overcome differences of gender, class, race, politics and religion. If Christ is 'all in all' and we are his body, then mutual love makes these distinctions of valued difference, not divisive barriers.

PRAYER
Universal God, as I am part of your body in the world, so may I claim your respectful love for all people, especially those who are different from me. Make us one in your grace. Amen.

---

*HSP (1740) RV 19 CH 504 HP 764 UMH 550

Who hath a right like us to sing,
  Us whom his mercy raises?
Merry our hearts, for Christ is King,
  Cheerful are all our faces:
Who of his love doth once partake
  Thence evermore rejoices;
Melody in our hearts we make,
  Melody with our voices.

We that a sprinkled conscience have
  We that in God are merry,
Let us sing psalms, the Spirit saith
  Joyful, and never weary,
Offer the sacrifice of praise,
  Hearty, and never ceasing,
Spiritual songs and anthems raise,
  Honour and thanks and blessing.

Be filled with the Spirit; Speaking to yourselves in psalms and hymns and spiritual songs, singing and making melody in your heart to the Lord.

Ephesians 5:18-19

As the question in the first line might suggest, the early Methodists had competition when they sang. As many meetings were held outdoors, there was ample opportunity for rival activities, among them riotous singing from drunken sailors. On one occasion while Charles Wesley was visiting Plymouth in June 1746, 'an whole army of soldiers and sailors stood behind [him] shouting and blaspheming'.[1]

Apart from folk carols, the story of singing within the church in pre-Wesley days could hardly be described as 'merry'. The Church of England used only metrical psalms and ancient canticles. Isaac Watts, the Independent, had created some splendid hymns just prior to the Wesleys, but Charles was really breaking new ground. He wrote in nearly one hundred different metres, many of them infectiously singable. Often he would take a popular song and write his own words to it.

POINT TO PONDER
In what ways can we express our 'merry hearts' outside the walls of the church today? Communicating our faith in a post-Christian age suggests that, like the Wesleys, we might try to understand and make use of our own popular culture.

---

*HSP (1749) RV 84A [1:6 He evermore 2:1-3 He that . . . hath/He that . . . is/Let him]

Happy one whom God doth aid!
God our soul, and body made,
God on us, in gracious showers,
Blessings every moment pours;
Compasses with angel-bands,
Bids them bear us in their hands;
Parents, friends, 'twas God bestowed,
Life and all descends from God.

He this flowery carpet spread,
Made the earth on which we tread;
God refreshes in the air,
Covers with the clothes we wear,
Feeds us in the food we eat,
Cheers us by his light and heat,
Makes the sun on us to shine:
All our blessings are divine.

Giving thanks always for all things unto God and the Father in the name of our Lord Jesus Christ.

Ephesians 5:20

A hymn bearing the marks of the Wesleys' earnest desire to instruct children. Regular rhythm and rhyming couplets may be an aid to memory, but the result is not always fine poetry, however informative it may be. John wrote that Charles, unlike Isaac Watts, always sought to bring children to the level of adults, rather than speak down to them. Perhaps it was their own mother's instruction in the Epworth rectory that had such a powerful influence on their approach to education, for she had taught her children in strikingly thorough and rational ways. John abstracted a prose work *Instructions for Children* in 1763, and this hymn seems to be a paraphrase of it.[1]

Its message is clear, and not confined to children: 'All our blessings are divine.' Happiness comes through all the gifts of mind, body and soul, the protection of all who care for us, the natural world, food and clothing, warmth and light and the sun which shines on us. For all of life's goodness, we should give God thanks.

PRAYER
Thank him, thank him, all his children thank him.
He is love, he is love.

---

*HC (1763) CH 223 [1:1 Happy man] RV 103

212 THE WHOLE ARMOUR OF GOD (1)

Soldiers of Christ, arise,
And put your armour on,
Strong in the strength which God supplies
Through his eternal Son;
Strong in the Lord of hosts,
And in his mighty power,
Who in the strength of Jesus trusts
Is more than conqueror.

Stand then in his great might,
With all his strength endued;
And take, to arm you for the fight,
The panoply of God;
That, having all things done,
And all your conflicts passed,
Ye may o'ercome through Christ alone,
And stand entire at last.

Be strong in the Lord, and in the power of his might. Put on the whole armour of God, that ye may be able to stand against the wiles of the devil. For we wrestle not against flesh and blood, but against principalities, against powers, against the rulers of the darkness of this world, against spiritual wickedness in high places.

Ephesians 6:10-12

This major poem of Wesley's has rarely been published as a whole. It originally had sixteen eight-line verses, blending the language describing the 'war in heaven' of Milton's *Paradise Lost* with the text from Ephesians.

The hymn is an extended meditation on Paul's own metaphor using the complete armour ('the panoply') of a Roman soldier as an image of all the qualities of faith with which Christians need to be armed in battle against the evil both within themselves and in a sinful world.

PRAYER
Help us to discern our real enemy – not our fellow men and women who, like ourselves, are frail human beings – but the force of evil which must be resisted wherever it manifests itself, within our own lives and within the whole of human society. Amen.

**The Character of a Methodist* (1742) RV 30 CH 258-260 HP 719 UMH 513

Leave no unguarded place,
No weakness of the soul;
Take every virtue, every grace,
And fortify the whole:
Indissolubly joined,
To battle all proceed;
But arm yourselves with all the mind
That was in Christ, your Head.

Let truth the girdle be
That binds your armour on,
In faithful firm security
To Jesus cleave alone;
Let faith and love combine
To guard your valiant breast,
The plate be righteousness divine,
Imputed and imprest.

Stand therefore, having your loins girt about with truth, and having on the breastplate of righteousness; And your feet shod with the preparation of the gospel of peace.
Ephesians 6:14-15

The first of these verses sets the framework of spiritual battle, but note how the humility of Christ is part of this. 'The mind that was in Christ' suggests Paul's words to the Philippians: 'Let this mind be in you, which was also in Christ Jesus . . . who made himself of no reputation and took upon himself the form of a servant . . .' (Philippians 2:5,7).

Then we move to the separate parts of the armour, which we bind on to ourselves by the integrity of truth. We are protected by the righteousness Christ has won for us, 'imputed' to us as the mark of our captain, and 'imprest' upon us, so that it becomes also the mark of our own character as soldiers of Christ.

PRAYER
Lord, give us the confidence to believe that those whom you enlist in your service, you fully equip for all the duties that lie ahead. May our feet be shod with your peace, so that with confidence we may carry through the battlefields of death the gospel of life. Amen.

**The Character of a Methodist* (1742) RV 30 CH 258-260 HP 719

But above all, lay hold
Of faith's victorious shield;
Armed with that adamant and gold
Be sure to win the field;
If faith surround your heart,
Satan shall be subdued,
Repelled his every fiery dart,
And quenched with Jesus' blood.

Your rock can never shake:
Hither, he saith, come up!
The helmet of salvation take,
The confidence of hope:
Hope for his perfect love,
Hope for his people's rest,
Hope to sit down with Christ above
And share the marriage feast.

Above all, taking the shield of faith, wherewith ye shall be able to quench all the fiery darts of the wicked. And take the helmet of salvation, and the sword of the Spirit, which is the word of God.

Ephesians 6:16-17

Once more Wesley's mind leaps to *Paradise Lost* for real drama. There, in the war in heaven, it is Satan who 'Came tow'ring, armed in adamant and gold' (*PL* 6:109-10). Now it is the 'soldier of Christ' whose shield of faith is made of adamant and gold, and who will subdue Satan himself with the power of Christ.

Then we move on to the helmet of salvation, which Paul has described elsewhere as the 'hope of salvation' (1 Thessalonians 5:8). Four times, the word 'hope' strikes home here, ending with the great feast in heaven.

PRAYER
God of majesty and power, teach us that there need be no limits to what we can tackle in your name. When forces of evil seem to be too strong for us, may we work with others to combat them, made strong by the armour of truth, faith, love and hope, through trust in Jesus, who showed that the power of love is stronger than the power of hatred. Amen.

**The Character of a Methodist* (1742) RV 30 CH 258-260

Pray, without ceasing pray,
(Your Captain gives the word)
His summons cheerfully obey,
And call upon the Lord;
To God your every want
In instant prayer display,
Pray always; pray, and never faint;
Pray, without ceasing pray.

Pour out your souls to God,
And bow them with your knees,
And spread your hearts and hands abroad
And pray for Zion's peace;
Your guides and comrades bear
Forever on your mind;
Extend the arms of mighty prayer
Ingrasping all mankind.

Praying always with all prayer and supplication in the Spirit, and watching thereunto with all perseverance and supplication for all saints.

Ephesians 6:18

All the qualities of faith, hope, love, truth and peace come by means of prayer. All and any sorts of prayer will suffice: the sudden, quick, darting prayer to God for what we need at the moment, the groan of pain when we cannot put into words our anguish for the hurts of the world, the silent meditation, or the shout of joy on a glorious morning. Note how, in this poem, the last two lines about the arms of prayer 'ingrasping' all humankind become a symbol of inclusiveness for all the people of the world.

MEDITATION

Brother Lawrence of the Resurrection speaks of constant prayer:

> . . . it consists of renouncing once and for all everything that we know does not lead to God, so that we might accustom ourselves to a continual conversation with him, a conversation free of mystery and of the utmost simplicity . . . to address ourselves to him at every moment, to ask his aid, to discern his will in doubtful things . . . in praising, adoring and loving God.[1]

May this be so for us.

**The Character of a Methodist* (1742) [2:5 and brethren bear] RV30 CH258-260 HP719 UMH 513

From strength to strength go on,
Wrestle, and fight, and pray,
Tread all the powers of darkness down,
And win the well-fought day;
Still let the Spirit cry
In all his soldiers: Come!
Till Christ the Lord descends from high,
And takes the conquerors home.

They go from strength to strength, every one of them in Zion appeareth before God.
Psalm 84:7

This last verse of 'Soldiers of Christ, arise' brings us back full circle, exhorting us, as the early Christians at Ephesus were exhorted, not to give up in the fight against powers of darkness, for we are taking part in a cosmic victory.

The spiritual war is waged in the world against all that limits the fullness of life for all creation. In our times we can think of the non-violent struggle of Gandhi for the liberation of India, of Martin Luther King for the dignity of blacks in America, and of Desmond Tutu, Nelson Mandela and many others against apartheid in South Africa. We also think of those who are trying to save our environment from forces of greed and exploitation. There are rising tides of ethnic violence in many parts of the world, increasing poverty and reduced social support in the so-called developed world. The list seems endless, and there is so much we are called to do.

When our institutions do our sinning for us, how, as Christians, do we make a difference in those institutions? There is desperate danger that in times like these we will hide ourselves in a private piety that does not embrace this world that God loves.

PRAYER
God of history, you share our joys and crushing sorrows, you hear the cries of the afflicted, you fill the hungry, and you set free the oppressed. We pray for an end to all injustice. Inspire us with the all-embracing love of God, challenge us with the sacrificial love of Jesus, empower us with the transforming love of the Spirit, that we and all God's people may live and be free! Amen.

**The Character of a Methodist* (1742) RV 30 CH 258-260 HP 719 UMH 513

THE NAME OF JESUS (1) 217

Jesus – the name high over all,
 In hell, or earth, or sky!
Angels and mortals prostrate fall,
 And devils fear and fly.

Jesus – the name to sinners dear,
 The name to sinners given!
It scatters all their guilty fear,
 It turns their hell to heaven.

Jesus – the prisoner's fetters breaks,
 And bruises Satan's head,
Power into strengthless souls it speaks,
 And life into the dead.

Wherefore God also hath highly exalted him, and given him a name which is above every name: That at the name of Jesus, every knee should bow, of things in heaven, and things in earth, and things under the earth; And that every tongue should confess that Jesus Christ is Lord.

Philippians 2:9-11

In many cultures of the ancient world, as in many aboriginal cultures today, a person's name evokes a person's whole being, and to use that name implies a special relationship. Thus, invoking the name of a god or gods is a powerful act. In this passage, the Greek title 'kurios' that Paul gives to Jesus has close affinities with the Jewish naming of God. The name of Jesus conveys the power of God.

How powerful this name of Jesus is! Wesley describes its cosmic effect in verse one, and then goes into detail in the other two verses. It is a name that sets people free from all that holds them captive – their guilty fear, their addictive sins, their sense of powerlessness. Here is good news today for all persons in or outside the church.

PRAYER
O God, fill me with your power, that my own weakness may be turned to strength, my fear be dispelled, and whatever prison I feel myself to be in, be opened to the liberation of your love. I ask this in the powerful name of Jesus. Amen.

HSP (1749) *CH 36 [1:3 angels and men before it UMH] HP 264 UMH 193

O that the world might taste and see
The riches of his grace!
The arms of love that compass me
Would all the world embrace.

O that my Jesu's heavenly charms
Might every bosom move!
Fly, sinners, fly into those arms
Of everlasting love.

Happy if with my latest breath
I may but gasp his name;
Preach him to all, and cry in death:
'Behold! Behold the Lamb!'

O taste and see that the LORD is good; happy are those who take refuge in him.
Psalm 34:8 (NRSV)

The Hebrew Scriptures express in vivid, sensuous imagery what it is like to experience the goodness of God. It satisfies our whole being. Human love has that same quality – all of us know it, some of us more than others. We know that God is in all human love also; this is part of the meaning of the incarnation. The warm hug of a loving friend, or child, or partner is the embrace of God.

If only others could share that love: the lonely single mother, the homeless man, the abused child, the person who is of different race or religion from me and from whom I sometimes distance myself, my estranged partner, my 'enemy' whoever that may be. And on the world scene, how much could be achieved by the compassion that springs from the love of Christ and commends his love to others.

PRAYER
Gracious God, you want to embrace the whole world in your love. Warm my heart, widen my embrace, and take these gifts and use them as Christ would have done. For his name's sake. Amen.

HSP (1749) *CH 34 HP 264 [1:3 all mankind = UMH] UMH 193

Most gracious Lord,
Thy kindest word
I joyfully obey,
Hold fast my confidence restored,
And cast my sins away.

No longer I
Lament and sigh
With guilty fear oppressed;
To me who on thy love rely
Whatever is, is best.

In each event
The kind intent
Of Love divine I see,
And mixed with joyful thanks present
My humble prayers to thee.

Then let thy peace
My heart possess;
By thy unspotted mind,
Preserve in perfect quietness
A soul to Jesus joined.

Have no anxiety about anything, but in everything by prayer and supplication with thanksgiving let your requests be made known unto God.

Philippians 4:6 (RSV)

In this meditation on the Philippians passage, Wesley identifies a trust in God's providence as the perfect antidote to anxiety. The title, taken from the second verse, adapts the well-known phrase of one of his favourite poets, the contemporary of his father, Alexander Pope: 'Whatever is, is right.'

In writing this as an old man of seventy-six, Wesley is not falling into fatalism; rather he still shows energy and delight and confidence in the future, because he feels himself one in spirit with the divine love. In life and in death, God will keep him in peace.

PRAYER
Let us remember, our God is a pure Spirit and delights to dwell in a calm tabernacle.
John Wesley

MS Scripture Hymns (1783) RV 223

A LOVING HEART

Who can a pastor's heart express,
The unutterable tenderness,
Beyond what fondest mothers prove,
The yearning pangs of softest love?
They only comprehend who know
Whence every grace and blessing flow,
Who feel, but never can explain,
The kindness of the Son of Man.

I appeal to you for my child, Onesimus, whose father I have become in my imprisonment. I am sending him back to you, sending my very heart.

Philemon 10, 12 (RSV)

The shortest book in the New Testament is a personal note sent by Paul to Philemon. It was a letter of reference, commending the runaway slave Onesimus to his former master, and asking Philemon to love the young man as a son rather than a slave. Paul, who sometimes seems a somewhat austere figure and who, as far as we know, had no family of his own, appears in this letter to be a man who was able to forge bonds of great affection beyond the limits of immediate kinship. Onesimus had become like a son to him.

It is interesting to note that the word 'kindness' originally stems from the same root as the word 'kinship'. The kindness Jesus showed was the kindness which treated all people as kinsfolk, as brothers and sisters, children of the same God. Sometimes people who have no immediate family, or couples who have never had children feel a certain emptiness in their lives, as though they have no-one to love in the close bonds of family life. A Chinese widow, who had been left childless and was therefore pitied by her neighbours, once commented, 'But I know why God has left my arms empty. It is so that I may put them around children who need my love.'

PRAYER
Lord, help me to find people whom I can love in the close bonds of a kind affection. Bless all my family ties, and help me to extend the circle of my loved ones to include those who feel unloved, for the sake of Jesus Christ, our Brother and your Son. Amen.

*SH (1796) [5-7 He only comprehends who knows/flows/Who feels 8 The bowels of]

Brightness of the eternal glory,
Image of our God expressed,
Jesus, let thy works adore thee,
God supreme forever blest!
Still upheld by their creator,
Heaven and earth thy power confess;
Lord of universal nature,
Take the universal praise.

God . . . hath in these last days spoken unto us by his Son, whom he hath appointed heir of all things, by whom also he made the worlds; Who being the brightness of his glory, and the express image of his person, and upholding all things by the word of his power, when he had by himself purged our sins, sat down on the right hand of the Majesty on high.

Hebrews 1:2-3

Wesley's verse, with heightened intensity, turns the complex language of the biblical text from Hebrews into a powerful, compact, joyful prayer of praise. Jesus is the very image of the supreme God, the Creator and Upholder of the whole universe. So he is worshipped not only by us, but by all his works. The whole universe sings his praise.

Peoples who live close to nature also express this 'universal praise'. The following prayer comes from the Dakota nation of the American plains.

PRAYER

Grandfather, Great Spirit,
you have always been, and before you nothing has been.
There is no one to pray to but you.
The star nations all over the heaven are yours,
and yours are the grasses of the earth.
You are older than all need, older than all pain and prayer.
Grandfather, Great Spirit,
fill us with light.
Give us strength to understand and eyes to see.
Teach us to walk the soft earth
as relatives to all that live.
Help us, for without you we are nothing.[1]

*SH (1796)

God of all power, and truth, and grace,
Which shall from age to age endure,
Whose word, when heaven and earth shall pass,
Remains and stands for ever sure;

That I thy mercy may proclaim,
That all the world thy truth may see,
Hallow thy great and glorious name,
And perfect holiness in me.

Give me a new, a perfect heart,
From doubt, and fear, and sorrow free;
The mind which was in Christ impart,
And let my spirit cleave to thee.

O that I now, from sin released,
Thy word may to the utmost prove,
Enter into the promised rest,
The Canaan of thy perfect love!

There remaineth therefore a rest to the people of God.

Hebrews 4:9

This is part of a very long hymn written in 1742 which John Wesley subsequently added to his sermon *Christian Perfection.* In prayer, the poet asks for 'a new and perfect heart'. There will be a real change in his life when he is no longer driven by his fears, held captive by doubts, shut in by sorrow. He names this glorious freedom of the Christian the realm of 'perfect love'.

As an image, Canaan may mean little these days. Set however in the context of the distant goal of the Israelites' Exodus and desert wanderings, it becomes the naming of our deepest heart's desire. The land of milk and honey is a metaphor for our own promised homecoming in the love of God.

PRAYER
Glory to God, whose power working in us can do infinitely more than we can ask or imagine. Glory to God from generation to generation, in the church and in Christ Jesus, for ever and ever. Amen.

HSP (1742) CH 380 *HP 726 [2:2 that all mankind]

Let the winds blow, and billows roll,
Hope is the anchor of the soul.
But can I by so slight a tie,
An unseen hope, on God rely?
Steadfast and sure it cannot fail,
It enters deep within the veil,
It fastens on a land unknown
And moors me to my Father's throne.

Which hope we have as an anchor of the soul, both sure and steadfast, and which entereth into that within the veil.

Hebrews 6:19

In the Jewish Temple, only the high priest could enter the inner sanctuary, or 'holy of holies', the place of the presence of God. For the writer of Hebrews, our hope in the certainty of God's promises rests on the entrance of Jesus on our behalf beyond the curtain, or veil, into that presence.

In writing a poem on this specific text, Wesley's imagination is fired by the nautical image of the anchor. He had taken many perilous sea journeys, particularly across the Irish Sea, and knows both the fragility of a drifting anchor ('so slight a tie') and the value of a secure mooring. A hundred years later, Priscilla Owen's popular hymn, 'Will your anchor hold in the storms of life' takes this same text and imagery as its starting point and echoes Wesley's language.

By its very nature, the object of hope is unseen, and therefore requires strong faith to sustain it. It is more than 'whistling in the darkness'. Only those who have been in desperate circumstances can understand its depths. These words are said to have been found on the walls of a German concentration camp:

I believe in the sun, even when it is not shining,
I believe in love, even when I feel it not,
I believe in God, even when God is silent.

PRAYER OF BENEDICTION
May the God of hope fill you with all joy and peace in believing, so that by the power of the Holy Spirit you may abound in hope. Amen.

---

*SH (1796)

Author of faith, eternal Word,
Whose Spirit breathes the active flame,
Faith, like its finisher and Lord,
Today as yesterday the same:

To thee our humble hearts aspire,
And ask the gift unspeakable;
Increase in us the kindled fire,
In us the work of faith fulfil.

By faith we know thee strong to save –
Save us, a present Saviour thou!
What'er we hope, by faith we have,
Future and past subsisting now.

The things unknown to feeble sense,
Unseen by reason's glimmering ray,
With strong, commanding evidence
Their heavenly origin display.

Faith lends its realising light,
The clouds disperse, the shadows fly;
The invisible appears in sight,
And God is seen by mortal eye.

Now faith is the substance of things hoped for, the evidence of things not seen.
Hebrews 11:1

This is one of a series of hymns on the nature of faith, inspired by Hebrews 11. There the writer uses an epic style to celebrate the heroes of ancient Israel, who lived by faith in a God whose purposes they could not yet fully discern or understand. Among them are well-known figures like Abraham and Sarah, but also surprises like Rahab, the prostitute of Jericho. All have their place in the saga of the people of God, of those who like ourselves aspire to life in the city of God, and live as pilgrims hoping for fulfilment of the promise.

In an age where science seems to many people to have undercut the rational basis for faith, the stories of God's faithful people are important. At a dark time in Jewish life, an Hasidic teacher reminded his people that, at those moments when it seems that all we can do is tell the story, telling the story is enough to work the miracle.

PRAYER
Invisible God, my senses are limited and my reason only a ray through the clouds; but faith in you clears my eyes and warms my heart so that I can see you and your purposes. Thank you for this gift. Amen.

HSP (1740) *CH 92 HP 662

WHOLE HEALING 225

Jesus, thy far-extended fame
  My drooping soul exults to hear;
Thy name, thy all-restoring name,
  Is music in a sinner's ear.

Sinners of old thou didst receive,
  With comfortable words and kind,
Their sorrows cheer, their wants relieve,
  Heal the diseased, and cure the blind.

And art thou not the Saviour still,
  In every place and age the same?
Hast thou forgot thy gracious skill,
  Or lost the virtue of thy name?

Faith in thy changeless name I have;
  The good, the kind physician, thou
Art able now our souls to save,
  Art willing to restore them now.

All my disease, my every sin,
  To thee, O Jesus, I confess;
In pardon, Lord, my cure begin,
  And perfect it in holiness.

Jesus Christ the same yesterday, and today, and for ever.

Hebrews 13:8

The links between physical and emotional health are so complex that we cannot separate them. Jesus saw them as inextricably intertwined; sometimes he forgave sin and then performed physical healing, as in the story of the man let down through the roof (Mark 2:9) and at other times, the physical healing came first (see John 5:2-16). In all cases he sought to restore wholeness.

The question behind this hymn is one that haunts us all. Can healing like this still happen today? Perhaps a better question is 'How can I (or the person I care about) be a whole person?' Charles, with good biblical authority and psychological wisdom, thinks that forgiveness – freedom from guilt – is the starting point.

AN IONA COMMUNITY PRAYER WITH LAYING ON OF HANDS
May the Spirit of the living God, present with us now, enter you, body, mind and spirit, and heal you of all that harms you, in Jesus' name. Amen.

HSP (1749) *CH 385 HP 148

Happy soul, who now renewed,
God in thee, and thou in God,
Only feels within thee move
Tenderness, compassion, love,
Love immense, and unconfined,
Love to all of humankind.

Happy soul, whose active love
Emulates the blest above,
In thy every action seen,
Sparkling from the soul within:
Thou to every sufferer nigh,
Hearest, not in vain, the cry
Of the widow in distress,
Of the poor and fatherless!
Raiment thou to all that need,
To the hungry deal'st thy bread,
To the sick thou giv'st relief,
Sooth'st the hapless prisoner's grief,
The weak hands thou liftest up,
Bid'st the helpless mourner hope,
Giv'st to those in darkness light,
Guid'st the weary wanderer right.

Happy are they who are generous to the poor.

Proverbs 14:21

Part of a long poem of one hundred and sixty-two lines based on the Beatitudes, the earlier part of the poem is filled with a deep meditation on sin and its repeated destructive effects in the human heart. After God removes that burden, the soul experiences the great happiness described in these verses. The change from gloom to joy is dramatic and ecstatic. The message, however detailed, is still simple: love received from God makes the believer so happy that it in turn results in an 'active love' that imitates the love of God as seen in the life of Christ.

PRAYER

God of love, preserve us from doing good only out of a sense of duty. May our love for you bring a sparkle into our lives and happiness into the lives of others, for your sake. Amen.

---

*HSP (1749) RV 135

Father, on me the grace bestow,
Unblamable before thy sight,
Whence all the streams of goodness flow;
Mercy, thine own supreme delight,
To me, for Jesus' sake, impart,
And plant thy nature in my heart.

Thy mind throughout my life be shown,
While, listening to the wretch's cry,
The widow's and the orphan's groan,
On mercy's wings I swiftly fly,
The poor and helpless to relieve,
My life, my all, for them I give.

Pure religion and undefiled before God and the Father is this, To visit the fatherless and widows in their affliction.

James 1:27

The key word in this meditation is 'mercy' – not just the vague concept but the very nature of God who nourishes, forgives and sustains all creation. To ask for this gift in ourselves is no small request, for if we take the hint from saints past and present whom we regard as being close to the nature of God, we usually find they have not come by this easily. They have had to share their own pain and live alongside others in equal or greater need. But Christ is there before them; that is where they find him, with the hungry, the thirsty, the naked, the sick and the prisoners. Such a life is religion at its best, its truest.

PRAYER

Nourishing God, you care for all your children. Give me the mind of Christ that I may listen as he listened, love as he loved, and do as he did among all those who are in any kind of need, through the grace of Jesus Christ our Lord. Amen.

*SH (1762) CH 354 HP 318

Let us plead for faith alone,
Faith which by our works is shown;
God it is who justifies,
Only faith the grace applies.

Active faith that lives within,
Conquers hell and death and sin,
Hallows whom it first made whole,
Forms the Saviour in the soul.

Only let us persevere
Till we see our Lord appear,
Never from the Rock remove,
Saved by faith which works by love.

For by grace are ye saved through faith; and that not of yourselves: it is the gift of God.

Ephesians 2:8

I will show thee my faith by my works.

James 2:18

Perhaps one of the most protracted arguments in the history of the church has been that concerning the relative merits of faith versus works. That they are two sides of the same coin may be obvious to us now, but both sides of the debate have held destructively entrenched positions. Even today there are people in the church who feel that if they are 'saved' they are excused from involvement in the world, while others may run out of compassion in their 'good works' because they have no spiritual resources.

The first two lines of this hymn carry a shock. 'Faith alone' we say, and are just settling into happy agreement when the next line wakes us up again as we are reminded that works are the necessary outcome of faith. The image of Christ as rock reminds us that the man who built his house on the rock was the one who heard the words of Jesus and *acted* on them. But it is love that holds the whole together; it is love that helps to avoid the situation when 'the helping hand strikes again' and itself becomes oppressive.

PRAYER
Lord Jesus Christ, you promised your presence to all who ask; may I so live by faith in you that all my actions reflect your love for others. Amen.

HSP (1740) PW 1, 352-3 [1:1 Plead we thus for faith alone] *UMH 385

Thou God of harmony and love,
Whose name transports the saints above
And lulls the ravished spheres;
On thee in feeble strain I call,
And mix my humble voice with all
The heavenly choristers.

Thine own musician, Lord, inspire,
And let my consecrated lyre
Repeat the psalmist's part;
His Son and thine reveal in me,
And fill with sacred melody
The fibres of my heart.

So shall I charm the listening throng,
And draw the living stones along,
By Jesus' tuneful name;
The living stones shall dance, shall rise,
And form a city in the skies,
The new Jerusalem.

Ye also, as lively stones, are built up a spiritual house, an holy priesthood, to offer up spiritual sacrifices, acceptable to God by Jesus Christ.

1 Peter 2:5

This is part of a charming hymn of invocation and personal dedication by a compulsive poet. At times Charles Wesley had felt both inner hesitation and external criticism, that 'making verse' was improper for one whose whole life should be devoted to God. By the grace of God, a wider sense of his vocation prevailed, and in this hymn it becomes a joyful, triumphant affirmation of the God whose nature is 'harmony and love'. In God's house, even the 'living stones' dance!

MEDITATION

Look at the exuberant words in this hymn – 'transports', 'ravished', 'charm', 'dance', 'rise'. Thank God and pray for all who use their musical talents in praise of God. Think of songs that bring you closer to God.

---

*PW 4, 243-4

THE MARKS OF FAITH

How can we sinners know
Our sins on earth forgiven?
How can our gracious Saviour show
Our names inscribed in heaven?

What we have felt, and seen,
With confidence we tell,
And publish now to all the world
The signs infallible.

His love, surpassing far
The love of all beneath,
We find within our hearts, and dare
The pointless darts of death:

Stronger than death or hell
The mystic power we prove;
And, conquerors of the world, we dwell
In heaven, who dwell in love.

That which was from the beginning, which we have heard, which we have seen with our eyes, which we have looked upon, and our hands have handled, of the Word of life . . . declare we unto you, that ye also may have fellowship with us.

1 John 1:1,3

These verses come from an eight-stanza poem with an unusual, urgent metre, which was somewhat changed by John Wesley in his *Collection of Hymns* in 1780 in order to make it a more easily singable hymn.

This is no poem of mere theory; it speaks from real experience. Look at all the single-syllable verbs – 'know', 'show', 'felt', 'seen', 'tell' – and the typically Wesleyan word, 'prove'. This is experimental religion, drawing on the 'mystic power' of the love of God, so that we feel forgiven, and already enjoy a foretaste of the life of heaven as we live in love.

PRAYER
Liberating God, you are part of all the worlds that are, yet you are also part of me. May I accept your sustaining gift of love as it nourishes me to bring forth good fruit. Amen.

HSP (1749) RV 141 *CH 93 [1:1-2 a sinner . . . his sins 1:3-4 my gracious Saviour show my name 2:3 And publish to the sons of men] HP 728 UMH 372

Thou God of truth and love,
We seek thy perfect way,
Ready thy choice to approve,
Thy providence to obey;
Enter into thy wise design,
And sweetly lose our will in thine.

Why hast thou cast our lot
In the same age and place,
Or why together brought
To see each other's face,
To join with softest sympathy,
And mix our friendly souls in thee?

Didst thou not make us one,
That both might one remain,
Together travel on,
And bear each other's pain,
Till both thine utmost goodness prove,
And rise renewed in perfect love?

Beloved, let us love one another, because love is from God; everyone who loves is born of God and knows God. Whoever does not love does not know God, for God is love.

1 John 4:7-8 (NRSV)

The word 'love' has many connotations. In the history of the church there have always been those who want to dissect its meaning, pointing out the difference between spiritual love and physical love. On the other hand, mystics have often visualised their relationship with God as a marriage, and their language reflects many elements of human desire, as well as the experience of 'falling in love'.

This hymn was at first a love poem from Charles Wesley to Sally Gwynne whom he later married. Theirs was a tender courtship, and the amazement of two persons in love ('why us?!') comes through in the first four lines of verse two. His dream was the union of their love within the love of God.

PRAYER
God, the source of all love, I thank you for all those whose lives have touched mine and through whom I have come to know what it is to love and be loved. Give me eyes to see loving actions, ears to hear loving words, and hands of strong compassion to join with others in building your kingdom of love and peace. Through Jesus Christ our Lord. Amen.

---

*HSP (1749) RV 144 CH 496 HP 374

Jesus, the Conqueror, reigns,
In glorious strength arrayed,
His kingdom over all maintains,
And bids the earth be glad.
Ye peoples all, rejoice
In Jesus' mighty love;
Lift up your heart, lift up your voice
To him who rules above.

Extol his kingly power,
Kiss the exalted Son,
Who died; and lives, to die no more
High on his Father's throne:
Our Advocate with God,
He undertakes our cause,
And spreads through all the earth abroad
The victory of his cross.

For whatsoever is born of God overcometh the world: and this is the victory that overcometh the world, even our faith.

1 John 5:4

In all these things we are more than conquerors through him that loved us.

Romans 8:37

The tragic history of Christendom shows how easy it has been to turn the victory of faith into an excuse for holy wars. But the victory of the cross is the very opposite of militarism; it is the love which by its vulnerability overcomes the world. To those who are victims of oppression and violence the affirmation of Christ's victory over evil comes as a liberating word. He accompanies them in their suffering and holds out to them the hope of ultimate freedom.

In January 1993 the phrase 'Operation Accompaniment' was used in Guatemala to describe teams of people who travelled alongside refugees returning to their homes after ten years of exile. They needed friends beside them to ensure their safe journey. Christ who undertakes our cause is such a friend, whose love is an arm of protection against all our enemies.

PRAYER

Lord Jesus, you overcame the powers of darkness and evil with a love stronger than death. May all who struggle this day against those powers draw strength from the assurance of their share in your final victory. Amen.

HSP (1749) *CH 268 HP 262

Weary souls who wander wide
From the central point of bliss,
Turn to Jesus crucified,
Fly to those dear wounds of his:
Sink into the purple flood;
Rise into the life of God!

Find in Christ the way of peace,
Peace unspeakable, unknown;
By his pain he gives you ease,
Life by his expiring groan;
Rise exalted by his fall,
Find in Christ your all in all.

O believe the record true,
God to you his Son hath given:
Ye may now be happy too,
Live on earth the life of heaven,
Live the life of heaven above,
All the life of glorious love.

And this is the record, that God hath given to us eternal life, and this life is in his Son.
1 John 5:11

'Bliss' is a word of mystics rather than philosophers. Charles Wesley is comfortable with the mystical writers and the poets of the previous century who used such language, as well as other phrases here like 'purple flood' (Dryden) and 'dear wounds' (Crashaw).

Today we can probably best use this hymn for meditation if we concentrate on the paradoxes, which Charles uses to bring us back to that 'central point of bliss' from which we all wander. In verse one there is the sink/rise antithesis. Verse two has the paradox of pain/ease, life/death, rise/fall which is summed up in Christ our 'all in all'. In verse three the contrast sets all the benefits of living on earth beside enjoying the delights of heaven.

POINT TO PONDER
It has been said that one can never reconcile paradoxes, only live in the tension between them. What am I being invited to experience through this hymn?

*RH (1747) CH 20 MHB 319

The schools of scribes, and courts of kings,
The learn'd and great he passes by,
Chooses the weak and foolish things,
His power and grace to testify;
Plain simple folk his call endues
With power and wisdom from above;
And such he still vouchsafes to use,
Who nothing know but Jesus' love.

Jesus . . . saw two brethren, Simon called Peter, and Andrew his brother, casting a net into the sea: for they were fishers. And he saith unto them, 'Follow me . . .'
Matthew 4:18-19

What sort of people did Jesus need to follow him? Fishermen, used to hard work in all weathers, men who had to be aware of their environment, good friends who could form a community – all these qualities would be fine, at least for a while. And later, we know that Jesus added tax collectors, and women, and many others whom society might regard as questionable. How strange that this medley of people were to be messengers of the kingdom!

Perhaps, as Wesley suggests, those who follow Christ need only to respond to the love of God, from whom they can receive the wisdom and power they need. Jean Vanier, who has set up L'Arche communities for mentally disabled persons in several countries, speaks of the special gifts of love which these people have. One assistant writes:

> When I first came . . . I was going to do so much. I wanted to work hard, and help, and show what I could do. Gradually I discovered there was little I could do. I couldn't use all my knowledge. The boys didn't even notice how smart I was. It was hard until the day I realised that they were glad I was here, just so we could be together. It wasn't what I could do. They liked me, just me.[1]

PRAYER
God, grant that I may see others through your clear eyes and understand them with your loving heart, so that I may value people for who they are and not for what they can do. For Christ's sake. Amen.

---

*PW 10, 157 [1:5 simple men]

THE ABSENT CHRIST (1) 235

Jesus, if still the same thou art,
    If all thy promises are sure,
Set up thy kingdom in my heart,
    And make me rich, for I am poor;
To me be all thy treasures given,
The kingdom of an inward heaven.

Thou hast pronounced the mourner blest;
    And lo, for thee I ever mourn:
I cannot – no, I will not rest,
    Till thou, my only rest, return;
Till thou, the Prince of Peace, appear,
And I receive the Comforter.

*

Blessed are the poor in spirit: for theirs is the kingdom of heaven. Blessed are they that mourn: for they shall be comforted.

Matthew 5:3-4

Whenever one hears that powerful word 'mourn' the associated idea is 'loss'. Usually we think of bereavement or physical loss: a partner, a child, a parent, a friend goes from us. Wesley writes here of another loss. Charles has apparently lost his sense of the presence of Christ: a frightening experience for one whose life is bound up with God. He is truly 'poor', impoverished in spirit. His response here is a Job-like challenge. He might well be shouting, 'Jesus, if all that you said, and all that is said about you is true, then come back to me again. I am mourning my loss of you, isn't that proof enough that I should be comforted by the Comforter?'

Many spiritual guides speak in some way of this form of spiritual poverty – 'the dark night of the soul' – as the experience of those who journey deeper into the heart of God. In tomorrow's meditation, we explore this further in another beatitude.

PRAYER
God, you made us for yourself and our hearts are restless until they find their rest in you. *St Augustine*

---

*HSP (1740) RV 14 CH 130 HP 529

THE ABSENT CHRIST (2)

Where is the blessedness bestowed
On all that hunger after thee?
I hunger now, I thirst for God;
See the poor fainting sinner, see,
And satisfy with endless peace,
And fill me with thy righteousness.

Ah Lord! if thou art in that sigh,
Then hear thyself within me pray.
Hear in my heart thy Spirit's cry,
Mark what my labouring soul would say,
Answer the deep, unuttered groan,
And show that thou and I are one.

Shine on thy work, disperse the gloom,
Light in thy light I then shall see;
Say to my soul: 'Thy light is come,
Glory divine is risen on thee,
Thy warfare's past, thy mourning's o'er:
Look up, for thou shalt weep no more!'

Blessed are they which do hunger and thirst after righteousness: for they shall be filled.

Matthew 5:6

This continues the poet's yearning for God begun yesterday in the first two verses of this hymn. Here are still the questioning tone and the proof that he qualifies as hungry and fainting with thirst. Only now (in verse two) there is some movement away from this desperate state.

The 'sigh' of despair becomes the 'cry' of the Spirit, speaking on behalf of the one who cannot even groan, and gradually the tone changes; confidence returns with the anticipation of an end to gloom and mourning. How the words 'shine' and 'light' and 'glory' lift the mood to one of jubilation (see Isaiah 40:2, 60:1, 60:20)!

PRAYER
Gracious and loving God, you never abandon your children but are always present whether we know it or not. Send your light on all those who live in the darkness of depression and hopelessness. Break through their gloom with the piercing beam of your love, that they may once more know joy. Amen.

---

*HSP (1740) RV 14 CH 130 HP 529

Ah! Lord, with trembling I confess,
A gracious soul may fall from grace;
The salt may lose its savoury power,
And never, never find it more.
Lest this my fearful case should be,
Each moment knit my soul to thee;
And lead me to thy mount above,
Through the low vale of humble love.

Ye are the salt of the earth: but if the salt have lost his savour, wherewith shall it be salted? it is thenceforth good for nothing, but to be cast out, and to be trodden under foot.

Matthew 5:13

This little poem functions rather like a precautionary injection taken before exposure to sickness. The 'gracious soul' is healthy, but open to the possibility of a 'fall from grace'. The idea of salt losing its saltiness forever stems from the mini-parable in the gospel. Elsewhere, Wesley insists that no time is too late to receive the grace of God.

The precautionary medicine is constant communion with Jesus to whom our soul is knit. This echoes the friendship of David and Jonathan ('the soul of Jonathan was knit with the soul of David, and Jonathan loved him as his own soul' 1 Samuel 18:1) and Paul's hope that believers might be 'knit together in love' (Colossians 2:2).

An early friend of the Wesley brothers was William Law. John Wesley, in selecting some parts of Law's work for republishing, chose the following passage on creative 'humble love':

> Let every day, therefore, be a day of humility; condescend to all the infirmities of your fellow-creatures, cover their frailties, love their excellencies, encourage their virtues, relieve their wants, rejoice in their prosperities, compassionate their distress, receive their friendship, overlook their unkindness, forgive their malice, be a servant of servants, and condescend to do the lowest office to the lowest of mortals.[1]

PRAYER
Keep me aware, O Lord, of my own fragility so that I may be more understanding of the frailty of others. Keep my heart so close-knit to your love for me that I may keep strong the bonds of my love for them. For your name's sake. Amen.

SH (1762) *(1796) MHB 480

Prayer is the language of the heart,
By humble faith to heaven addressed,
Above the studied rules of art,
And more in groans than words expressed,
Groans by the wrestling Spirit bestowed,
Groans which affect the heart of God.

Father, the prayer thou dost require
Through Jesus I present to thee,
In vehemence of inflamed desire,
In faith's resigned simplicity,
In hope thy promised grace to prove,
In speechless eloquence of love.

When you are praying, do not heap up empty phrases.

Matthew 6:7 (NRSV)

A deceptively simple meditation on these words of Jesus from the Sermon on the Mount. The first verse is in the form of a statement: 'Prayer is . . .' The second is itself a prayer to God, an offering of desire, faith and hope that extends beyond rational thought, beyond words, to the 'speechless eloquence of love'. We know something of what that means when we have looked silently into the loving eyes of a friend, or sat in helpless love at the bedside of a sick child.

The liturgy of the Anglican *Book of Common Prayer* was the constant companion of Charles Wesley throughout his life, and its language permeated his own private prayers. But he acknowledges that there are times when no words are sufficient to express our innermost yearning – the groaning of our hearts in times of great distress.

Paul teaches that the Spirit takes our inarticulate cries of distress and turns them into intercessions (Romans 8:28). How else could we truly pray for others and for ourselves except through the Spirit's interpreting the language of our hearts?

PRAYER

Listening God, give me simplicity of faith and urgency of passion, that I may pray for your broken and hurting world with all my heart, through the name of Jesus. Amen.

---

*MS Matthew RV 161

THE LORD'S PRAYER (1)

Father of earth and sky,
Thy name we magnify.
O that earth and heaven might join
Thy perfections to proclaim,
Praise the attributes divine,
Fear, and love thy awful name!

When shall thy Spirit reign
In every heart alone?
Father, bring the Kingdom near,
Honour thy triumphant Son,
God of heaven, on earth appear,
Fix with us thy glorious throne.

Our Father which art in heaven, Hallowed be thy name. Thy kingdom come.
Matthew 6:9-10

The prayer which Jesus taught his disciples is a model for all our prayers. It begins by reaching up to heaven in sublime adoration of the eternal God. Then it comes down to earth in simple admission of our basic human need and in confession of our sin. Finally, it soars up again in confidence of God's final victory.

On this framework, Charles Wesley has constructed a hymn which appeared only in the early editions of his works. Perhaps one reason why this paraphrase is not better known is because the change in language has given words like 'fear' and 'awful' a different connotation in modern speech. But they are a reminder that worship must always begin in awe, which should create such reverence that it can be compared almost to fear. 'Woe is me, for I am undone,' cried Isaiah in the temple when he saw the glory of the Lord. When we approach the presence of the living God in that spirit of humility, we pray with sincerity that God's name be honoured and loved, that God's kingdom come.

The hymn, like the Lord's Prayer itself, emphasises the link between heaven and earth, a link forged most strongly as we pray and work for the coming of God's kingdom.

PRAYER
God, as my prayer ascends to heaven to glorify your name, may it also be grounded here on earth in sympathy with all who are in need, for they are your people and this is your kingdom, now and forever. Amen.

SH (1762) [2:2 heart of man] *(1796)

THE LORD'S PRAYER (2)

Thy good and holy will,
Let all on earth fulfil;
We with minds angelic vie,
Saints below with saints above,
Thee to praise and glorify,
Thee to serve with perfect love.

This day with this day's bread
Thy hungry children feed;
Fountain of all blessings, grant
Now the manna from above,
Now supply our bodies' want,
Now sustain our souls with love.

Thy will be done in earth, as it is in heaven. Give us this day our daily bread.
Matthew 6:10-11

The theme of the link between heaven and earth is continued in another image characteristic of Charles Wesley, of saints below almost competing with the saints above in striving to obey the will of God. There is something reassuring in this sense of the continuity of the community of prayer, through which our lives, with all their imperfections, can nevertheless be linked with godly men and women who have gone before us and have now attained the state of perfection.

Wesley emphasises the corporate nature of this prayer. The petition for daily bread is not solely an expression of our personal need. It is offered on behalf of all who are hungry, whether that be hunger for basic food for the body, or a yearning for that love which alone can nourish the soul. In these days we are made acutely aware of the plight of millions of people in our world who suffer from physical malnutrition. We need to be equally aware of that spiritual famine which now afflicts the affluent nations of the world, 'not a famine of bread, nor a thirst for water, but of hearing the words of the LORD' (Amos 8:11). We bring both famished bodies and starved souls into our prayer, as we pray not only for ourselves but for the need of the whole world.

PRAYER
Grant, O God, that I who have never known an empty stomach may ever remember those who have never known a full one; that I who have never known poverty may never forget those who have never known anything else; that I, to whom so much has been given, may ever remember those who have so little; and that, remembering these things, I may ever seek to minister to their needs in every way I can, for thy love's sake. Amen. *Nadir Dinshaw*

SH (1762) [1:3 Men with] *(1796)

THE LORD'S PRAYER (3)

Our trespasses forgive,
And when absolved we live,
Thou our life of grace maintain;
Lest we from our God depart,
Lose thy pardoning love again,
Grant us a forgiving heart.

In every fiery hour
Display thy guardian power,
Near in our temptation stay,
With sufficient grace defend,
Bring us through the evil day,
Make us faithful to the end.

Father, by right divine,
Assert the kingdom thine;
Jesus, power of God, subdue
Thine own universe to thee;
Spirit of grace and glory too,
Reign through all eternity.

Forgive us our debts, as we forgive our debtors. And lead us not into temptation, but deliver us from evil: For thine is the kingdom, and the power, and the glory, for ever.
Matthew 6:12-13

Three brief sentences from the Lord's Prayer have here become three pregnant verses of a Wesley hymn. The first expresses the whole concept of absolution for those who confess their faults, and who show gratitude for that forgiveness by living a life of love. The second vividly describes the protecting power of God, who can defend us against all enemies of the soul. The third verse lifts the whole prayer into a Trinitarian context, as it gives glory to God the Father, the Son and the Holy Spirit.

So Wesley has enlarged the simple prayer which Jesus taught us, addressed to our Father, into a comprehensive expression of Christian faith and corporate worship that acknowledges the One in Three, who reigns over both earth and heaven.

PRAYER
God, may I be not only forgiven for my sins, but also set free from them. Then grant that I may show to others the generous spirit you have shown to me, through Christ our Lord. Amen.

SH (1762) *(1796)

LIVING IN THE PRESENT

The past no longer in my power,
The future who shall live to see?
Mine only is the present hour,
Lent, to be all laid out for thee.
Now, Saviour, with thy grace endowed
Now let me serve and please my God.

Why should I ask the future load
To aggravate my present care?
Strong in the grace today bestowed,
The evil of today I bear;
And if tomorrow's care I see,
Fresh grace shall still suffice for me.

Take therefore no thought for the morrow: for the morrow shall take thought for the things of itself. Sufficient unto the day is the evil thereof.

Matthew 6:34

Living in the present moment is one of the most difficult of spiritual disciplines. We tend to spend so much of our time either looking back on the past or looking forward, often apprehensively, to the future. Yet this present moment is the only reality we have. Wesley's verse takes up the thought that to dwell in the immediate moment does not necessarily relieve us of all anxiety or pain, but it does ensure that we are not bearing a heavier load than is required of us. And, however great the burden of the moment, the grace of God is always greater to enable us to bear it.

PRAYER
Saviour, help me not to care so much about yesterday,
that I care too little about today,
And help me not to peer so anxiously into tomorrow
that I fail to perceive your presence with me now.
Give me the faith that can rejoice that yesterday,
today and forever, you are always the same.
Amen.

---

*SH (1796)

When undistinguishing I prayed
For worldly good, instead of bread,
  I fondly asked a stone;
But for a stone, my loving God
Hath true Bread on me bestowed
  By giving me his Son.

Is there anyone among you who, if your child asks for bread, will give a stone?
Matthew 7:9 (NRSV)

Charles Wesley seems to have enjoyed playing with words. There is almost a teasing note in this brief reference to an illustration Jesus used in his teaching about prayer. Jesus was reminding the people that, whatever we might ask for, God will never give us what will harm us. Like a good father, he wants to give only good gifts to his children. So however 'fondly', and the word here is used in the old sense of 'foolishly', we might think we know what we want, God will only give us what is best for us. Wesley plays with the parable by making the son ask for a stone when he really needs bread, but the bread he receives is the broken bread that is the Son of God.

A preacher once used this parable in a children's address. To make it come alive for them, he produced some small bread rolls, including among them a stone of the same colour, but slightly larger. Then he told the children to choose the roll they would most like to have. Most of them pointed to the bigger one, but one boy (who happened to be the preacher's son) said, 'I'd rather you chose for me, Dad, because you know what the catch is!' It has been said that true prayer is not telling God what we want to receive but asking God what he wants to give.

PRAYER
O God, if in my foolishness I am seeking after the wrong things, please give me those things necessary for my soul's health, for the love of your Son, Jesus Christ. Amen.

*PW 10, 201

Let the rain descend, the flood
And vehement wind assail,
Built on an eternal God
The house can never fail:
Built on Christ the rock it stands,
Stablished in obedience sure,
They who keep their God's commands,
Shall as their God endure.

Who on Jesus' love rely,
And keep his word of grace,
We the rain and storm defy,
And floods of wickedness:
Troubles pouring from above,
Mortals, fiends, like floods and wind
Never can the house remove,
The soul on Christ reclined.

Everyone then who hears these words of mine and acts on them will be like a wise man who built his house on a rock.

Matthew 7:24-25 (NRSV)

Physical hardships of wind and weather when they travelled on horseback seemed not to trouble the Wesleys. Neither were they discouraged by organised opposition from drunken mobs. But as the Methodist movement grew they did become concerned about the widely scattered Societies, which were receiving poor pastoral care, and not surprisingly, had some members who could not hold on to their first profession of faith. An entry in Charles Wesley's journal for 12th October 1756 speaks of some people in Leeds who were following a former Methodist preacher, Mr Edwards. He was now leaving the Society to set up his own church. Next day, Charles writes in his journal:

> The word at Birstal was clothed with power, both to awaken and to confirm. My principal concern is for the disciples, that their houses may be built on the rock, before the rains descend. I hear in most places the effect of the word; but I hearken after it less than formerly, and take little notice of those who say they receive comfort, or faith, or forgiveness. Let their fruits show.

The hymn was probably written a few years later. Characteristically it takes the parable and turns it into a small sermon of encouragement, in which the message is driven home: the safety of the house on the rock is for those 'who keep their God's commands'. Hearing the words of Christ and agreeing with them is not enough. 'Let their fruits show.'

PRAYER
Save me, O God, from having only a fragile faith. May I build on the firm foundation of Christ, the rock of my salvation. Amen.

---

*SH (1762) RV 162 [1:7-8 Man who keeps his . . ./Shall as his 2:6 Men and . . .]

Poorest of earth, with comfort see
Thy God more indigent than thee –
He had not where to rest;
But if thou in his footsteps tread,
He bids thee lean thy weary head
On thy Redeemer's breast.

Ye rich who bear the Christian name,
Behold with self-abasing shame
Your God by heaven adored;
Ye who increased with goods appear,
O how unlike your Pattern here,
Your poor, afflicted Lord!

All hail, thou suffering Son of Man,
Who freely did'st for me sustain
The depth of poverty;
I bless my self-denying Lord,
More destitute than beast or bird,
And come to follow thee.

A scribe then approached and said, 'Teacher, I will follow you wherever you go.' And Jesus said to him, 'Foxes have holes, and birds of the air have nests; but the Son of Man has nowhere to lay his head.'

Matthew 8:19-20 (NRSV)

Matthew sets this short conversation after a series of healing stories. First to be healed by Jesus is the Jewish stranger, the leper; then the servant of the foreigner, a Roman centurion; and finally the close family member, Peter's mother-in-law. It is not surprising that the scribe wanted to be a follower of Jesus. But Jesus warns him, without any sense of self-pity, that this would mean no easy life.

The tender-hearted Wesley feels pity for all poor people. Coping with perennial poverty can bring a bone-deep weariness of body and of soul. To persons working long hours for inadequate pay, living on social assistance or struggling to find employment, it might be a comfort to know that their God was also poor, and to learn that he invited all tired and weary people to come and rest in him. This ought also to shame those of us who, claiming to follow Christ, yet live a life of extravagance and ease.

PRAYER
As I travel in your footsteps, O Christ, forgive me that I carry so much baggage with me, and teach me your simplicity of life. Amen.

---

*PW 10, 215 [1:1 Poorest of men]

AT LYING DOWN (1)

How do thy mercies close me round!
For ever be thy name adored!
I blush in all things to abound;
The servant is above his Lord!

Inured to poverty and pain,
A suffering life my Master led;
The Son of God, the Son of Man,
He had not where to lay his head.

But, lo, a place he hath prepared
For me, whom watchful angels keep;
Yea, he himself becomes my guard,
He smooths my bed, and gives me sleep.

And Jesus saith unto him, The foxes have holes, and the birds of the air have nests; but the Son of man hath not where to lay his head.

Matthew 8:20

That God protects us in the night as well as in the day is a great comfort to those who fear the night. Psalm 91 includes the comforting words 'There shall no evil befall thee . . . for he shall give the angels charge over thee.' Wesley takes this care to tangible domestic lengths when he thinks of God who 'smooths my bed' and prepares a resting place for me, not only in eternity, but here and now, as each night brings the blessing of sleep.

But Christ, like countless homeless people today, did not even have a regular place to sleep. Charles, the servant-poet, is embarrassed to realise that God's gifts – the mercies that encompass him – make his life so much more comfortable than that of his master – Christ.

AN AFRICAN PRAYER FOR REFUGEES
O brother Jesus, who as a child was carried into exile, remember all those who are deprived of their home or country, who groan under the burden of anguish and sorrow, enduring the burning heat of the sun, the freezing cold of the sea, or the humid heat of the forest, searching for a place of refuge. Cause these storms to cease, O Christ. Move the hearts of those in power that they may respect the men and women whom you have created in your own image; that the grief of refugees may be turned into joy. Amen.[1]

HSP (1740) *CH 218 HP 562

Jesus protects; my fears, begone!
What can the Rock of Ages move?
Safe in thy arms I lay me down,
Thy everlasting arms of love.

While thou art intimately nigh,
Who, who shall violate my rest?
Sin, earth, and hell I now defy;
I lean upon my Saviour's breast.

I rest beneath the Almighty's shade,
My griefs expire, my troubles cease;
Thou, Lord, on whom my soul is stayed,
Wilt keep me still in perfect peace.

Me for thine own thou lov'st to take,
In time and in eternity;
Thou never, never wilt forsake
A helpless soul that trusts in thee.

I will both lay me down in peace, and sleep: for thou, LORD, only makest me dwell in safety.

Psalm 4:8

A skilful weaving of biblical passages develops the theme of the security of the loving embrace of Christ. The phrase 'rock of ages' reminds us of Toplady's hymn, 'Rock of Ages, cleft for me', which was written some thirty years later. Wesley took the phrase from the Hebrew of Isaiah 26:4, 'the Lord JEHOVAH is everlasting strength'. The preceding verse, 'Thou wilt keep him in perfect peace, whose mind is stayed on thee: because he trusteth in thee' lies behind the last two lines of Wesley's verse three, while Psalm 91:1 speaks of those who 'abide under the shadow of the Almighty'.

Perhaps all these references are too much! Simply pondering on Wesley's hymn and the following prayer should be sufficient to lead us into a peaceful sleep.

PRAYER

Christ stands before you, and peace is in his mind. Sleep in the calm of all calm. Sleep in the guidance of all guidance. Sleep in the love of all loves: Sleep, beloved, in the God of life. Amen. [1] *Iona Community*

HSP (1740) *CH 218 [4:4 helpless worm] HP 562

To whom should thy disciples go,
Of whom should they be taught, but thee?
Thy Spirit doth thy meaning show;
O might he show it now to me,
And give my heart to understand
The new, the old, supreme command.

Blessing thou dost to sinners give,
Not sacrifice from us require;
Thou will'st that we should still receive,
Should after all thy mind aspire,
And moulded in thine image prove
Thy first great attribute is love.

Go ye and learn what that meaneth, I will have mercy, and not sacrifice.

Matthew 9:13

The starting point for these verses is the scene in which the Pharisees criticise Jesus for keeping bad company. Matthew has just left his job in order to follow Jesus. Now they are eating a meal together in Matthew's house, joined by a number of Matthew's old friends and associates, 'publicans and sinners'. When his disciples report to Jesus the criticism of the company he keeps, he is annoyed by this preoccupation with respectability rather than with reconciliation. Far more important than keeping the rules is the restoring of right relationships. There is a good precedent for the generous hospitality he is showing to those whom some would regard as sinners. He quotes the prophet Hosea: 'For I [God] desired mercy, and not sacrifice; the knowledge of God more than burnt offerings' (Hosea 6:6).

Jesus sends his critics away to go and think about what this means. Wesley takes up the challenge himself and reminds us that Christ is teaching a new law of love, which is also the heart and summary of the old law. So it is not the offering of sacrifices that God requires, but the unreserved gift of love.

PRAYER

God of all wisdom, grant me the understanding to discover what are my own foolish preoccupations with rules, and where they obstruct the living of your greater law of love. Through Jesus Christ our Lord. Amen.

---

*MS Matthew RV 164B

PEACE TO THIS HOUSE

Peace to the house I enter now!
If sent with thy commission, thou
Shalt answer, Lord, for me;
Peace to the peaceable impart,
Set up thy kingdom in their heart
Through faith which is in thee.

When ye come into an house, salute it. And if the house be worthy, let your peace come upon it: but if it be not worthy, let your peace return to you.
Matthew 10:12-13

Travelling as preachers throughout the British Isles, the Wesley brothers on numerous occasions enjoyed the hospitality of a private home. Not surprisingly therefore, Charles wrote more than one text on this same theme of blessing the home. At a time when the Societies often met in each other's homes for prayer, singing and preaching, it was only right to declare the peace of God to the house and the people in it.

At the core of the message here is the sense of hospitality to those messengers whom Jesus sends. Without doubt, every house and every family needs the gift of peace; every family overcome by violence, or loneliness, or alienation needs this benediction of the peace of God. But hospitality is something more.

Hospitality assumes a welcome – a peace answering peace. One of the 'rules' of the Order of the Sisters of St Joseph expresses it clearly: 'Hospitality is an expression of our spirit of simplicity and cordial charity.' Anyone staying in their retreat house receives just that: a simple bed and desk in a quiet room, simple food, and an unobtrusive sense of warmth.

Peace to this house!

PRAYER
O God, make the door of this house wide enough to receive all who need human love and fellowship, narrow enough to shut out all envy, pride and strife. God, make the door of this house the gateway to thine eternal kingdom.
St Stephen's Wallbrook, London

---

*PW 10, 235 [1:4 the son of peace 1:5 his heart]

THE SERPENT AND THE DOVE

Saviour, my double want I feel,
  By fear, by innocence betrayed,
By prudence false, and blindful zeal;
  In pity hasten to my aid.
With wisdom pure of worldly art,
  With harmless, undesigning love
Meeken, yet fortify, my heart,
  And blend the serpent with the dove.

Behold, I send you forth as sheep in the midst of wolves: be ye therefore wise as serpents, and harmless as doves.

Matthew 10:16

Round the balcony of Wesley's Chapel in City Road, London, runs a sculpted frieze with the repeated motif of a dove bearing an olive branch, encircled by a serpent with its tail in its mouth. It was a symbol chosen by John Wesley himself to represent the winged Spirit carrying its message of peace, surrounded by the wise serpent who carries within its body an antidote to its own potential poison. For Wesley this signified the twin mission of evangelism and healing, both enterprises dear to his heart.

The twin symbolism attracted the attention of his brother Charles too. In this verse he plays with the paradoxes suggested by the innocence of the dove and the subtlety of the serpent. He sees the same paradoxes present in his own nature. The apparently opposing qualities of innocence and subtlety need not be mutually destructive. They can serve both to make the soul strong and to keep it humble.

PRAYER

Jesus, I know that there are many paradoxes in my own life too. Teach me when to show the wisdom of the serpent and when to be as gentle as the dove. Help me never to be falsely prudent or blindly zealous but in all things to display an 'undesigning' love. Amen.

---

*SH (1796)

Saviour from sin, I wait to prove
  That Jesus is thy healing name;
To lose, when perfected in love,
  Whate'er I have, or can, or am.
I stay me on thy faithful word:
The servant shall be as his Lord.

Didst thou not die that I might live
  No longer to myself, but thee,
Might body, soul, and spirit give
  To him who gave himself for me?
Come then, my Master and my God!
Take the dear purchase of thy blood.

Thine own peculiar servant claim,
  For thine own truth and mercy's sake;
Hallow in me thy glorious name;
  Me for thine own this moment take,
And change, and throughly purify;
Thine only may I live and die.

It is enough for the disciple to be like the teacher, and the slave like the master.
Matthew 10:25 (NRSV)

This is a prayer for that perfection which Jesus promises as a possibility particularly to one who is most conscious of sin. The hymn adopts an almost challenging tone – 'Prove that it is possible, however hard it is for me to believe it,' the writer seems to say. Only if I allow the Lord to take complete control of my life will I become all that he wants me to be. Note in the last verse the bold extension of the phrase 'Hallowed be thy name.' God's name will be truly hallowed when I live in a way worthy of my master.

PRAYER
Gracious God, you alone know how conscious I am of my own sinfulness. Release the goodness hidden in my life, illuminate the dark contradictions, and in your great mercy, forgive what is wrong. Claim me as your own that I may hallow your name through all my days. Through Jesus Christ our Lord. Amen.

---

*HSP (1742) CH 364 HP 747

Stupendous love of God most high!
He comes to meet us from the sky
  In mildest majesty;
Full of unutterable grace
He calls the weary burden'd race:
  Come all for help to me.

Weary of passions unsubdued,
Weary of vows in vain renewed,
  Of forms without the power,
Of prayers and hopes, complaints and groans,
My fainting soul in silence owns
  I can hold out no more.

Fulfil thine own intense desire,
And now into my heart inspire
  The power of faith and love;
Then Saviour, then to thee I come,
And find on earth the life, the home,
  The rest of saints above.

Come unto me, all ye that labour and are heavy laden, and I will give you rest.
Matthew 11:28

These words of Jesus to those who carry heavy loads have comforted many people who have grown weary on the journey of life. Wesley himself here confesses a sense of spiritual exhaustion in trying to run the straight race in his own strength. He prays for the refreshment of Christ's indwelling power, knowing that then he will be able to keep going along the path of faith and reach the final goal, together with all those who have learned to 'run and not be weary, to walk, and not faint' (Isaiah 40:31).

PRAYER
Grant me, O most sweet and loving Jesus, to rest in thee, above all creatures, above all health and beauty, above all glory and honour, above all power and dignity, above all knowledge and subtlety, above all riches and arts, above all joy and gladness . . . For surely my heart cannot truly rest, nor be entirely contented, unless it rest in thee.
Thomas à Kempis

---

*PW 10, 253-4

Rise all who seek the crucified,
The God that once for sinners died,
With lifted voice and heart adore.
Chasing our griefs, and sins, and fears,
The Sun of Righteousness appears,
Appears, to set in blood no more.

This day the scripture is fulfilled,
The Father now his Son hath sealed,
And owned him for his Son with power;
God from the belly of the earth
Hath called him forth to second birth,
Nor let the greedy deep devour.

Cast for our sins into the deep,
His life hath saved the sinking ship,
His life for ours a ransom given;
But lo! on the third joyful morn
Our Jonas doth for us return,
Emerging from his tomb to heaven.

For as Jonas was three days and three nights in the whale's belly; so shall the Son of man be three days and three nights in the heart of the earth.

Matthew 12:40

Believing that Jesus was the fulfilment of God's covenant with Israel, the early Christians searched their Scriptures – our Old Testament – for words and events that could be seen as pointers to him. Two of these scriptural images are evoked here – the story of the rebellious prophet Jonah, and the picture of the rising sun. Both were depicted frequently on the walls of Roman catacombs where Christians buried their loved ones in the hope of resurrection.

As Jonah was cast overboard to save a sinking ship, so Jesus is thought of as dying to save our 'sinking ship' – our fallen humanity. And as Jonah was saved from the whale's belly to preach good news in Nineveh, so Christ, rising again as the sun of God's righteousness, sheds light and life on the whole earth.

PRAYER OF BENEDICTION
As you rose from the tomb, O Christ, lift me from the darkness and gloom of my griefs and fears and bring me to new life. Amen.

*HLR (1746) PW 4, 45

Sequestered from the noisy crowd
  Fain would I pray apart,
Confess my sins and wants to God,
  And pour out all my heart.
Now let me leave the world beneath,
  Now to the mount repair,
Sink at my Saviour's feet, and breathe
  My latest breath in prayer.

And when he had sent the multitudes away, he went up into a mountain apart to pray.
Matthew 14:23

Looking at the story of the earthly ministry of Jesus, one sees that all the words and deeds are punctuated by prayer. The pressure of people who needed him, the demand for healing, the discussion and relationships among his close friends – all these could only be sustained if he could get away, often, it seems, to a mountain, to spend time alone with God.

In this short poem, Wesley, following the example of his master, yearns for the same opportunity. His own life was one of busy travelling, preaching, corporate prayer, writing, encouraging and examining the fledgling Methodist classes, so private prayer was essential. He wants to be on the mountainside with Christ, to fall at his feet, to tell him what is wrong with his life, and to pour out his wants.

In many ways, prayer is a state of being as much as of doing. About a hundred years ago, in a letter from China, a Wesleyan missionary wrote to a friend about his powerful guidance from God while he was in a state of 'prayerful passivity'.[1] Others write of prayer as 'creative brooding', 'pondering', 'nurturing' and 'meditating'. We all need the resuscitation that comes through breathing in the breath of life, and returning that breath to our creator.

PRAYER
God, you are everywhere, in all things. Giver of the breath of life, may I listen to you in the beat of my heart and the breath of my lungs; may I sense your presence in sight and sound and feeling and touch. When I have done wrong, when the world overwhelms me, and my heart is full of longings, may I pour them out to you on your holy mountain, in the privacy of prayer. Amen.

---

*SH (1796)

Jesus, to thee I would look up,
    Tossed in a storm of passion,
Thou art the Anchor of my hope,
    Thou art my strong salvation.
Pity and save a soul, distressed
    Till I the port recover;
O that I in thy wounds might rest,
    Till all the storm is over.

Great is the storm that works within,
    Jesus, his grace is greater,
Thou art above the power of sin,
    Thou art the God of Nature;
Speak, and at thy supreme command
    Trouble and sin shall leave me,
Stir up thy strength, stretch out thine hand,
    Say 'It is I', and save me.

When the disciples saw him walking on the sea, they were troubled, saying, It is a spirit; and they cried out for fear. But straightway Jesus spake unto them, saying, Be of good cheer; it is I; be not afraid.

Matthew 14:26-27 (read also verses 22-33)

These verses are part of a longer poem in which Wesley reflects on two miracle stories in Matthew's Gospel, where Jesus and his disciples are caught in a storm at sea. Fear is the dominant emotion of the disciples in each of the stories, and on each occasion Jesus, by actions and words, calms their fear and stills the sea. Charles Wesley, for whom the tempest is a stormy emotional turmoil, appeals with confidence to the same Jesus for help in his distress. Keeping the nautical imagery, he uses the statement from Hebrews 6:19 that hope is 'a sure and steadfast anchor of the soul' and Jesus becomes the anchor – the one who will hold him firm 'till all the storm is over'.

PRAYER
O God of nature, you hold all things in your care. Calm my fears as you calmed the sea, and bring me peace of heart and mind. Amen.

MS *RV 130

256 AFTER A RECOVERY

Son of God, if thy free grace
  Again hath raised me up,
Called me still to seek thy face,
  And given me back my hope;
Still thy gracious help afford,
And all thy loving-kindness show;
Keep me, keep me, dearest Lord,
  And never let me go!

By me, O my Saviour, stand
  In sore temptation's hour;
Save me with thine outstretched hand,
  And show forth all thy power;
O be mindful of thy word,
Thine all-sufficient grace bestow:
Keep me, keep me, dearest Lord,
  And never let me go!

When Peter was come down out of the ship, he walked on the water, to go to Jesus. But when he saw the wind boisterous, he was afraid; and beginning to sink, he cried, saying, Lord, save me. And immediately Jesus stretched forth his hand and caught him, and said unto him, O thou of little faith, wherefore didst thou doubt?
Matthew 14:29-31

The sea of faith was not all plain sailing even, for Charles Wesley. There were times of bodily illness or depression which caused his usually exuberant spirit to sink. In this hymn written 'after a recovery', he expresses in tangible terms the sense of Christ's coming to his rescue. The refrain, repeated in each verse, acts as a reminder that God's strong arm is always there to raise us up again, the moment we cry for help.

A child playing with her grandfather was trying to hold him by the wrist. He easily broke free. Then he grasped her wrist, and, wriggle as she might, nothing could break his hold upon her. 'Remember,' he said to her, 'it is not our hold on God that matters; it is God's hold on us.'

PRAYER
The winds are often rough and our own weight presses us downwards.
Reach forth, O Lord, thy hand, thy saving hand, and speedily deliver us.
John Wesley

---

*HSP (1742) CH 180 HP 720

That mighty faith on me bestow
  Which cannot ask in vain,
Which holds, and will not let thee go,
  Till I my suit obtain;
Till thou into my soul inspire
  The perfect love unknown,
And tell mine infinite desire:
  'Whate'er thou wilt, be done!'

And, behold, a woman of Canaan . . . cried unto him, saying, Have mercy on me, O Lord, thou son of David; my daughter is grievously vexed with a devil . . . Jesus answered and said unto her, O woman, great is thy faith: be it unto thee even as thou wilt.

Matthew 15:22,28

The gospel stories give us many examples of persistence in prayer. The most striking of them is the account of the foreign woman who encountered Jesus during his journey through one of the districts of Tyre and Sidon. Though she called him Lord, and recognised him as the Son of David, she herself was a Canaanite of a different faith from the Jews. Nevertheless, she pleaded with Jesus to help her daughter who was grievously ill. At first Jesus seems to rebuff her, but she persists in her pleading. Her faith is rewarded and her daughter is healed.

This is the kind of persistence Wesley wants to bring into his own prayers. It is the determination Jesus commended in his parables. Like the man who wakes up his neighbour during the night because he has run out of bread, or like the widow who wearies the judge by her constant appeals, we are to pray with urgency, never giving up until we know that our prayers have been answered according to God's will.

PRAYER
Gracious God, inspire my soul to desire such gifts as are in accordance with your purposes, and then give me the energy to pray persistently for them, believing that you will indeed hear my prayer, and grant me above all the gift of perfect love. For Jesus' sake. Amen.

---

*SH (1796)

Give me the faith which can remove
    And sink the mountain to a plain;
Give me the childlike praying love,
    Which longs to build thy house again;
Thy love, let it my heart o'erpower,
And all my simple soul devour.

My talents, gifts, and graces, Lord,
    Into thy blessèd hands receive;
And let me live to preach thy word,
    And let me to thy glory live;
My every sacred moment spend
In publishing the sinners' friend.

Enlarge, inflame, and fill my heart
    With boundless charity divine:
So shall I all my strength exert,
    And love them with a zeal like thine;
And lead them to thy open side,
The sheep for whom their Shepherd died.

If ye have faith as a grain of mustard seed, ye shall say unto this mountain, Remove hence to yonder place; and it shall remove.

Matthew 17:20

It is told of St Francis of Assisi that in the first days of his discipleship he heard, as it were, Christ speaking to him with the words: 'Restore my house.' Taking this summons literally, he spent many days rebuilding a ruined chapel nearby. One day at his task, he realised that this action was symbolic of a more important task. He was being called to build up the house of 'living stones' (1 Peter 2:5), to bring Christ's love to the poor. It is possible for the church, too, in its concern about its own structures, to lose sight of the heart of the gospel: its message of love for all God's people.

PRAYER
Lord, renew my faith, receive my gifts, rekindle my love, that I may share in the rebuilding of your church in the lives of your people. Amen.

HSP (1749) *CH 421 HP 767 UMH 650

The golden rule she still pursued,
And did to others as she would
Others should do to her:
Justice composed her upright soul,
Justice did all her thoughts control,
And formed her character.

Affliction, poverty, disease
Drew out her soul in soft distress,
The wretched to relieve:
In all the works of love employed,
Her sympathising soul enjoyed
The blessedness to give.

Her Saviour in his members seen,
A stranger she received him in,
An hungry Jesus fed,
Tended her sick, imprisoned Lord,
And flew in all his wants to afford
Her ministerial aid.

A nursing mother to the poor,
For them she husbanded her store,
Her life, her all bestowed;
For them she laboured day and night,
In doing good her whole delight,
In copying after God.

I was hungry and you gave me food, I was thirsty and you gave me something to drink, I was a stranger and you welcomed me, I was naked and you gave me clothing, I was sick and you took care of me, I was in prison and you visited me.

Matthew 25:35-36 (NRSV)

Among the early Methodists were persons whose lives were the very personification of the gospel. In this hymn written for the funeral of Mrs Mary Naylor, Charles Wesley gives us a portrait of a woman whose practical ministry to the poor made her in his eyes a model of Christian discipleship. Such goodness, Wesley declares, is godlike.

PRAYER

Lord, give me a sympathising love that enables me to see your presence among those who are in need, and to minister to them in your name. Amen.

(from *A Song for the Poor,* ST Kimbrough, NY 1993 p.43; orig. in *Journal* 2, 339-41)

THE WRONG COMPANY

'So high, so holy and so great,
Why doth your Lord with sinners eat?
  Unfold his strange design.'
A Pharisee inquires in vain,
Faith only can the depth explain
  Of charity divine.

God over all, for ever blessed,
Whose presence is the heavenly feast,
  For us his throne he leaves,
His love the Man of Grief constrains
And makes him live with publicans
  And makes him die with thieves!

And when the scribes and Pharisees saw him eat with publicans and sinners, they said unto his disciples, How is it that he eateth and drinketh with publicans and sinners?
Mark 2:16

Keeping the wrong company has been problematic in every age and place. Society has always assumed that its leaders, in order to be leaders at all, should not lower themselves in the social scale by making friends of those beneath them. But as Mark here goes on to record, perhaps with a touch of irony, Jesus said he came not to the good, but to those who were considered 'sinners'. Wesley's last two lines bring the point into sharper focus and forbid us to give easy answers. Not only did Jesus mix with sinners; he died with thieves. Only faith can understand that depth of love.

PRAYER
Lord Jesus Christ, because you broke bread with the poor,
you were looked on with contempt.
Because you broke bread with the sinful and outcast,
you were looked on as ungodly.
Because you broke bread with the joyful,
you were looked on as a winebibber and a glutton.
Because you broke bread in the upstairs room,
you sealed your acceptance of the way of the cross.
Because you broke bread on the road to Emmaus,
you made scales fall from the disciples' eyes.
Because you broke bread and shared it,
we will do so too, and ask your blessing.[1]
Iona Community

PW10, 458

Who follow Christ in good delight,
The soul they in his name invite:
Sinner, thy hand extend,
In alms and prayer thy faith to show,
Extend thy hand to grasp a foe,
And turn that foe to friend.

[Jesus] saith unto the man, Stretch forth thine hand. And he stretched it out: and his hand was restored whole as the other.

Mark 3:5

'You cannot shake hands with a closed fist,' commented Indira Gandhi when she was Prime Minister of India. The handshake has always been a sign of friendship, an indication that the people greeting one another are unarmed and prepared to come close without threat or fear. The extending of 'the right hand of fellowship' has even become a liturgical act, a way of welcoming a new member into the church, or an alternative way of exchanging the 'kiss of peace'.

Michael Lapsley, an Anglican priest now living in South Africa, lost both his hands when a letter bomb sent to him during the freedom struggle exploded as he opened it. Striving to carry on his work, he once commented that he never realised before what 'manual' work the priesthood requires. The blessing in baptism, the offering of the Eucharist, the anointing with oil, the simple touch of comfort – all require a priest to stretch out a hand. Prayer and praise are often accompanied by hands uplifted to God.

Charles Wesley's verse celebrates these manual acts and encourages us to stretch out our hands, not only to those whose fellowship we already enjoy, but to those whom we would make our friends. Abraham Lincoln once astounded America by appointing one of his arch-enemies to an important post in his government. Asked by a shocked supporter why he did this, he replied, 'Madam, do I not destroy my enemies when I make them my friends?'

PRAYER
Take my hands, and let them move
At the impulse of thy love. *Frances Ridley Havergal*

PW10, 464 [6 turn him to a friend]

Jesus, the word bestow,
The true immortal seed;
Thy gospel then shall greatly grow,
And all our land o'erspread;
Through earth extended wide
Shall mightily prevail,
Destroy the works of self and pride,
And shake the gates of hell.

Its energy exert
In the believing soul;
Diffuse thy grace through every part
And sanctify the whole;
Its utmost virtue show
In pure consummate love,
And fill with all thy life below,
And give us thrones above.

Behold, there went out a sower to sow: And it came to pass, as he sowed, some fell by the way side . . . and other [seed] fell on good ground, and did yield fruit that sprang up and increased . . . The sower soweth the word.

Mark 4:3-4,8,14

By blending the parable of the sower with Peter's words to the church in Asia Minor (1 Peter 1:23), a prayer of universal mission emerges. The dominant image is that of a growing seed – the seed of the good news. Whereas Jesus tells the story of a nameless 'sower', Charles transforms that sower into Jesus himself, who plants the word which then grows to fill our lives with his love.

Experience suggests that words by themselves are not all that is needed to spread the good news of the gospel. 'Don't tell me – show me!' Eliza Doolittle sings in *My Fair Lady*. The energy to demonstrate in deed as well as in word what the love of God means to us and to others will only be given to us as we allow that love to penetrate every part of our lives and become our whole motivation.

PRAYER
Almighty Father, you have called . . . [us] to share in the work of your kingdom; so empower us by the Holy Spirit, that in faith and holiness we may proclaim to all the good news of your salvation; through Jesus Christ our Lord. Amen.
The Wesley Community Collect

PW 13, 22 *HP 768

Waiting at their Saviour's feet,
  Till Jesus bids them rise,
They alone are truly great
  Who greatness dare despise;
Court the dignity supreme
  Obedient to their Master's call,
Seek the praise that comes from him
  By ministering to all.

On the way they had argued with one another who was the greatest. He sat down, called the twelve, and said to them, 'Whoever wants to be first must be last of all and servant of all.'

Mark 9:34-35 (NRSV)

Mark goes on to tell the story of Jesus gathering a child in his arms and telling the disciples that in welcoming such a child in his name (because of regard for who and what Jesus is) they are welcoming himself. Commentators suggest this is another expression of the reversals of the commonly accepted ideal of first and last. In other words, as Wesley paradoxically suggests, those who are truly great are those who despise greatness.

Wesley goes on to affirm that we find our greatest dignity in assuming the humility of Christ himself. The one who serves others is of a higher status in God's eyes than the one who expects to be served. This indeed is a reversal of the way people are generally regarded in our world, where those of the highest rank expect to have servants rather than to be servants themselves.

PRAYER
God, give me the strength to resist the temptation to seek status on the world's terms. Help me instead to follow your way of service and to recognise in those who serve me the dignity that Christ confers on all God's children, for his sake. Amen.

---

*PW 11 27 [1:1 his Saviour's 1:2 bids him 1:3 He alone is 1:4 dares 1:5 courts 1:6 to his 1:7 seeks]

Master, can thy followers be
Excluded from thy care,
Tossed on life's tempestuous sea,
And sinking in despair?
Now command the storm to rest,
Hush the wind, the sea reprove,
Spread throughout this troubled breast
A calm of faith and love.

And there arose a great storm of wind, and the waves beat into the ship, so that it was now full. And he was in the hinder part of the ship, asleep on a pillow: and they awake him, and say unto him, Master, carest thou not that we perish?

Mark 4:37-38

The angry question of the anxious fishermen-disciples caught in an unexpected life-threatening storm carries all the frustration of those who feel abandoned in a crisis. The tone of Wesley's poem is somewhat milder, for he is relying on knowledge the disciples did not have: Jesus will save them. So the opening lines apply that knowledge to our own troubled circumstances. He who saved the disciples in a real storm will surely save us in the storms of life.

The Chinese sign for worry combines the signs for 'tiger' and 'thought', meaning thoughts in the grasp of a tiger. In writing of this state of anxiety, William Cornaby, who lived as a missionary through the troubled days of the 1900 Boxer Rising in China, says: 'Worry is acted atheism! It is a difficulty or a set of difficulties to be borne alone as though we had no heavenly father.'[1] After such a diagnosis, there is comfort in the words of Thomas à Kempis:

> Jesus says: Trust in me, and put thy confidence in my mercy. When thou thinkest thyself furthest off from me, oftentimes I am nearest to thee. When thou judgest that almost all is lost, then oftentimes the greatest gain of reward is close at hand. All is not lost when a thing falleth out against thee. I can quickly succour thee, and turn all thy heaviness into joy.

PRAYER

Loving God, you alone know all my troubles. You alone can save me. Calm my anxiety as you calmed the sea, bring peace to my heart, and give me faith in your unfailing providence. Amen.

SH (1762) *(1796)

All things are possible to them
That can in Jesus' name believe:
Lord, I no more thy truth blaspheme,
Thy truth I lovingly receive;
I can, I do believe in thee;
All things are possible to me.

The most impossible of all
Is that I e'er from sin should cease;
Yet shall it be, I know it shall,
Jesus, look to thy faithfulness!
If nothing is too hard for thee,
All things are possible to me.

Jesus said unto him, 'If you can believe, all things are possible to the one who believes.'

Mark 9:23 (adapt.)

Jesus, Peter, James and John, returning from the Mount of Transfiguration, are met by needy parents. Having found that the other disciples cannot heal their epileptic child, they appeal directly to Jesus. The father is bold, but hesitant in his plea: 'Lord, I believe; help thou mine unbelief.'

Wesley sustains this same tone of bold challenge to Jesus in this remarkable hymn which is wrapped in the words 'possible/impossible'. See how the last lines of each verse vary, yet build on the same message, 'all things are possible to me.' See too how Wesley demands, 'Jesus, look to thy faithfulness', or in other words, a confident 'Don't forget what you promised. I believe; now do your part.'

Reread the Mark story, imagining you are one of the parents of the demented child. Do you find echoes of their experience in your own life? Do you waver between faith and unbelief? Are you prepared to pray with the same persistence a) on behalf of others, b) for your own salvation?

PRAYER
Lord, I believe; help thou my unbelief. Amen.

HSP (1749) [1:1 to him] CH 389 *HP 723

ALL THINGS ARE POSSIBLE (2)

Though earth and hell the word gainsay,
The word of God can never fail;
The Lamb shall take my sins away,
'Tis certain, though impossible;
The thing impossible shall be;
All things are possible to me.

All things are possible to God,
To Christ, God's power in human form,
To me, when I am all renewed,
When I in Christ am born again,
And witness, from all sin set free,
All things are possible to me.

Jesus looked at them and said, 'For mortals it is impossible, but for God all things are possible.'

Matthew 19:26 (NRSV)

The African theologian Tertullian, writing in the early third century, claimed that the resurrection was 'certain because it is impossible'. Inspired by the same words of Jesus, that while it must seem impossible for anyone weighed down with riches to enter the kingdom of heaven, nothing is impossible for God, Charles Wesley marvels here that Christ is able to do the impossible and set him free from sin.

This was the favourite hymn of George Loveless, one of the 'Tolpuddle Martyrs', six agricultural workers who were deported to Australia in 1834 because of their determination to get a fair wage for their work. Public outcry brought them back after two years, a victory for the right of workers to form trade unions.

PRAYER
Pray for those who struggle for justice in many parts of the world today, that they may be encouraged by the thought that there is no limit to the possibilities for good, because all things are possible to God.

---

*HSP (1749) [2:2 the power of God in man] CH 389 HP 723

Commendable excess
Of generous faith and love!
O could I thus my zeal express,
My gratitude approve;
Pour out the precious balm
And rendering him his own,
Whate'er I have, whate'er I am,
Expend on Christ alone.

And being in Bethany in the house of Simon the leper, as he sat at meat, there came a woman having an alabaster box of ointment of spikenard very precious; and she brake the box, and poured it on his head.

Mark 14:3

Mark, Matthew and John place this story at the beginning of the Holy Week events. Each of them reports Jesus as saying, 'Wherever the gospel is preached in the whole world, what she has done will be told in memory of her . . .' Yet there is confusion between them as to who the woman actually was! It seems fitting that Wesley should have at least two meditations on the story. In this poem he characteristically does more than just put the incident into verse; he uses this woman as a model of what he would like to become. Writing this in the 'age of reason', he commends the emotional extravagance of the woman's gesture which he, despite the prevailing culture, longs to emulate.

In the north of England, there is a group of women who occasionally begin their celebration of the sacrament of the Lord's Supper with this story of the anointing of Jesus. This formal reciting of the story 'in memory of her' is an appropriate complement to the account of the other supper on the night before Jesus died

PRAYER
Christ, whose feet were caressed with perfume and a woman's hair, you humbly took basin and towel and washed the feet of your friends. Wash us also in your tenderness as we touch one another, that, embracing your service freely, we may accept no other bondage in your name. Amen.[1] *Elaine Morgan*

---

*PW 11, 69

Who would not eagerly desire
 That envied infant's place?
Jesus, I to thine arms aspire,
 And pant for thy embrace;
My ruined innocence regive,
 My lost simplicity,
And then with arms of love receive
 A little child in me.

He took a little child and put it among them; and taking it in his arms, he said to them, 'Whoever welcomes one such child in my name welcomes me.'

Mark 9:36-37 (NRSV)

The search for lost innocence! The search for the comfort of loving arms! The search for the lost child inside ourselves! Two-thirds of all the self-help books on sale today address these fundamental needs. Wesley touches centre in this one-verse meditation on the scripture passage. Note how he moves straight into a dialogue in the first two lines, as though Mark is actually present in person to tell him this tale.

Poets before and after Wesley searched for lost innocence and the simplicity of childhood. Henry Vaughan (1621-95) opens a poem with the lines:

Happy those early dayes! when I
Shin'd in my Angel infancy . . .
But felt through all this fleshly dresse
Bright shoots of everlastingness. ('The Retreate': 1-2;19-20)

Similarly, the opening section of Wordsworth's ode, 'Intimations of Immortality' repeats this theme; he writes looking back on his childhood: 'But yet I know, where'er I go,/That there hath passed away a glory from the earth' (17-18).

Wesley thinks it is possible to return to that state of being a 'little child', for did not Jesus require this as a condition of the kingdom? With the help of God I can be as open and trusting as the child I once was before I learned too much about the world.

PRAYER SUGGESTION
If you had a church childhood, try to remember your favourite children's hymns. If you remember them, say them aloud; if not, find the hymnbook in which they appeared. Alternatively, try to recall and then ponder on childhood moments of trust and safety.

---

*PW 11, 27

Who is this tender-hearted Friend,
That doth for children care,
That doth my little ones defend,
And in his bosom bear?
The arms, within whose soft embrace
My sleeping babes I see,
They comprehend unbounded space,
And grasp infinity!

[Jesus said]: Suffer the little children to come unto me . . . And he took them up in his arms, put his hands upon them, and blessed them.

Mark 10:14,16

As an almost doting father, Charles Wesley wrote many anxious letters to his wife about the health and well-being of their family. In this poem he relates the words of Christ to his own children – 'my babes'. One can almost see him arriving home after a tiring journey, tiptoeing to the bedside of sleeping Sally or Samuel and imagining Christ's arms around them. Being the evangelist-poet he was, he could not stop there; the unbounded space of the universe is embraced by those same arms.

At the sixth Assembly of the World Council of Churches in Vancouver in 1983, a poster was used to celebrate the theme 'Jesus Christ, the Life of the World'. It is a cartoon of a slender, happy man, trying to grasp a giant globe of the world. He leans his face on it with love, and his arms almost embrace it. Looking at it one has to smile, for the task is so great, yet the man is so happy. This is the Christ, whose arms encompass my little ones and our large world as well.

PRAYER

Parent God, who loves each single soul as though it were the whole world, and the whole world as though it were a single soul, embrace with the arms of your mercy the little ones I love, and help me to reach out in compassion to the great world you stretched out your arms to save. Through Christ our Lord. Amen.

SH (1762) *(1796)

What is the fruit which Christ requires?
Promises vain, or good desires,
Our outward services?
These are but leaves which fade and die,
Nor can the want of grace supply,
Nor can the Saviour please.

But faith, and hope of joys above,
True virtue, Lord, and real love
Are pleasant to thy taste;
Good works, and meek humility,
These are the fruits required by thee,
Which shall forever last.

When they came from Bethany, he was hungry. Seeing in the distance a fig tree in leaf, he went to see whether perhaps he would find anything on it. When he came to it, he found nothing but leaves, for it was not the season for figs.
Mark 11:12-13 (NRSV)

A simple meditation on this story which Mark and Matthew describe as an incident in the life of Jesus, and which Luke treats as a parable with a rather more encouraging ending.

Wesley uses this story to remind us of the proper outcome of our Christian discipleship. He seems to be following Paul who lists the fruits of the Spirit as 'love, joy, peace, longsuffering, gentleness, goodness, faith, meekness, temperance: against such there is no law' (Galatians 5:22-23). They are qualities which form a good checklist of our own spiritual maturity.

PRAYER
Teach me, O God, so to use all the circumstances of my life today that they may bring forth in me the fruits of holiness . . .
Let me use disappointments as material for patience;
Let me use success as material for thankfulness;
Let me use suspense as material for perseverance;
Let me use danger as material for courage;
Let me use reproach as material for longsuffering;
Let me use praise as material for humility;
Let me use pleasure as material for temperance;
Let me use pains as material for endurance.
John Baillie

*PW 11, 42

WHOLE DELIGHT

The sovereign God affects*
Our whole delight to be,
And every worshipper rejects
When void of charity:
No other sacrifice
Can for this want atone,
But love the place of all supplies,
But love is all in one.

Our God is love supreme;
And who in love abide,
They dwell in God, and God in them
Substantially resides:
His spirit lives and reigns
In every loving one,
His throne of grace in saints maintains
His everlasting throne.

The scribe said to him . . . 'You are right in saying that God is one, and beside him there is no other. And to love God with all your heart, all your understanding, and all your strength, and to love your neighbour as yourself – that means far more than any whole-offerings and sacrifices.' When Jesus saw how thoughtfully he answered, he said to him, 'You are not far from the kingdom of God.'

Mark 12:32-34 (REB)

What seems to be a verbal sparring match between the lawyers and Jesus takes on a new tone of honesty in this short dialogue. The lawyer not only agrees with Jesus' summary of the law of Moses, he adds the words of Hosea (6:6): God desires 'mercy, and not sacrifice; and the knowledge of God more than burnt offerings'. In Luke's version, this exchange is followed by the parable of the Good Samaritan.

Wesley takes all this and adds to it words from the first letter of John, that God is the source of self-giving human love. By extension, God's 'throne of grace' in us is 'everlasting', as God is everlasting. Wesley can then make the bold assertion that in those who love, God 'substantially resides', that is, in those whose 'whole delight' is in God's love, there is found the very reality of God's own self.

PRAYER
Sovereign God, forgive us for the times when we bring you our prayers and our worship and yet have no love in our hearts. May your love live in us so that it truly becomes 'all in one' with our actions and we become 'all in One' with you. Amen.

---

*PW 11, 57 [2:2-3 in love abides/He dwells . . . God in him]

---

* from the Latin *affectare:* to strive after

By the needy widow taught
  Blush, ye rich, who little give;
Poorest you who offer naught;
  Learn the poorest to relieve;
God declares the giver blessed:
  Trust his providential word,
Cast your mite into the chest,
  Cast yourselves upon the Lord.

Jesus sat over against the treasury, and beheld how the people cast money into the treasury: and many that were rich cast in much. And there came a certain poor widow, and she threw in two mites . . . [Jesus] saith unto them, Verily I say unto you, that this poor widow hath cast more in, than all they which have cast into the treasury: For all they did cast in of their abundance; but she of her want did cast in all that she had, even all her living.

Mark 12:41-44

Following as it does an attack by Jesus on those who 'devour widows' houses, and for a pretence make long prayers', this story is seen by some modern commentators as an attack on the exploitation of widows, rather than the traditional reading of it as a lesson that we should give sacrificially to the church.

Wesley's short poem on the text is somewhere between these two interpretations. He asks us to learn from the widow who was prepared to give all. Such generosity requires total commitment of life and livelihood. The word 'cast' is important for it suggests here not only throwing in money, but throwing in ourselves – or rather, an abandoning of self-interest in the service of God (1 Peter 5:7). It is an attack on caution, on the careful giving of only what we can afford in time and money. We will never know whether the poor widow had to give all in order to satisfy the greedy needs of the religious establishment. We do know that she, and others like her, are blessed by God and stand as signposts to a larger life.

PRAYER
God, grant me generosity of spirit and material possessions as I put aside my calculated plans for the future and trust more completely that as I follow your way, I will be in your providential care. Amen.

*PW 11, 59

O thou, whom once they flocked to hear,
Thy words to hear, thy power to feel;
Suffer the sinners to draw near,
And graciously receive us still.

They that be whole, thyself has said,
No need of a physician have;
But I am sick, and want thine aid,
And ask thine utmost power to save.

Scribes and Pharisees murmured against his disciples, saying, Why do ye eat and drink with publicans and sinners? And Jesus answering said unto them, They that are whole need not a physician, but they that are sick. I came not to call the righteous, but sinners to repentance.

Luke 5:30-32

The setting is a great feast given for Jesus and his friends by Levi the tax collector, who had just accepted Jesus' invitation to follow him. This is one of those occasions when we could wish to hear the tone of Jesus' voice. Perhaps there is here more than a touch of irony? Jesus knew the self-righteousness of the religious elite to be a great barrier to life change, and genuine righteousness.

It seems that the requirement for being a follower of Christ is to know that one is a sinner and to be open to receive forgiveness.

Charles Wesley's preoccupation with counting himself among the 'sinners' can best be seen in this light; as a passport to following Christ. In the last two lines of verse two, in simple, almost conversational language he states his problem: 'But I am sick'; he needs help. Today, persons in twelve-step recovery programmes for alcohol, drug, and other addictions take the first step by recognising they need help and cannot make it alone. This is the beginning of the journey to wholeness.

PRAYER
Gracious God, so often I slip into a feeling of self-satisfaction that becomes a barrier to real goodness. I need your help to know myself and to be able to confess what is wrong. Keep me always in your love. Amen.

---

*HSP (1749) CH 384 HP 150

Thy power, and truth, and love divine,
The same from age to age endure;
A word, a gracious word of thine,
The most inveterate plague can cure.

Helpless howe'er my spirit lies,
And long has languished at the pool,
A word of thine shall make me rise,
Shall speak me in a moment whole.

Eighteen, or eight and thirty years,
Or thousands are alike to thee:
Soon as thy saving grace appears,
My plague is gone, my heart is free.

Make this the acceptable hour;
Come, O my soul's physician, thou!
Display thy justifying power,
And show me thy salvation now.

Now there is at Jerusalem . . . a pool [where] lay a great multitude of impotent folk, of blind, halt, withered, waiting for the moving of the water . . . And a certain man was there, which had an infirmity thirty and eight years.

John 5:2-3,5 (read to verse 16)

Some things stand out in this story. We never know the invalid's name, but he seems to be in a hopeless situation. Jesus noticed him specially among a crowd of others, and he asked what was a very realistic question: 'Do you want to be made whole?' After being ill for thirty-eight years, the change to health would mean major challenges. When the man explained why he had been inactive for so long, Jesus inspired him to take a step for himself, and he was healed.

In the poem – which echoes the man's request – Charles Wesley himself becomes the man at the pool speaking to Jesus. This is a well-tried form of meditation available to all of us. The anonymous person is you or me. The miracle of physical healing becomes for all of us a parable, an invitation to personal spiritual healing by the 'soul's physician'.

PRAYER
Jesus, healer of women and men, I recognise my need. Your word can 'speak me a moment whole . . .' and set me free immediately, even from my sins of long-standing. Speak the word now. Amen.

---

*HSP (1749) CH 384 HP 150

Forgive my foes? It cannot be;
My foes with cordial love embrace?
Fast bound in sin and misery,
Unsaved, unchanged by hallowing grace,
Throughout my fallen soul I feel
With mortals 'tis impossible.

Great searcher of the mazy heart,
A thought from thee I would not hide;
I cannot draw th' envenomed dart,
Or quench this hell of wrath and pride,
Jesus, till I thy Spirit receive,
Thou know'st, I never can forgive.

Come, Lord, and tame the tiger's force,
Arrest the whirlwind in my will,
Turn back the torrent's rapid course,
And bid the headlong sun stand still,
The rock dissolve, the mountain move,
And melt my hatred into love.

Forgive, and ye shall be forgiven.

Luke 6:37

Only those who have struggled with the power of the emotion of hatred can fully respond to these words. For whatever reason – betrayal, abandonment, deliberate attack, deceit, abuse – the destructive power of 'the enemy' does not end with the injury itself, it compounds itself. The memory of the injustice lingers on; the effects are still present with terrifying reality.

By using images of natural power – the force of the tiger, the whirlwind, the rushing torrent, the 'headlong sun' in its inevitable course – Wesley captures that feeling of being overwhelmed by hatred. It feels like the dart of a poisoned arrow, spreading infection in what was once a healthy body. It has taken over. In that state, the idea of forgiveness is laughable! 'Forgive my foes?' Embrace them with love? And yet, that is what Christ commands. However unlikely it sounds, that is also the remedy for the mountain of pain; God alone can melt it into love.

PRAYER
O God, searcher of my mazy heart, I cannot save myself. Help me! Root out the hatred that is consuming my life, and give me the mind of Christ, enabling me to forgive those who have injured me, as he forgave his enemies. Amen.

*SH (1762) [1:6 With man it is] SH (1796) RV 171

STANDING STILL

Father, that I thy child may be,
That I may thy salvation see,
  Assist me to stand still,
Thy kind instructions to receive,
What to reject and what believe,
  And how perform thy will.

I trust thy mercy to restrain
My blind, implicit faith in man,
  My rash, prejudging haste,
And every hindrance to remove,
That fully I may all things prove,
  And find the Good at last.

Fast let me hold the good I find,
No longer tossed by every wind,
  With every specious tale;
But built on the Foundation sure,
The word which always shall endure,
  The rock that cannot fail.

He is like a man which built an house, and digged deep, and laid the foundation on a rock: and when the flood arose, the stream beat vehemently upon that house, and could not shake it: for it was founded upon a rock.

Luke 6:48

From all accounts, Charles was an affectionate, sensitive man, having the temperament of a poet, a trusting nature, and to the end of his life, a daily schedule that would have exhausted many people. He made mistakes in judgement, was too gullible, and in 'prejudging haste' came to some wrong conclusions. This poem shows his awareness of these weaknesses in his character. No wonder he prays for a firm foundation, built on the word of God, firm and all-enduring!

PRAYER
Patient God, slow me down; make me stand still, so I may hear your wise word and understand your will. In the name of Jesus. Amen.

*UPCW 3, 206-7

Jesus takes the sinner's part,
 Her whom Pharisees condemn;
Searcher of his creature's heart
 Turns the charge from her to them,
Bids their haughtiness give place,
 Thrice commends whom they reprove,
Triumphs in his work of grace,
 Praises her superior love.

Know, ye zealots proud and blind,
 Ye who profligates despise,
Profligates, when Christ they find,
 More than you, the Saviour prize;
Precious balm on Christ they pour,
 Lavish what they most esteem,
Glad his costliest gifts restore,
 Nothing count too dear for him.

My head with oil thou did'st not anoint: but this woman hath anointed my feet with ointment.

Luke 7:46 (read verses 36-50)

We are in the house of the Pharisee, Simon, who has invited Jesus to supper. In the middle of the meal a woman arrives, uninvited of course, who is notoriously labelled 'a sinner'. She creates an emotional scene which horrifies Simon and his friends. But Jesus responds to her with love.

This little poem shows Wesley's appreciation of the dynamics of the situation, and perhaps his delight that the zealous Simons of the world have the tables turned on them, as Jesus 'Turns the charge from her to them . . . Thrice commends whom they reprove.' They did not offer the simple courtesy of washing his feet; they did not kiss him, neither did they anoint his head.

PRAYER
Loving God, you have made all your children in your image. Give me the Christlike courage to be steadfast in my companionship with all people who need my presence. Give me the vision to see the face of Christ in each person, to listen attentively and learn with humility, that I may receive as well as give. Amen.

---

*Gospel of Luke UPCW 2, p.102

Martha's faith in active life
   Was laudably employed,
Tending Christ with zealous strife,
   She served the eternal God;
Mary waiting at his feet
   The life contemplative expressed,
Let the happy sisters meet,
   For joined they both are blessed.

Martha received him into her house. And she had a sister called Mary, which also sat at Jesus' feet, and heard his word.

Luke 10:38-39

It is relatively easy to create caricature sketches of Martha and Mary: Mary, sitting waiting at Jesus' feet, and Martha, the household manager who did all the work.

Wesley's claim that the two sisters make two parts of a whole shows special insight. In any group of people, there are those who have gifts which complement others, as Paul pointed out in reference to spiritual gifts in the body of Christ (1 Corinthians 12). So Wesley names the importance to one another of the two Christian lifestyles, the active and the contemplative.

A helpful model for keeping this kind of balance in life is the circular one of the North American Indian medicine wheel. Whatever one's natural starting point, the task in life is to complete the circle. Thus the Marys learn to be more active, like the Marthas, and the Marthas learn the value of contemplation.

But labelling people can be misleading. Though Martha's personality seems always associated with this story, it must be noted that on another occasion, her perceptive, visionary side allowed her to see and to confess that Jesus was the Christ, the Son of God (John 11:27). To her he spoke the great words: 'I am the resurrection and the life.'

PRAYER
May my actions be inspired by prayer, my prayer made sincere by service. Amen.

---

*Gospel of Luke UPCW 2, p.123

O love divine, how sweet thou art!
When shall I find my longing heart
All taken up by thee?
I thirst, I faint, and die, to prove
The greatness of redeeming love,
The love of Christ to me.

God only knows the love of God;
O that it now were shed abroad
In this poor stony heart!
For love I sigh, for love I pine:
This only portion, Lord, be mine,
Be mine this better part!

O that I could for ever sit
With Mary, at the Master's feet!
Be this my happy choice:
My only care, delight, and bliss,
My joy, my heaven on earth, be this–
To hear the Bridegroom's voice!

[Martha] had a sister called Mary, which also sat at Jesus' feet, and heard his word.
Luke 10:39

This hymn expresses a yearning for union with Christ, the very source of love. This mystical desire has been expressed through human experiences of longing to be with the loved one. In the home at Bethany Mary chose the opportunity of spending time with Jesus above all other duties or pastimes. John the Baptist compared his own waiting for Jesus to the eager expectancy of a best man at a wedding, who shares in the bridegroom's joy. It is a joy available to us too, as we wait in Christ's presence.

PRAYER
Lord Jesus Christ, help me to choose, above all other joys, the joy of being in your presence and finding in your love the fulfilment of all the other loves in my life. Amen.

---

*HGF (1746) PW 4, 341-2 RV 63 MHB 434

280 AFTER PREACHING TO THE NEWCASTLE COLLIERS (1)

See how great a flame aspires,
Kindled by a spark of grace!
Jesu's love the nations fires,
Sets the kingdoms on a blaze.
To bring fire on earth he came;
Kindled in some hearts it is:
O that all might catch the flame,
All partake the glorious bliss!

When he first the work begun,
Small and feeble was his day:
Now the word doth swiftly run,
Now it wins its widening way;
More and more it spreads and grows
Ever mighty to prevail;
Sin's strongholds it now o'erthrows,
Shakes the trembling gates of hell.

'I came to cast fire upon the earth; and would that it were already kindled!'
Luke 12:49 (RSV)

The writer of the letter of James warns his readers to watch what they say, for wrong words spoken by the tongue (only a small part of the body) are like a fire which can burn the whole Christian community (James 3:5). Wesley's word is equally dynamic, but he sees it as a powerful, positive force. This is the fire of the love of Jesus which changes and purifies human hearts, the flame of the Spirit that came in living tongues at Pentecost.

The hymn is one of four written 'After preaching to the Newcastle colliers'. It has been suggested that Wesley's opening 'See' may have been prompted by the open fires that burned beside the collieries. But that is just the starting point for seven 'fire' words which start with a spark, continue in a blaze, and have potential for setting all ablaze in a flame of bliss.

PRAYER
Almighty and loving God, whose will it is that all your children should know you, so fill my heart with the fire of your love that others may also catch the flame. Amen.

---

*HSP (1749) RV 79 CH 209 HP 781 UMH 541

AFTER PREACHING TO THE NEWCASTLE COLLIERS (2)

Saints of God, your Saviour praise!
He the door hath opened wide;
He hath given the word of grace,
Jesu's word is glorified;
Jesus, mighty to redeem,
He alone the work hath wrought,
Worthy is the work of him,
Him who spake a world from naught.

Saw ye not the cloud arise,
Little as a human hand?
Now it spreads along the skies,
Hangs o'er all the thirsty land:
Lo! the promise of a shower
Drops already from above;
But the Lord shall shortly pour
All the spirit of his love!

And it came to pass at the seventh time, that he said, Behold, there ariseth a little cloud out of the sea, like a man's hand.

1 Kings 18:44

The first section of this hymn spoke of fire; today's second verse uses the image of rain. Both symbols of the Spirit, they point to the sense of immediacy and imminence which permeates Wesley's view of the kingdom. In both we are required to look and observe the signs of the coming blessing.

Just as the spark turns to blazing fire, so the cloud will turn to a downpour. The God who created a world from nothing is the same God who gives this word of grace. Perhaps when we think nothing is happening we are not looking in the right place. The Spirit moves in strange ways, and unexpected places. Where love is, God is. In the care of a single parent for his child, in the persistence of a woman who works in difficult circumstances to feed her family, in nursing homes and prisons and city streets, signs of the kingdom can be seen. Keep looking!

PRAYER
Spirit of truth, keep me alive to your working in my own life, and help me to see the signs of your presence in the life of the world. Amen.

---

*HSP (1749) [1:1 Sons of God (UMH = Saints)] RV 79 CH 209 HP 781 UMH 541

Nor time nor means my Lord can need
To accomplish thy own work in me;
Speak, and my soul from sin is freed,
Is loosed from its infirmity.
My heart and spirit rectify,
Remove my nature's bent to ill,
And while thou dost the rule apply,
Conform me to thy perfect will.

O that I now my heart could raise
Transferred from earth to things above,
And only live to spread thy praise,
To magnify thy healing love!
O that in every word and thought
And deed I might thy glory show,
Who hast on me such wonders wrought,
That all may thy salvation know.

And, behold, there was a woman which had a spirit of infirmity eighteen years, and was bowed together, and could in no wise lift herself up. And when Jesus saw her, he called her to him and said unto her, Woman, thou art loosed from thine infirmity.
Luke 13:11-12

Only Luke, the physician, tells this story of Jesus healing an unnamed woman bent double through a long-term illness. Wesley invites us to use this cameo as a metaphor for our own bondage to sin – the infirmity from which we need to be 'loosed'. Like the woman, we are 'bent to ill' and need the help of one who can bring a straightening 'rule' to our lives, can 'raise' us up. Then our hearts as well as our bodies will be raised, and, like the woman, we shall be uplifted in praise to God.

PRAYER
O God our deliverer, at whose feet we are free to lay down our heavy burden: we bring before you those whose tasks are backbreaking . . . those who live uneasy in their bodies . . . those whose spirits are crushed . . . who cannot dance free. Make them hear of joy and gladness, that the bones which you have broken may rejoice.[1]
Janet Morley

---

*UPCW 2 p.144

Come, sinners, to the gospel feast,
Let every soul be Jesu's guest;
Ye need not one be left behind,
For God hath bid all humankind.

Sent by my Lord, on you I call,
The invitation is to all;
Come, all the world; come, sinner, thou!
All things in Christ are ready now.

Do not begin to make excuse,
Ah! do not you his grace refuse;
Your worldly cares and pleasures leave,
And take what Jesus has to give.

Excused from coming to a feast!
Excused from being Jesu's guest!
From knowing *now* your sins forgiven,
From tasting *here* the joys of heaven!

Go then, my angry master said,
Since these on all my mercies tread,
Invite the rich and great no more,
But preach my gospel to the poor.

A certain man made a great supper, and bade many: And sent his servant at supper time to say . . . Come; for all things are now ready.

Luke 14:16-17 (read to verse 24)

Shared meals are one of the strongest images in the New Testament. Christ is often found eating with friends and strangers, including many who were social outcasts. In this parable, the feast includes all those guests who are normally excluded. Wesley uses this as a metaphor for the love of God, given freely to all, but especially to the poor and the marginalised people of the world.

PRAYER
Hospitable God, you invite me to your banquet, and I am often distracted by all my cares and worries. Give me grace to come, and let my problems fall into their rightful place. Amen.

---

*RH (1747) RV 72 [1:4 bidden all mankind] CH 2 HP 460 UMH 339 & 616

Come, then, ye souls, by sin oppressed,
Ye restless wanderers after rest,
Ye poor, and maimed, and halt, and blind,
In Christ a hearty welcome find.

Sinners my gracious Lord receives,
Harlots and publicans and thieves,
Drunkards and all the hellish crew,
I have a message now to you.

The worst unto my supper press,
Monsters of daring wickedness,
Tell them my grace for all is free,
They cannot be too bad for me.

Tell them their sins are all forgiven,
Tell every creature under heaven
I died to save them from all sin;
And force the vagrants to come in.

This is the time; no more delay!
This is the acceptable day;
Come in, this moment, at his call,
And live for him who died for all.

Go out quickly into the streets and lanes of the city, and bring in hither the poor, and the maimed, and the halt, and the blind . . . Go out into the highways and hedges, and compel them to come in, that my house may be filled.

Luke 14:21,23

Ina 'Mum' Roelents, founder of a drop-in centre for street women in downtown Vancouver, Canada, tells a modern parable which illustrates the message of this hymn, 'Tell them my grace for all is free/They cannot be too bad for me.' It is the story of a prostitute, Tina, who had been on the streets since she was thirteen. The girl was murdered. 'I guess I must head for hell,' Tina thought, 'That's where all those street preachers and TV evangelists said I would go.' But when she got to hell, she was told she was not wanted. Discouraged, for she had always been rejected, Tina tried the handle of another door, and 'slipped through into light and beauty beyond anything she had known on earth'. Here her friends met her, telling her she was safe, for she was in heaven. Wesley asserts that none can be too bad for heaven.

PRAYER
Lord, help us to welcome others, not in spite of their sin but because of your love. For Christ's sake. Amen.

---

*RH (1747) RV 72 CH 2 HP 460 UMH 339 & 616

Surely if we ought, we may
Every moment watch and pray:
Simply I receive thy word,
Merciful, almighty Lord.
Thou who gavest the command,
Nothing can thy will withstand;
And if I believe in thee,
Nothing is too hard for me.

Then Jesus told them a parable about their need to pray always and not to lose heart. He said, 'In a certain city there was a judge who neither feared God nor had respect for people. In that city there was a widow who kept coming to him and saying, "Grant me justice against my opponent." '

Luke 18:1-3 (NRSV) (read to verse 8)

Perhaps Luke is right in believing that this is a parable about prayer, but the powerfully persistent widow insists on nudging us to other forms of action too, for as Wesley writes, 'Nothing can thy will withstand.' The woman's energy in arguing with the judge eventually moves him to action. Certainly he does not do so for moral reasons, but only because he is worn down by her persistence.

Rigoberta Menchu, Nobel Peace Prize winner of 1992, comes from Guatemala where in her early twenties she saw the murder of her husband, her brothers and her mother and father. Her biographer writes:

> Like the widow of the parable of Jesus, Rigoberta would not give up seeking and demanding that the just rights of her people be heard in the court of the world's heart and mind. Barely five feet tall she has become a little pest in the hallowed halls of International Human Rights hearings. She has been a pest to the church . . . a pest to the Government and the Military of Guatemala . . . Let those who would act as judge and oppressor in Central America take heed to the words of the judge in the parable of Jesus, when, in a state of utter exhaustion, he conceded: 'I must give this widow her just rights, or she will persist in coming and worry me to death.'[1]

PRAYER
In a world that prizes instant results teach me, O God, the patience of persistent prayer, that will not let go until your will is done on earth as in heaven. Amen.

SH (1762) *(1796).

Thy faithfulness, Lord, each moment we find,
So true to thy word, so loving and kind;
Thy mercy so tender to all the lost race,
The vilest offender may turn and find grace.

O let me commend my Saviour to you,
I set to my seal that Jesus is true;
You all may find favour who come at his call;
O come to my Saviour! His grace is for all.

To save what was lost, from heaven he came;
Come, sinners, and trust in Jesus's name;
He offers you pardon, he bids you be free:
'If sin be your burden, O come unto me!'

Then let us submit his grace to receive,
Fall down at his feet, and gladly believe;
We all are forgiven for Jesus's sake;
Our title to heaven his merits we take.

The Son of man is come to seek and to save that which was lost.

Luke 19:10

Three years before he wrote this hymn, Charles was visiting ten condemned prisoners in Newgate Gaol 'with a heavy heart'. He writes in his diary of 10 July 1738: 'I could hardly hope there was mercy for those whose time was so short. But in the midst of my languid discourse, a sudden spirit of faith came upon me, and I promised them all pardon, in the name of Jesus Christ, if they would then, as at the last hour, repent, and believe the gospel.'

We may on occasion find ourselves called to bring comfort to others in extreme circumstances. Even in everyday situations we are often aware of another's longing to hear words of acceptance and forgiveness. One woman may feel she has made a mess of life by poor choices; a man may regret what he feels was a failure of years ago. Spoken or unspoken, the question is: 'Can I ever be forgiven?' Fortunately I do not have to judge myself or others. 'The mercy I feel, to others I show', because God's answer, and thus my answer, is a confident, unequivocal 'Yes.'

PRAYER
May I feel in myself this day, and share with others, the joy of sins forgiven. Amen.

HGEL (1741) CH 5 *HP 805

Sinners, to you the source we show
  From whence all human discord springs,
That origin of evil know,
  That direful lust of earthly things,
And ask your Lord, in instant prayer,
The root out of your hearts to tear.

Your life on needful things depends,
  Not on superfluous treasures vain:
A little serves for nature's ends;
  And if a world of wealth ye gain,
Ye nothing gain with all your care
But food to eat and clothes to wear.

Take care! Be on your guard against all kinds of greed; for one's life does not consist in the abundance of possessions.

Luke 12:15 (NRSV)

These words of Jesus, as recorded by Luke, follow his refusal to be a judge between a man and his brother in their quarrel over the family inheritance. After this warning Luke tells the parable of the rich man who was doing so well that he decided to extend his barns and relax in happy retirement, only to be struck down by death.

Greed for material possessions is one of the greatest causes of human strife. Wesley recommends a radical remedy for such sin: in urgent prayer, ask God to root out from the heart all forms of lust. Whilst Wesley recognises the need for essential commodities such as food and clothing, he pleads that a little is enough.

In today's society, consumerism has become almost a compulsion, an addiction, what someone has called a 'shop till you drop' mentality. Unequal distribution of the world's goods means that gluttony and starvation exist side by side – these are ills that make for violence. We all need to learn to live simply so that others may simply live. As this change works in us, we discover that the way of justice for others is also a way to a fuller life for ourselves.

PRAYER
Great God, root out all that is selfish in me. Give me a new heart, so that I find the ground of my being in what nourishes me and all the world. Amen.

---

*Gospel of Luke UPCW 2, p. 137

Father, behold thy son
In Christ I am thy own;
Stranger long to thee and rest,
See the prodigal is come;
Open wide thine arms and breast
Take the weary wanderer home.

Thine eye observed from far,
Thy pity looked me near:
Me thy body yearned to see
Me thy mercy ran to find,
Empty, poor and void of thee,
Hungry, sick, and faint, and blind.

Thou on my neck didst fall,
Thy kiss forgave me all:
Still the gracious words I hear,
Words that made the Saviour mine,
'Haste, for him the robe prepare,
His be righteousness divine!'

Thee then, my God and King,
My Father, thee I sing!
Hear, well-pleased the joyous sound,
Praise from earth and heaven receive;
Lost, I now in Christ am found,
Dead, by faith in Christ I live.

And he arose, and came to his father. But when he was yet a great way off, his father saw him and had compassion, and ran, and fell on his neck and kissed him . . . For this my son was dead, and is alive again; he was lost, and is found.

Luke 15:20,24

The parable of the prodigal son is so familiar that it can lose some of its impact. In this, one of the earliest hymns that he wrote, Charles enlivens our vision by 'becoming' the son at the point when he meets his father. By making the first and last verses almost the same he conveys the idea of homecoming; by the lost/found and dead/live antitheses he dramatically marks the change that has happened in his own life, as in the prodigal's.

POINT TO PONDER

How few words are spoken, and how many gestures are used to express forgiveness and welcome to the returning sinner. Make the story your own.

---

*HSP (1739) [2:3 thy bowels] CH 184 RV 2

Sinners, obey the gospel word;
Haste to the supper of the Lord!
Be wise to know your gracious day;
All things are ready, come away!

Ready the Father is to own
And kiss his late-returning son;
Ready your loving Saviour stands,
And spreads for you his bleeding hands.

Ready the Spirit of his love
Just now the stone heart to remove;
To apply, and witness with the blood,
And wash and seal each child of God.

The Father, Son and Holy Ghost
Is ready, with their shining host;
All heaven is ready to resound:
The dead's alive, the lost is found!

For this my son was dead, and is alive again; he was lost, and is found. And they began to be merry.

Luke 15:24

Again, a meal is a celebration and an expression of the love of God. In blending the parable of the great supper in Luke 14 with that of the prodigal son, Wesley does more than use the meal as the common metaphor. He turns his poem on the word 'ready': God in the three persons of the Trinity is always ready to welcome us to the table.

Wanting to come home to God after a long absence may make us feel guilty. We may feel like those who have forgotten to keep in touch with their parents, and wonder about their welcome. Wesley reminds us how wrong we are! The feast is ready in our honour; we are sure of God's love waiting to celebrate our homecoming.

PRAYER
Lord, make us ready to respond to your invitation, as you are ready to receive us as your guests. Amen.

HSP (1749) *CH 9 [3:2 the stony to 3:4 seal the sons] MHB 326

COME, FOR ALL THINGS ARE NOW READY (2)

Come, then, ye sinners, to your Lord,
In Christ to paradise restored;
His proffered benefits embrace,
The plenitude of gospel grace:

The godly grief, the pleasing smart,
The meltings of a broken heart;
The tears that tell your sins forgiven,
The sighs that waft your souls to heaven;

The guiltless shame, the sweet distress,
The unutterable tenderness;
The genuine meek humility;
The wonder, 'Why such love to me?'

The o'erwhelming power of saving grace,
The sight that veils the seraph's face,
The speechless awe that dares not move,
And all the silent heaven of love!

Now I rejoice, not that ye were made sorry, but that ye sorrowed to repentance . . . For godly sorrow worketh repentance to salvation.

2 Corinthians 7:9-10

Wesley lists numerous 'benefits' of God's grace, some apparently contradictions – 'pleasing smart', 'guiltless shame', 'sweet distress'. Even our experience of shame and suffering can be counted among our blessings. Our tears and our sense of guilt become means of grace if they bring us to repentance. Then we can experience a love that is beyond all words as we bow in reverent gratitude before God.

PRAYER
Mysterious, forgiving God, only you know what I do and fail to do. You know what is wrong with my life, and how I avoid you because I feel guilty. Overwhelm me with your love, so that I may feel forgiven and live thankfully and joyfully in that love. Amen.

HSP (1749) *CH 9 MHB 325

Returned into thy kingdom, Lord,
For good remember me,
And tell a penitent restored,
I soon shall be with thee.

The offering of a broken heart
Thou never wilt despise,
But while my soul and body part,
Accept the sacrifice.

My spirit humbly I commend,
To thy redeeming care,
My last important moments spend
In penitence and prayer.

And if I may not testify
On earth my sins forgiven,
Yet I, the poorest outcast I
May praise thy love in heaven.

And [the malefactor] said unto Jesus, Lord, remember me when thou comest into thy kingdom. And Jesus said unto him, Verily I say unto thee, Today shalt thou be with me in paradise.

Luke 23:42-43

The eighteenth century in England was a time when hangings were public entertainment, when a person could be put to death for minor crimes such as stealing sheep, and when few seemed to care.

Frank Baker suggests that by the time this hymn was written, the Wesleys themselves may have had some part in turning public opinion against this barbarism.[1] From their earliest days in the Holy Club at Oxford, they had always taken seriously Christ's command to visit those in prison. As well as bringing practical help, they gave spiritual comfort. Charles wrote a number of hymn-prayers for prisoners, of which this is one.

Using the story of the thief on the cross and Jesus' last words to him, Charles shows fundamental, pastoral compassion. Society may shun, but Christ and Christ's followers do not.

PRAYER
God of justice and love, you seek the liberation of us all. Comfort those who are in prison for whatever reason, give them hope in their darkness, courage in their times of fear, and friends to offer your love, through Jesus Christ. Amen.

---

*Prayers for Condemned Malefactors (1785) RV 229

LIVING WATER

Jesus, the gift divine I know,
   The gift divine I ask of thee;
The living water now bestow,
   Thy Spirit and thyself, on me;
Thou, Lord, of life the fountain art;
O could I find thee in my heart!

Thee let me drink, and thirst no more
   For drops of finite happiness;
Spring up, O Well, in heavenly power,
   In streams of pure perennial peace,
In joy that none can take away,
In life which shall for ever stay.

If you knew the gift of God and who it is that is saying to you, 'Give me a drink', you would have asked him, and he would have given you living water. Those who drink of the water that I will give them will never be thirsty . . . [It] will become in them a spring of water gushing up to eternal life.

John 4:10,14 (NRSV)

Imagine the conversation between Jesus and the Samaritan woman at the well – this revealing talk which starts in an apparent succession of misunderstandings, as Jesus speaks figuratively and the woman speaks literally. Charles Wesley interrupts the flow of the dialogue and, becoming the third person in the conversation, claims Christ's attention by saying that (unlike the woman) he does know the gift of God and is at this moment asking for it.

But like the woman and like most of us he has not arrived at a peaceful state. He is still adding little drops of 'finite happiness' by his own effort, when he could be receiving a fountain of power and peace and joy and everlasting life that is there for the asking. Whatever those drops are for you and for me; a little more money, another relationship, a holiday, a well-planned life, all these reasonable drops do not add up to a satisfying whole if we are drawing from the wrong well.

PRAYER
Fountain of life, come to my heart and flood its empty, longing spaces with love for you and for all the world. Amen.

---

*SH (1762) CH 354 HP 318

See a soul with pardon blessed,
  Freely saved by grace alone!
Knowing Christ, she cannot rest,
  Till she makes her Saviour known.
Changed by one almighty word,
  Earthly things she leaves behind,
The Apostle of the Lord,
  Lord of her, and all mankind.

'Sinners come by faith and see
  A celestial Man unknown,
One who hath revealed to me
  All I have in secret done;
Virtue doth from him proceed,
  All my life and heart he showed.
Is not this the Christ indeed?
  Is not this the omniscient God?'

The woman left her water jar and went back to the city. She said to the people, 'Come and see a man who told me everything I have ever done!'

John 4:28-29 (NRSV)

The title 'Apostle' has too often been limited to the twelve male disciples whom Jesus chose to accompany him in his ministry. But here Charles Wesley applies the title to one of the women who comes into the company of Jesus and who, even without being given any special commission, goes out herself to tell others of her experience in meeting him and of her conviction that he is the Messiah.

The remarkable feature of this story is that the woman is a foreigner, of dubious reputation and of a different faith from the Jews. Yet Jesus went out of his way to talk with her, to ask her help and to engage in serious theological discussion with her. In the course of their conversation, she realises that he knows her story and her bad reputation, yet he treats her with gracious acceptance and respect, a clear example of grace freely given and of pardon received.

PRAYER
Christ, both stranger and friend, help us to overcome the barriers of gender and race and religion that separate us from others, so that we may share with them the good news of our encounter with your love. Amen.

---

*UPCW 2, 229-30

Holy Lamb, who thee confess,
Followers of thy holiness,
Thee they ever keep in view,
Ever ask: 'What shall we do?'

Governed by thy only will,
All thy words we would fulfil,
Would in all thy footsteps go,
Walk as Jesus walked below.

While thou didst on earth appear,
Servant to thy servants here,
Mindful of thy place above,
All thy life was prayer and love.

Such our whole employment be,
Works of faith and charity;
Works of love on all bestowed,
Secret intercourse with God.

Then said they unto [Jesus], What shall we do, that we might work the works of God?
John 6:28

This hymn has been compared to an exquisite mosaic pavement. Each line is like a separate tile that fits smoothly into the whole picture. There is no rough edge nor broken fragment. Yet each phrase adds its own colour to the whole. The lines and verses, said Dr Benjamin Gregory, are 'knit together in love'.

The image of a mosaic is an appropriate one for this hymn about the family and the church. Charles Wesley believed that every member has a distinctive contribution to make to the whole pattern of the church's life. All must be engaged in works of outgoing love, nourished by lives of inward spirituality.

PRAYER
Thou art never weary, O Lord, of doing us good. Let us never be weary of doing thee service. Amen. *John Wesley*

FH (1767) *CH 515 [4:3 on man bestowed] MHB 598

Early in the temple met,
Let us still our Maker greet;
Nightly to the mount repair,
Join our praying Pattern there.

There by wrestling faith obtain
Power to work for God again,
Power his image to retrieve,
Power like thee, our Lord, to live.

Vessels, instruments of grace,
Pass we thus our happy days
'Twixt the mount and multitude,
Doing or receiving good.

Glad to pray and labour on,
Till our earthly course is run,
Till we, on the sacred tree,
Bow the head and die like thee.

Jesus taketh with him Peter, and James, and John, and leadeth them up into an high mountain apart by themselves . . . And when he came to his disciples, he saw a great multitude about them.

Mark 9:2,14

It is sometimes suggested that there are two different ways of seeing God. There are those who choose the contemplative life, spending most of their time in prayer. There are others who are engaged in active service, spending all their energy in good works of one kind or another.

Jesus showed how essential it is that we do both. His disciples noted the way he habitually drew away from the crowds for a short time for a period of private prayer. It must have been a rare privilege for the three who were closest to him to be allowed sometimes to accompany him on those vigils. Then they found their faith strengthened, their anxiety relieved and their energy renewed for service to the needy multitude.

Note the amazing last verse of Wesley's hymn. Prayer does not protect us from suffering nor from an ultimate death. But it prepares us to face both with a courage born of trust.

PRAYER
Lord, may I seek thee in the quiet place so that I may serve thee in the market-place. Amen.

---

*FH (1767) CH 515 MHB 598

MY ONLY WAY

Thou, O my God, thou only art
The Life, the Truth, the Way;
Quicken my soul, instruct my heart,
My sinking footsteps stay.

Of all thou hast in earth below,
In heaven above, to give,
Give me thy love alone to know,
In thee to walk and live.

Fill me with all the life of love;
In mystic union join
Me to thyself, and let me prove
The fellowship divine.

Jesus saith unto him, I am the way, the truth, and the life.

John 14:6

It is a pity that Jesus' words to Thomas are sometimes quoted in an exclusive context as though he were speaking to people of other faiths and warning them that there was no other way of walking with God save with Christ alone. But Charles Wesley here emphasises the positive words which Jesus spoke personally to Thomas, the disciple who seems to have found faith difficult and who felt himself at times sinking under the weight of his own doubts.

In Morecambe, one of the beautiful bays on the north-west coast of England, there is a path that leads across from one part of the coast to another, but it passes through dangerous sinking sands. To travel safely one needs to walk with a guide who knows the territory and can keep to a safe path. This is the kind of picture conjured up by these verses from one of Wesley's morning hymns. Here Charles the disciple asks that Christ will guide him along each step of the way, refreshing him day by day with the assurance of God's love. With such a guide he has no need to be afraid of sinking. Christ will be walking beside him, pointing out the way and sharing with him a life of love and constant companionship.

PRAYER
Lord Jesus, I ask you to be my companion as I go through life. I want to walk with you along your way; I want to learn from you all that you can teach me about God; and I want to share my whole life with you in an ever-deepening love for you and for all whom you love. Amen.

HSP (1740) *PW 1, 225 MHB 464

Saviour and Prince of Peace,
Thy saying we receive:
Thou wilt not leave us comfortless,
Thine own thou wilt not leave.
Poor helpless orphans we
Awhile thine absence mourn,
But we thy face again shall see,
But thou wilt soon return.

No longer visible
To eyes of flesh and blood,
Come, Lord, to us thyself reveal,
O come and show us God.
Because thou liv'st above,
Let us thy Spirit know,
And in the glorious knowledge prove
Eternal life below.

I will pray the Father, and he shall give you another Comforter, that he may abide with you for ever; even the Spirit of truth . . . I will not leave you comfortless: I will come to you.

John 14:16-18

'I am too old to be an orphan,' wrote a middle-aged man when his father died. When Jesus left the disciples, they must have felt much of the same bewildering sense of abandonment. The wonderful change from the despair of the crucifixion to the joy of knowing Christ was alive was muted again, as they mourned the loss of Christ after his ascension. There was only the strange promise that he would send his Spirit.

In this in-between time Wesley places the pilgrim followers of Christ. We have seen, and yet we wait to 'know and feel'. As a prayer of petition to Christ it is full of confidence that, through the Spirit, God, the Three-in-One will be at home in our hearts.

PRAYER
Hasten the day of your coming with power into my life, O Holy Spirit. Make real to me the presence of God through the love of Christ, that I may share in their eternal life even here and now. Amen.

Hymns of Petition and Thanksgiving for the Praising of the Father (1746) *PW 4, 177

O that with humbled Peter, I
Could weep, believe, and thrice reply,
  My faithfulness to prove!
Thou knowest, for all to thee is known,
Thou knowest, O Lord, and thou alone,
  Thou knowest, that thee I love.

O that I could, with favoured John,
Recline my weary head upon
  The dear Redeemer's breast!
From care and sin and sorrow free,
Give me, O Lord, to find in thee
  My everlasting rest.

Thy only love do I require,
Nothing on earth beneath desire,
  Nothing in heaven above:
Let earth and heaven and all things go,
Give me thine only love to know,
  Give me thine only love.

[Jesus said to Peter the third time]: Simon, son of Jonas, lovest thou me? Peter was grieved because he said unto him the third time, Lovest thou me? And he said unto him, Lord, thou knowest all things; thou knowest that I love thee.

John 21:17

In these reminders of the stories of Peter and John we have scenes of loving intimacy: Peter's protestation of love, cancelling out his three former denials, and John's closeness to Jesus at the Last Supper (John 13:23).

The last verse expresses the desire for love itself. Wesley repeats the words 'heaven' and 'earth' to emphasise that everything else can go. The last two lines are particularly moving, for the shorter line actually contains the larger message. The paradox of the double 'nothing' immediately followed by the double 'give me' is especially effective as it reaches its climax in the last bold request.

PRAYER SUGGESTION
Read slowly these gospel incidents. Then close your eyes and imagine yourself to be Peter or John, or an onlooker. What comes to mind? How do you feel?

---

*HGF (1746) PW 4, 341-2 RV 63

HYMN TO THE SON (1)

O filial Deity!
Accept my newborn cry;
See the travail of thy soul,
Saviour, and be satisfied;
Take me now, possess me whole,
Who for me, for me, hast died.

Of life thou art the tree,
My immortality!
Feed this tender branch of thine,
Ceaseless influence derive;
Thou the true, the heavenly vine,
Grafted into thee I live.

Of life the fountain thou,
I know, I feel it now;
Faint and dead no more I droop:
Thou art in me; thy supplies,
Every moment springing up,
Into life eternal rise.

To those who are victorious I will give the right to eat from the tree of life that stands in the garden of God.

Revelation 2:7 (REB)

For with you is the fountain of life.

Psalm 36:9 (REB)

Written within the first three weeks of his conversion, Charles brings to this all the passion of that experience. As the tender newborn child in a first cry of life gasps in the air and turns to its mother for milk, so the newborn Charles cries out and seeks nourishment from Christ.

The fruit of the tree gives life because it grows in paradise (Genesis 3:3). Jesus speaks of himself as the vine and of us as the branches (John 15:1-5). Charles feels that now he is grafted on to the vine. His earlier separation from Christ has been changed into an organic unity with him. So, too, he has the fountain of living water within, that refreshes him continuously, now and through all eternity.

PRAYER
Loving Jesus, nourish me, soul and body, with all your goodness, so that I may grow in you. Daily refresh my spirit at your spring of living water. Amen.

HSP (1739) *CH 186 MHB 97

HYMN TO THE SON (2)

Thou the good Shepherd art,
From thee I ne'er shall part;
Thou my Keeper and my Guide,
Make me still thy tender care;
Gently lead me by thy side,
Sweetly in thy bosom bear.

Thou art my daily Bread;
O Christ, thou art my Head!
Motion, virtue, strength, to me,
Me thy living member, flow;
Nourished I, and fed by thee,
Up to thee in all things grow.

He shall feed his flock like a shepherd: he shall gather the lambs with his arm, and carry them in his bosom, and shall gently lead those that are with young.

Isaiah 40:11

In

yesterday's hymn, the newborn spiritual child finds nourishment in Christ, the tree of life and the water of life. Wesley now breaks the pattern of food images at this point to introduce the good shepherd, before returning to Jesus as bread in the fifth verse. Charles understood that a child needs love as well as food. In Isaiah's prophecy the young lambs are fed, but also protected and carried in the arms of God, the good shepherd. This is the only safe place for the person new in faith.

As the growing child needs daily bread, so Charles affirms Jesus as the bread of life. But what is all this nourishment for? Wesley turns to Ephesians, which inspires us to grow up, beyond childhood, in the love of Christ (Ephesians 4:11-16).

PRAYER
Jesus, you give protection and food to all who need your care. Challenge us to grow in love all the days of our years and all the years of our lives, so we may become as you are. Amen.

HSP (1729) *CH 186 MHB 97

Come, let us with our Lord arise,
Our Lord, who made both earth and skies:
Who died to save the world he made,
And rose triumphant from the dead;
He rose, the Prince of life and peace,
And stamped the day for ever his.

This is the day the Lord has made,
That all may see his love displayed,
May feel his resurrection's power,
And rise again, to fall no more,
In perfect righteousness renewed,
And filled with all the life of God.

Then let us render him his own,
With solemn prayer approach his throne,
With meekness hear the gospel word,
With thanks his dying love record,
Our joyful hearts and voices raise,
And fill his courts with songs of praise.

This is the day which the LORD hath made; we will rejoice and be glad in it.
Psalm 118:24

This hymn is intended to teach children part of the Apostles Creed (especially in verse one) and to encourage a proper response to the Christian Sunday. See how the child is encouraged to get up ('come . . . arise') in the first line, and how this action is linked to Christ's rising throughout the first two verses. The meekness Charles saw as a childlike quality is not false humility, but an openness to the world of wonder and wisdom and truth.

Each generation, in reconsidering its use of Sunday, has different reasons for needing a day of rest; but for Christians the primary reason for keeping Sunday special is that it is the celebration of the day of resurrection.

PRAYER
Risen and ever-living God, be present with people of all ages who join in worship on the Lord's day. Grant them meekness to hear your word with open hearts and minds, that they may rediscover your truth for our own time. Amen.

Hymns for Children (1763) RV 106 [2:2 power displayed] *HP 575

ON HIS BIRTHDAY

Away with my fears,
The glad morning appears,
When an heir of salvation was born!
From Jehovah I came,
For his glory I am,
And to him I with singing return.

In a rapture of joy
My life I employ,
The God of my life to proclaim;
'Tis worth living for this,
To administer bliss
And salvation in Jesus's name.

My remnant of days
I spend in his praise,
Who died the whole world to redeem;
Be they many or few
My days are his due,
And they all are devoted to him!

My soul shall be joyful in the LORD: it shall rejoice in his salvation.

Psalm 35:9

This, a hymn Charles Wesley wrote on his birthday, is only part of twelve verses, all of which sustain the same exuberant tone. John Wesley also made it a practice to mark his own birthday by noting in his journal the state of his physical and spiritual progress. On 28 June 1788, a few months after his brother's death, he writes, 'I this day enter on my eighty-fifth year; and what cause I have to praise God, as for a thousand spiritual blessings, so for bodily blessings too.' Then he adds the last verse of this hymn.

Birthdays are for all of us a good time for reflection, a time to recollect all the elements which make up our lives. If you keep a journal, read through the entries of the last year at one reading, then close the book and in a short paragraph, or list, or poem, write down what particular blessings you have received during this past year and commit the remaining years, 'the remnant' as Charles puts it, into the hands of God.

PRAYER

Let it be the one business of my life to glorify thee, by every word of my tongue, by every work of my hand; by professing thy truth, and by engaging all persons, so far as in me lies, to glorify and love thee. *John Wesley*

---

*HSP (1749) CH 221

FOR THE ANNIVERSARY DAY OF ONE'S CONVERSION (1)

O for a thousand tongues to sing
  My dear Redeemer's praise,
The glories of my God and King,
  The triumphs of his grace!

My gracious Master and my God,
  Assist me to proclaim,
To spread through all the earth abroad
  The honours of thy name.

Jesus – the name that charms our fears,
  That bids our sorrows cease;
'Tis music in the sinner's ears,
  'Tis life, and health, and peace.

He breaks the power of cancelled sin,
  He sets the prisoner free;
His blood can make the foulest clean,
  His blood availed for me.

Make a joyful noise unto God, all ye lands: Sing forth the honour of his name: make his praise glorious.

Psalm 66:1-2

This hymn, the first in so many Methodist hymnbooks from 1780 onwards, is really part of a much longer work which begins with a doxology: 'Glory to God, and praise and love/Be ever, ever given!' Several verses speak of Charles' own conversion experience in the same tone of amazed joy.

The sense of 'life, and health, and peace' is granted through calling on the powerful name of Jesus. This is the reversal of evil charms. The real effects are seen in verse four – the shattering of addiction to destructive acts.

Over a period of some years, two very different friends told of the power of these words for their own lives. Each of them had had the experience of knowing they were forgiven, and having the power of their addiction broken. This is joy indeed!

PRAYER
Almighty God, I need your life, and health, and peace. I need your power to see and then overcome all those things in my life that control me, and keep me in darkness and fear. Come, Lord Jesus, Come!

---

*HSP (1740) RV 17 CH 1 HP 744 UMH 57 VU 326

304 FOR THE ANNIVERSARY DAY OF ONE'S CONVERSION (2)

He speaks; and, listening to his voice,
New life the dead receive;
The mournful, broken hearts rejoice;
The humble poor believe.

Hear him, ye deaf; his praise, ye dumb,
Your loosened tongues employ;
Ye blind, behold your Saviour come;
And leap, ye lame, for joy!

Look unto him, ye nations, own
Your God, ye fallen race!
Look and be saved, through faith alone,
Be justified by grace.

In Christ, our Head, you then shall know,
Shall feel, your sins forgiven,
Anticipate your heaven below,
And own that love is heaven.

The blind receive their sight, and the lame walk, the lepers are cleansed, and the deaf hear, the dead are raised up, and the poor have the gospel preached to them.
Matthew 11:5

It was to the home of a Mr Bray that Charles says he was taken, just before Pentecost in the year 1738. Charles was not only sick and near death with pleurisy, he was distraught in mind. On the actual day of Pentecost (21st May) he said, 'I waked in hope and expectation of Christ's coming.' Later, as he dozed, he heard the words: 'In the name of Jesus Christ of Nazareth, arise and believe, and thou shalt be healed of all thy infirmities.'

He later realised the words were spoken by a woman he knew, who felt called by Christ to say them. The incident is described in the first two lines of this part of the hymn; the effect – the promise of knowing and feeling forgiveness – in the last verse.

The biblical healing images in verse two come from the prophet's vision of the day of God in Isaiah 35. They were quoted by Jesus to bring hope to John the Baptist in his lonely prison. In their present tense they remind Wesley and ourselves of the transforming power of Jesus' presence in lives in every age.

PRAYER
Lord, help me to listen to your words with my heart as well as with my head, so that their healing power might touch the depths of my being, and stir me into new life. For your name's sake. Amen.

---

*HSP (1740) RV 17 CH 1 [4:1 With me, your chief] HP 744 UMH 57 VU 326

Sing to the great Jehovah's praise;
All praise to him belongs;
Who kindly lengthens out our days
Demands our choicest songs.

His providence has brought us through
Another various year;
We all with vows and anthems new
Before our God appear.

Father, thy mercies past we own,
Thy still-continued care;
To thee presenting, through thy Son,
Whate'er we have or are.

Our lips and lives shall gladly show
The wonders of thy love,
While on in Jesus' steps we go
To see thy face above.

Our residue of days or hours
Thine, wholly thine, shall be,
And all our consecrated powers
A sacrifice to thee.

If thou wilt walk in my ways, to keep my statutes and my commandments, as thy father David did walk, then I will lengthen thy days.

1 Kings 3:14

New Year's Day is often a time of new resolutions. The Wesleys were conscious that it was also a time of corporate thanksgiving and rededication. These verses, part of a longer hymn, are arranged in the form of a command – 'sing', a reflection on the past and the present, and, in the closing lines, a dedication for the year to come. Charles echoes the words of Paul, that our 'reasonable service' is to present our bodies as a 'living sacrifice' to God (Romans 12:1).

PRAYER
. . . We beseech thee, give us that due sense of all thy mercies, that our hearts may be unfeignedly thankful, and that we show forth thy praise, not only with our lips but in our lives; by giving up ourselves to thy service, and by walking before thee in holiness and righteousness all our days.
Book of Common Prayer, from *A General Thanksgiving*

HNYD (1750) & *HP 360

FOR A LOVE FEAST

Let us join – 'tis God commands –
Let us join our hearts and hands;
Help to gain our calling's hope,
Build we each the other up:
God his blessing shall dispense,
God shall crown his ordinance,
Meet in his appointed ways,
Nourish us with social grace.

Hence may all our actions flow,
Love the proof that Christ we know;
Mutual love the token be,
Lord, that we belong to thee:
Love, thine image, love impart!
Stamp it on our face and heart!
Only love to us be given!
Lord, we ask no other heaven.

By this everyone will know that you are my disciples, if you have love for one another.
John 13:35 (NRSV)

The early Christians often gathered together for what was called an 'agape', a love feast. This was a simple meal, during which they shared their faith with one another and also shared their food with the poor. The custom was revived by the Moravians and later adopted by the people called Methodists. Though they still went to their Anglican parish church for the Communion Service, they would gather in their own homes or preaching houses for their love feast. Special 'loving cups' were used, two-handled vessels so that members might drink water together and share cake as a token of their love for one another. During the feast they would sing hymns celebrating their fellowship and encouraging one another in the faith.

This hymn is one of many that Charles Wesley wrote for such an occasion, stressing that a personal experience of God's grace inevitably has a social effect.

PRAYER
Christ, help us so to love one another in the fellowship of your church that others will recognise that we have indeed been in the company of Jesus. Amen.

HSP (1740) *CH 507-8 MHB 713

To thee, benign and saving power
 I consecrate my lengthened days,
While marked with blessings, every hour
 Shall speak thy co-extended praise.

How shall I teach the world to love,
 Unchanged myself, unloosed my tongue?
Give me the power of faith to prove,
 And mercy shall be all my song.

Be all my added life employed
 Thy image in my soul to see;
Fill with thyself the mighty void,
 Enlarge my heart to compass thee!

Prepare, and then possess my heart,
 O take me, seize me from above;
Thee do I love, for God thou art;
 Thee do I feel, for God is love.

Those who love me will keep my word, and my Father will love them, and we will come to them and make our home with them.

John 14:23 (NRSV)

Written after his return from Georgia in the spring of 1738, this urgent prayer-poem shows Wesley's state of mind before his spiritual search reached its climax in May of that year. Having just recovered from a serious illness, he believed that if God had saved his life, it must be to some purpose; hence the rededication.

Like many people, Charles found it hard to break through from an earnest desire to know God, to the experience itself. Head and heart knowledge are not the same thing. The final lines, while suggesting that the feeling of God's love for him is growing more intense, are such a balanced poetic scheme that it still seems very controlled. But no-one can doubt the urgent sincerity of his prayer: 'Come . . . seize me.'

PRAYER
Come then, my Hope, my Life, my Lord, and fix in me thy lasting home. Amen.

HSP (1739) *RV 114

BEFORE WORK (1)

Forth in thy name, O Lord, I go,
My daily labour to pursue,
Thee, only thee, resolved to know
In all I think, or speak, or do.

The task thy wisdom hath assigned
O let me cheerfully fulfil,
In all my works thy presence find,
And prove thine acceptable will.

Preserve me from my calling's snare,
And hide my simple heart above,
Above the thorns of choking care
The gilded baits of worldly love.

[Simon said unto Jesus]: Master, we have toiled all the night, and have taken nothing: nevertheless at thy word I will let down the net.

Luke 5:5

One of the most cheerful workers in the history of Christian spirituality was the Carmelite, Brother Lawrence of the Resurrection (c. 1605-1691). His humble way of doing all things in the presence of God made him feel that even uncongenial jobs were a joy. He was sure of his own incompetence but that, with God, things would turn out well. It is said that when he was in his monastery kitchen:

> for which [work] he had a naturally strong aversion; having accustomed himself to doing everything there for the love of God, and asking God's grace to do his work, he found he had become quite proficient . . . during the fifteen years he had worked in there.[1]

All the conversations which have come down to us in his writings, *The Practice of the Presence of God,* show this childlike trust.

The third verse of Wesley's hymn has rarely been put in contemporary hymnbooks, but it is worthy of meditation. Stress at work can come from many sources: pressure from above, unrealistic expectations and ambitions, genuine or perceived need for more money; all of these might be our 'calling's snare'.

MEDITATION
Consider what may be the snares in your particular kind of work. Imagine what it might be like if you were really finding God to be present in all you do.

---

*HSP (1749) RV 77 CH 315 HP 381 UMH 438 VU 416

Thee may I set at my right hand,
Whose eyes mine inmost substance see,
And labour on at thy command,
And offer all my works to thee.

Give me to bear thy easy yoke,
And every moment watch and pray,
And still to things eternal look,
And hasten to thy glorious day.

For thee delightfully employ
Whate'er thy bounteous grace hath given,
And run my course with even joy,
And closely walk with thee to heaven.

I have set the LORD always before me; because he is at my right hand, I shall not be moved.

Psalm 16:8

The tone of cheerfulness set in the first part of the hymn continues in today's meditation. Both the confidence of the Psalmist, and Christ's own words that he will bear our heavy burdens (Matthew 11:28-30) are the driving biblical sources here.

In the last verse the words 'delightfully' and 'bounteous' create a sense of buoyancy; an effective juxtaposition with the third line's 'even joy' which has its source in Paul's speech to the Ephesians (Acts 20:24). The phrase is striking, for often we think of joy as a transient emotion.

Those who have been part of the Iona Community in Scotland have found important the small rubric at the end of the morning worship, which declares, 'We remain standing to leave, the work of our day flowing directly from our worship.' This really happens: the whole community – guests as well – shares in the cleaning and tidying up as a prelude to any other programme which may be planned for the day.

PRAYER
This is the day that God has made; we will rejoice and be glad in it.
We will not offer to God offerings which cost us nothing.
Go in peace to love and serve the Lord.
We will seek peace and pursue it.
In the name of the Trinity of Love, one God in perfect community. Amen.[1]
End of Morning Worship, Iona Community

---

*HSP (1749) RV 77 HP 381 UMH 438 VU 416

Servant of all, to toil each day
  Thou didst not, Lord, refuse;
Thy majesty did not disdain
  To be employed for us.

Son of the carpenter, receive
  This humble work of mine;
Worth to my meanest labour give,
  By joining it to thine.

End of my every action thou,
  In all things thee I see;
Accepted my hallowed labour now,
  I do it unto thee.

Thy bright example I pursue,
  To thee in all things rise;
And all I think, or speak, or do
  Is one great sacrifice.

I am among you as one who serves.

Luke 22:27 (NRSV)

This poem is in simple metre with regular rhyme. It was originally two separate hymns, written by Wesley, as the title suggests, to be sung by labourers at the beginning of their working day. George Eliot gives a fine portrait of such a person in Adam Bede, a carpenter, in her novel of the same name. In modern collections, the two hymns are generally put together as one.

George Herbert (1593-1633) was one of the favourite poets of Susanna Wesley, the mother of John and Charles, and therefore his poetry was part of their childhood. This hymn is reminiscent of Herbert's prayer on the intrinsic value of everyday work, 'The Elixir':

Teach me, my God and King,
In all things thee to see,
And what I do in anything,
To do it as for thee.

MEDITATION
Rewrite this hymn in your own prose as a prayer for working days.

---

*HSP (1739) CH 312-313 [1:1 to toil for man] MHB 575 HP 383

Jesus, united by thy grace
And each to each endeared,
With confidence we seek thy face,
And know our prayer is heard.

Still let us own our common Lord,
And bear thine easy yoke,
A band of love, a threefold cord,
Which never can be broke.

O make us of one spirit drink;
Baptise into thy name;
And let us always kindly think,
And sweetly speak the same.

Touched by the lodestone of thy love,
Let all our hearts agree,
And ever toward each other move,
And ever move toward thee.

Two are better than one, because they have a good reward for their labour . . . and a threefold cord is not quickly broken.

Ecclesiastes 4:9,12

Friendship has been described by the writer Sallie McFague as the 'free, reciprocal, trusting bonding of persons committed to a common vision'.[1] As friends we look to each other for companionship and support, but as mutual friends of 'our common Lord' Jesus we also 'seek [his] face'. That means we join hands and look outward rather than inward. God's vision becomes ours as we work together.

The image of the powerful lodestone drawing the compass needle was captured by John Owen, the seventeenth century divine. He writes:

> The heart of a believer affected with the glory of Christ is like the needle touched with the lodestone. It can no longer be quiet, no longer be satisfied in a distance from him. It is put into continual motion towards him.[2]

PRAYER
Holy Spirit, counsellor and friend, in countless ways you draw me to yourself like a magnet, yet I keep pulling in other directions. Still you call me back. Help me to recognise the true centre of my life. Amen.

HSP (1742) CH 490 *HP 773

And are we yet alive,
And see each other's face?
Glory, and thanks to Jesus give
For his almighty grace!
Preserved by power divine
To full salvation here,
Again in Jesus' praise we join,
And in his sight appear.

What troubles have we seen,
What mighty conflicts past,
Fightings without, and fears within,
Since we assembled last!
Yet out of all the Lord
Hath brought us by his love,
And still he doth his help afford,
And hide our life above.

And Israel said unto Joseph, Now let me die, since I have seen thy face, because thou art yet alive.

Genesis 46:30

For over two hundred years, delegates to Methodist Conferences have started their deliberations with this hymn. While some still sing these opening words with great seriousness, others are slightly amused. Compared to the persecutions and natural hazards faced by the early Methodist preachers who were at times in danger of death itself, the question may seem a bit superfluous today when public apathy is a greater trial than physical danger. On the other hand, there are still many parts of the world where people face martyrdom for their faith.

The biblical background is worth our attention. The old and almost blind Jacob (Israel), who thought his son dead, finds to his joy that after all these years Joseph is alive and well. What a dramatic meeting that must have been! Charles Wesley recognises that same emotion of amazed joy when friends and colleagues are able to come together again after a long absence. What an occasion to say thank-you to God for keeping us all safe.

PRAYER
O God, who has ordered this wonderful world, who knows all things in earth and heaven, so fill my heart with trust in you, that by night and by day, at all times and in all seasons, I may without fear commit those who are dear to me to your never failing love, for this life and the life to come. Amen.

---

*HSP (1749) RV 86 CH 466 HP 707 UMH 553

Blest be the dear uniting love,
That will not let us part;
Our bodies may far off remove,
We still are joined in heart.

Joined in one spirit to our Head,
Where he appoints we go;
And still in Jesus' footsteps tread,
And do his work below.

Closer and closer let us cleave
To his belov'd embrace;
Expect his fullness to receive,
And grace to answer grace.

Partakers of the Saviour's grace,
The same in mind and heart,
Nor joy, nor grief, nor time, nor place,
Nor life, nor death can part.

And of his fullness have all we received, and grace for grace.

John 1:16

Friendship is one of life's greatest treasures, but when friends have to be away from each other, life feels empty. On Christmas Eve 1943, from his prison cell in Nazi Germany, Dietrich Bonhoeffer wrote to his friends:

> Nothing can fill the gap when we are away from those we love, and it would be wrong to try and find anything. We must simply hold out and win through. That sounds very hard at first, but at the same time it is a great consolation, since leaving the gap unfilled preserves the bonds between us. It is nonsense to say God fills the gap; God does not fill it, but keeps it empty so that our communion with another may be kept alive, even at the cost of pain.[1]

Wise words. Charles develops a similar thought by suggesting that common purpose in following and being embraced by Jesus, our mutual friend, will help us to feel 'joined . . . in mind and heart' in a way that nothing can part. The last two lines – with echoes of the last two verses of Romans 8 – are particularly comforting.

PRAYER
For all those I love, wherever they may be, I pray that you, God, will keep them in your care in this life and the life to come. Amen.

---

*HSP (1742) CH 520 HP 752 UMH 566

FRIENDS APART (1)

Lift up your hearts to things above,
Ye followers of the Lamb,
And join with us to praise his love
And glorify his name.

To Jesus' name give thanks and sing,
Whose mercies never end;
Rejoice! Rejoice! the Lord is King;
The King is now our friend!

O let us stir each other up,
Our faith by works to approve,
By holy purifying hope,
And the sweet task of love.

Those who love a pure heart and are gracious in speech will have the king as a friend.
Proverbs 22:11 (NRSV)

'Lift up your hearts: We lift them up unto the Lord,' say the minister and congregation in the Sursum Corda of the Communion Service. Perhaps it is this dialogue that is in the back of Wesley's mind as he writes this hymn 'for Christian friends'. The nature of the early Methodist movement was such that friends were often far away, so means had to be found to keep in touch. The conversation could continue by prayer – they were to remember each other before God at five o'clock each day.

Hymns provided another, tangible reminder of a fellowship that was not bound by the limits of time and space. Singing familiar hymns, distant friends would be reunited in spirit, in the unending 'strain of praise' (John Ellerton).

PRAYER
Companionable God, who in sending Jesus to live on earth showed yourself our friend, we thank you for all those who love us and whom we love. Grant us understanding that distance is no barrier to love, for you transcend time and space and even death itself. Amen.

HSP (1749) *CH 525 HP 820

Love us, though far in flesh disjoined,
Ye lovers of the Lamb,
And ever bear us on your mind,
Who think and speak the same.

You on our minds we ever bear,
Whoe'er to Jesus bow,
Stretch out the arms of faith and prayer
And lo! we reach you now.

Mercy and peace your portion be,
To carnal minds unknown,
The hidden manna, and the tree
Of life, and the white stone.

Live till the Lord in glory come,
And wait his heaven to share!
He now is fitting up our home –
Go on! we'll meet you there!

[The Spirit says to the churches:] To everyone who conquers, I will give permission to eat from the tree of life that is in the paradise of God . . . To everyone who conquers I will give some of the hidden manna, and I will give a white stone . . .

Revelation 2:7,17 (NRSV)

The hymn is set in the form of a dialogue between friends separated by distance but united in faith. They respond to one another in alternate verses, promising to bear one another up in their prayers.

In their greetings, the friends use the code language of the Book of Revelation. James Martin, a Canadian scholar commenting on this book, tells how he loves walking on the beach, looking for that one special white stone which represents his heart's desire. That and the tree of life and the hidden manna are all mysterious gifts of grace which God has prepared for the faithful.

The final parting has an almost domestic ring. God is 'fitting up our home' rather like a housewife preparing to receive her guests. There at last we shall all be at home together.

PRAYER

Pray especially today for those far distant from you, reaching across the divide to bring them into God's presence with you.

HSP (1749) *CH 525

A PRAYER FOR LABOURERS (1)

Jesus, thy wandering sheep behold!
See, Lord, with tenderest pity see
The sheep that cannot find the fold,
Till sought and gathered in by thee.

Lost are they now, and scattered wide,
In pain, and weariness, and want;
With no kind shepherd near to guide
The sick, and spiritless, and faint.

Thou, only thou, the kind and good
And sheep-redeeming Shepherd art:
Collect thy flock, and give them food,
And pastors after thine own heart.

For thus saith the Lord God; Behold, I, even I, will both search my sheep, and seek them out. As a shepherd seeketh out his flock in the day that he is among his sheep that are scattered . . . I will bring them to their own land, and feed them.

Ezekiel 34:11-13

To feel the impact of these verses, one needs to read from the beginning of this chapter of Ezekiel. Starting from the ancient image of ruler as shepherd, the prophet denounces those who, in positions of power, should have supported the people in their care, and instead have betrayed their trust.

The picture of Christ the Good Shepherd draws on this Hebrew image. Good rulers show compassion and seek to bring justice to all. This is a model for all followers of Jesus, especially today when, once more, society is tempted to turn its back on so many needy people.

PRAYER
Lord, give compassion to all whom you have called to serve others as rulers, pastors and teachers; give them wise and understanding hearts, fill them with a true love of your people, make them holy and keep them humble that they may serve you faithfully, through Jesus Christ our Lord. Amen.

HSP (1742) *HP 772

Give the pure word of general grace,
  And great shall be the preachers' crowd;
Preachers, who all the sinful race
  Point to the all-atoning blood.

Open their mouth, and utterance give;
  Give them a trumpet-voice, to call
A world, who all may turn and live,
  Through faith in him who died for all.

Thy only glory let them seek;
  O let their hearts with love o'erflow!
Let them believe, and therefore speak,
  And spread thy mercy's praise below.

Mercy for all be all their song,
  Mercy which every soul may claim,
Mercy which doth to all belong,
  Mercy for all in Jesus' name.

Scripture says, 'I believed and therefore I spoke out,' and we too, in the same spirit of faith, believe and therefore speak out.

2 Corinthians 4:13 (REB)

'Preach faith until you have it; and then preach faith because you have it' was the advice given to John Wesley in the days when he was seeking the assurance of faith. Here Charles Wesley prays particularly for those called to the ministry of preaching, that their words may come from a heart full of faith and overflowing with love. As a German proverb puts it, 'Only what comes from the heart goes to the heart.'

The message, he insists, must be one of universal grace. Notice how the word 'all' resounds throughout the hymn, like the ringing note of a summoning trumpet. The theme of the message too must be a constant one. 'Mercy', the word repeated in every line of the last verse, is what preaching is all about: this is what the preacher has to offer as the good news; this is what people yearn to hear, the compassionate, forgiving love of God for all.

PRAYER
Lord, have mercy upon me as I seek to proclaim your mercy for all. Amen.

HSP (1742) *HP 772 [2:3 On all the world to turn]

The people that in darkness lay,
In sin and error's deadly shade,
Have seen a glorious gospel day
In Jesus' lovely face displayed.

Thou only, Lord, the work hast done,
And bared thine arm in all our sight;
Hast made the reprobates thine own,
And claimed the outcasts as thy right.

Thy single arm, almighty Lord,
To us the great salvation brought;
Thy Word, thy all-creating Word,
That spake at first the world from nought.

For this (no longer sons of night)
To thee our thankful hearts we give;
To thee, who call'dst us into light;
To thee we die, to thee we live.

The people that walked in darkness have seen a great light.

Isaiah 9:2

To be an underground coal miner in the barbaric conditions of eighteenth century mines must have seemed like being in the deepest bowels of the earth. Wesley offered to the tough colliers of Bristol, who were regarded as outcasts in their society, the good news of the gospel, as well as his own compassion. To give others dignity in the sight of God, to call them from their spiritual and literal darkness into the light of the love of God, and to remove the 'sons of night' label that the world gave them, was bringing the gospel literally right down to earth.

PRAYER

Remind us, O God, that all your children are our brothers and sisters, that no situation, no person is beyond your love and care. Give us the compassion and sensitivity to be your word of light to others in unconventional ways and hidden places, that we may receive as well as give your love. To you be all the praise. Amen.

HSP (1740) *CH 195 MHB 379

Earth rejoice, our Lord is King!
Mortals all, his praises sing;
Sing ye in triumphant strains,
Jesus the Messiah reigns!

Though the hosts of night blaspheme,
More there are with us than them;
God with us, we cannot fear;
Fear, ye fiends, for Christ is here!

Lo, to faith's enlightened sight,
All the mountain flames with light!
Hell is nigh, but God is nigher,
Circling us with hosts of fire.

Christ the Saviour is come down,
Points us to the victor's crown,
Bids us take our seats above,
More than conquerors in his love.

Behold, an host encompassed the city both with horses and chariots. And his [Elisha's] servant said unto him, Alas, my master! how shall we do? And he answered, Fear not: for they that be with us are more than they that be with them . . . And, behold, the mountain was full of horses and chariots of fire round about Elisha.
2 Kings 6:15-17

'Methodists' in the 1740's were no strangers to riots. Some were attacked by mobs, preachers were stoned, houses set on fire, and even the magistrates were sometimes hostile. Wesley's own title for this hymn shows it is a remedy for such dangerous times. When under attack, sing! Sing words that invoke that other apparently hopeless situation, when Elisha the prophet was miraculously saved from the hosts of the king of Syria. Sing words that speak of the ultimate triumph of Christ!

PRAYER
Almighty God, who by your grace surrounds us with so great a cloud of witnesses, may we, encouraged by the example of your servants, persevere and run the race you set before us, until at last, through your mercy, we attain with them to your eternal joy; through Jesus Christ our Lord. Amen.[1] *Anglican Church of Canada*

HSP (1740) *HP 811 [1:2 Sons of men 2:1 sons of night]

Ye servants of God, your Master proclaim,
And publish abroad his wonderful name;
The name all-victorious of Jesus extol;
His kingdom is glorious, and rules over all.

God ruleth on high, almighty to save,
And still he is nigh, his presence we have;
The great congregation his triumph shall sing,
Ascribing salvation to Jesus our King.

'Salvation to God who sits on the throne!'
Let all cry aloud, and honour the Son;
The praises of Jesus the angels proclaim,
Fall down on their faces, and worship the Lamb.

Then let us adore, and give him his right:
All glory and power, all wisdom and might,
All honour and blessing, with angels above,
And thanks never-ceasing, and infinite love.

I will extol thee, my God, O king; and I will bless thy name for ever and ever. Every day will I bless thee; and I will praise thy name for ever and ever.

Psalm 145:1-2

What appears at first sight to be a general hymn of praise actually addressed dangerous situations in the 1740s. In addition to the menace of civil war, there was the threat to life and limb occasioned by a wave of anti-Methodist agitation. Two verses, omitted here, deal specifically with these dangers, but the hymn as a whole is a call to praise (extol), under any and all circumstances, the one in whom we shall celebrate the final victory of 'infinite love'.

Offering praise as a response to danger may seem rather unusual, but it has a long tradition in the church. Martyrs from Rome to Belsen to Central America have sung praise to God, even in death. On a less dramatic level, we are attracted by people whose buoyant gratitude to God seems to be the very core of their spirituality. Real praise, even in puzzling, painful and grief-ridden times, is the solid rock on which we can rebuild our lives.

PRAYER

Say or sing the hymn quietly as a personal act of praise and as a prayer for the church throughout the world.

HTTP (1744) [3:3 Our Jesus's praises] *HP 278 UMH 278 VU 342

Talk with me, Lord, thyself reveal,
While here o'er earth I rove;
Speak to my heart and let it feel
The kindling of thy love.

With thee conversing I forget
All time, and toil, and care;
Labour is rest, and pain is sweet
If thou, my God, art here.

Here then, my God, vouchsafe to stay,
And bid my heart rejoice;
My bounding heart shall own thy sway,
And echo to thy voice.

Thou callest me to seek thy face;
'Tis all I wish to seek;
To attend the whispers of thy grace,
And hear thee inly speak.

When thou saidst, Seek ye my face; my heart said unto thee, Thy face, LORD, will I seek.

Psalm 27:8

This hymn recalls the story of the conversation between the two disciples and the risen Jesus on the road to Emmaus, but there are other strands which add a rich texture to the meditation. The singular pronoun in Wesley's original version links these verses to a passage in Milton's *Paradise Lost,* where Eve talks to Adam in the Garden of Eden. She tells him:

With thee conversing I forget all time,
All seasons and their change, all please alike. [*PL* IV, 639-40]

These lines, with their sentiment many lovers will recognise, strengthen the tone of daring intimacy that Wesley suggests for our relationship with God. We are lovers and friends of Jesus.

MEDITATION
In what way does meeting a person 'face to face' enrich your relationship with that person? How can your relationship with God be more like a conversation between friends?

---

*HSP (1740) CH 205 HP 542

Far from thy mad fantastic ways,
I here have found a resting place
 Of poor wayfaring men;
Calm as the hermit in his grot,
I here enjoy my happy lot,
 And solid pleasures gain.

Along the hill or dewy mead
In sweet forgetfulness I tread,
 Or wander through the grove;
As Adam in his native seat,
In all his works my God I meet
 The object of my love.

I see his beauty in the flower;
To shade my walks and deck my bower,
 His love and wisdom join;
Him in the feathered choir I hear,
And own, while all my soul is ear,
 The music is divine!

O LORD, how manifold are thy works! in wisdom hast thou made them all: the earth is full of thy riches.

Psalm 104:24

On a week's holiday retreat at St Anne's Hill, Chertsey in the spring of the year 1751, Charles is delighted by all he sees and hears. His first line echoes Gray's *Elegy Written in a Country Churchyard*, which had been circulated in magazines during the previous year. He too has come 'far from the madding crowd' of the world.

Off the west coast of Canada are dotted various islands; some are only a short boat-ride from the city, but all have that marvellous feeling of isolation that only an island can give. A local church runs a camp on one of these islands, and every summer over five hundred people who would never otherwise have a holiday go there for a week. Swallows nest on the verandas, eagles float overhead, herons stand motionless on the shore, and above all the silence of the great stars by night. God's presence is tangible in this lovely world – this marvellous place of healing and new beginnings.

PRAYER
Great God, I see your works in the wonders of nature; give me a thankful heart. Amen.

---

*FH (1767) RV 206

Jesus, in whom the weary find
Their late, but permanent repose,
Physician of the sin-sick mind,
Relieve my wants, assuage my woes;
And let my soul on thee be cast,
Till life's fierce tyranny be past.

Loosed from my God, and far removed,
Long have I wandered to and fro,
O'er earth in endless circles roved,
Nor found whereon to rest below:
Back to my God at last I fly,
For O the waters still are high.

Selfish pursuits, and nature's maze,
The things of earth, for thee I leave;
Put forth thy hand, thy hand of grace,
Into the ark of love receive,
Take this poor fluttering soul to rest
And lodge it, Saviour, in thy breast.

[Noah] sent forth a dove . . . but the dove found no rest for the sole of her foot . . . then he put forth his hand, and took her, and pulled her in unto him into the ark.
Genesis 8:8-9

Physical weariness comes to us all, but there is another sort of weariness, that of life's struggle – for survival, for recognition, for health, for happiness, for a sense of being at home in the world. This weariness is what Wesley is talking about.

In addition to the dove sent out from the ark by Noah, in the back of Charles Wesley's mind may be Milton's fallen angels, who rove in endless circles looking for a place to rest. Our own wandering after too many of the wrong things may seem to us sometimes like an evil possession – a compulsion to keep going, to keep active, to keep looking for the land beyond the rainbow. Wesley is suggesting that our home is in God, and that Christ rescues us, if only we are willing to settle in that ark of a stabilising love.

PRAYER
God, you made us for yourself, and our hearts are restless till they find their rest in you. Amen. *Augustine of Hippo*

HSP (1740) *PW 1, 249 [1:2 late and permanent] MHB 357

See, sinners, in the gospel-glass,
The Saviour, friend of humankind!
Not one of all th'apostate race
But may in him salvation find;
His thoughts, and words, and actions prove –
His life and death – that God is love!

See where the God-incarnate stands,
And calls his wandering creatures home!
He all day long spreads out his hands:
'Come, weary souls, to Jesus come!
Ye all may hide you in my breast;
Believe, and I will give you rest.'

'Ah! do not of my goodness doubt,
My saving grace for all is free;
I will in no wise cast them out
That come as sinners unto me;
I can to none myself deny;
Why, sinners, will ye perish, why?'

I held out my hands all day long to a rebellious people, who walk in a way that is not good, following their own devices.

Isaiah 65:2 (NRSV)

The voice of the open-armed, pleading God of Isaiah takes form in Wesley's hymn as the voice of Christ, arms outstretched on the cross offering love to all. Christ's invitation is here described as one of unconditional love, free and welcoming, especially to those who are tired and weary. None need fear rejection, for the Christ who died on the cross cannot deny his own nature, which is love.

The invitation is to all people who, seeing themselves in the mirror of the gospel story, glimpse the possibility of change in their lives. See! Look! Experience the goodness of God.

PRAYER

Gracious and loving God, who showed in the life and death of Christ the extent to which your loving will go, release me from despair at my failures and fear of rejection, that, trusting in the welcoming arms of Christ, I may find my safety in you. Amen.

HGEL (1741) *CH 30 [1:2 the friend and Saviour of mankind 3:3-4 cast him out/That comes a sinner] cf MHB 312

Sinners, believe the gospel word,
  Jesus is come your souls to save!
Jesus is come, your common Lord;
  Pardon ye all in him may have,
May now be saved, whoever will;
This man receiveth sinners still.

See where the lame, the halt, the blind,
  The deaf, the dumb, the sick, the poor,
Flock to the Friend of humankind,
  And freely all accept their cure.
To whom doth he his help deny?
Whom in his days of flesh pass by?

Did not his work the fiends expel?
  The lepers cleanse, and raise the dead?
Did he not all their sickness heal?
  And satisfy their every need?
Did he reject his helpless clay?
Or send them sorrowful away?

The blind receive their sight, and the lame walk, the lepers are cleansed, and the deaf hear, the dead are raised up, and the poor have the gospel preached to them.
Matthew 11:5

John the Baptist, discouraged, rejected, and locked away in Herod's prison, sends two followers to ask Jesus if he really is the expected Messiah. This great question is answered by Jesus in practical terms – the evidence is in the healing of the needy, the good news heard by the poor. Wesley encourages us to put the reply of Jesus in a series of strong, rhetorical questions. Just see how he welcomes all who most need a friend and how he meets that need!

PRAYER
Loving, ever-living, faithful and healing Christ, I pray that you will heal me and those for whom I now pray by name . . . in body, mind and spirit. Amen.

HGEL (1741) *CH 31 cf MHB 312

AGAINST HOPE, BELIEVING IN HOPE (1)

My God! I know, I feel thee mine,
And will not quit my claim
Till all I have is lost in thine,
And all renewed I am.

I hold thee with a trembling hand,
But will not let thee go
Till steadfastly by faith I stand,
And all thy goodness know.

Jesus, thine all-victorious love
Shed in my heart abroad;
Then shall my feet no longer rove,
Rooted and fixed in God.

Love can bow down the stubborn neck,
The stone to flesh convert;
Soften, and melt, and pierce, and break
An adamantine heart.

I will take away the stony heart out of your flesh, and I will give you an heart of flesh. And I will put my spirit within you, and cause you to walk in my statutes, and ye shall keep my judgements, and do them.

Ezekiel 36:26-27

In the collection where this twelve-verse hymn first appeared, it was given the title above. Wesley borrows the expression from Paul in Romans 4:18, to compare his yearning for the experience of a renewed spirit and a holy life with the trust of Abraham in the faithfulness of God to fulfil the promise of an heir.

The passionate opening line states his conviction that he too is called by God. But to live each day in the steadfastness of faith requires more than a formal knowledge of God's will. To be 'rooted and fixed in God' is to be possessed by an inner motivation, a direction of the heart. Charles focuses his prayer with the graphic image from the Hebrew prophet Ezekiel: through the promised Spirit, the heart can cease to be stony – uncaring, 'adamantine' (impenetrably hard as a diamond) – and become flesh, marked by a tenderness that carries the imprint of love.

PRAYER
Spirit of holiness, motivate me from within to love and do your will. Amen.

HSP (1740) *CH 351 HP 740 UMH 422

O that in me the sacred fire
Might now begin to glow,
Burn up the dross of base desire,
And make the mountains flow!

O that it now from heaven might fall,
And all my sins consume!
Come, Holy Ghost, for thee I call,
Spirit of burning, come!

Refining fire, go through my heart,
Illuminate my soul;
Scatter thy life through every part,
And sanctify the whole.

My steadfast soul, from falling free,
Shall then no longer move;
But Christ be all the world to me,
And all my heart be love.

But who may abide the day of his coming? and who shall stand when he appeareth? for he is like a refiner's fire.

Malachi 3:2

Desire to be lost in God is one of the strongest themes of mystical writers. Wesley's desire also is nothing less than complete personal transformation; this he sums up in the prayer of the last two lines, that 'Christ be all the world to me,/And all my heart be love.' As so often in his writing, Wesley's strongest image of love is that of fire – the fire that purifies, refines and illuminates. But in these verses, too, there is the striking reference to a fear of 'falling free'. As a sage once said to a young seeker after truth, 'So long as you know where your own soul is tethered, you are free to explore the whole universe in search of the immensity of God's love.'

PRAYER
For this cause I bow my knees unto the Father of our Lord Jesus Christ . . . that Christ may dwell in your hearts by faith; that ye, being rooted and grounded in love, may be able to comprehend with all saints what is the breadth, and length, and depth, and height; And to know the love of Christ, which passeth knowledge, that ye might be filled with all the fullness of God. *Ephesians 3:14,17-19*

HSP (1740) *CH 351 HP 740 UMH 422

O thou that dost in darkness shine,
With clearest evidence divine
Inform me who thou art;
Appear the true, and living Way,
That thee I simply may obey,
And love with all my heart.

A thousand different paths I view,
But which to shun and which pursue
Still unresolved I stand
Till thou thy secret counsel show,
Direct me after thee to go,
And reach me out thy hand.

Thou know'st my feebleness of mind,
My will perverse, my passions blind,
My reason immature;
But thou, O God, if thee alone
My guide infallible I own,
Shalt make my footsteps sure.

O send out thy light and thy truth: let them lead me.

Psalm 43:3

Making decisions is not always easy. In this poem, written when he was seventy-seven years old, Wesley pleads for God's 'unerring light', that somehow out of the darkness of indecision, out of the 'thousand different paths' open to him, one will become clear.

In his uncertainty he acknowledges that he still cannot sort out the problem by himself, for too many things get in the way – perverse will, immature reason, blind desire and lack of ability to think. He then seeks the presence of God who is the 'true and living Way', and who will 'not let me miss my way'. With this infallible Guide, he will walk safely.

PRAYER
Lead me, Lord, lead me in thy righteousness;
Make thy way plain before my face. Amen.

UPCW 3, 205-6

Open, Lord, my inward ear,
And bid my heart rejoice;
Bid my quiet spirit hear
Thy comfortable voice;
Never in the whirlwind found,
Or where earthquakes rock the place,
Still and silent is the sound,
The whisper of thy grace.

From the world of sin, and noise,
And hurry I withdraw;
For the small and inward voice
I wait with humble awe;
Silent am I now and still,
Dare not in thy presence move;
To my waiting soul reveal
The secret of thy love.

Truly my soul waiteth upon God: from him cometh my salvation.

Psalm 62:1

Those of us who practise meditation or have regular prayer time come to know the value of silence. Waiting on God is just that: waiting and listening with an internal ear that is deaf to the sound of traffic, radio, tape recorder, TV and internal chatter. In writing this hymn-poem, Charles Wesley puts himself in the mystical tradition of all those who have waited on God – sometimes in the darkness, sometimes for a long time.

The hymn recalls the story of Elijah (1 Kings 19:1-8) who, fleeing into the Sinai wilderness to escape from the wrath of Queen Jezebel, turned to God in prayer. Doing as God told him, he stood on the holy mountain waiting for the Lord to pass by. The Lord was not in the wind, not in the subsequent earthquake, not in the fire. But after the wind came 'a sound of sheer silence'. It was in the silence that he could hear God.

PRAYER
Mysterious God, you call to me in my silence and sometimes I do not hear. As I pray the words of this poem may I make them truly my own, and as I live my life today keep me aware of the mystery of your presence. Amen.

HSP (1742) CH 348 *HP 540

WAITING ON GOD (2)

Show me, as my soul can bear,
The depth of inbred sin;
All the unbelief declare,
The pride that lurks within;
Take me, whom thyself hast bought,
Bring into captivity
Every high aspiring thought
That would not stoop to thee.

Lord, my time is in thy hand,
My soul to thee convert;
Thou canst make me understand,
Though I am slow of heart;
Thine in whom I live and move,
Thine the work, the praise is thine;
Thou art wisdom, power, and love,
And all thou art is mine.

Search me, O God, and know my heart: try me and know my thoughts: And see if there be any wicked way in me, and lead me in the way everlasting.

Psalm 139:23-24

These verses follow yesterday's understanding of God's voice speaking in the silence. Opening up one's life in prayer means that one can see more clearly what is wrong. But, as any good counsellor knows, total exposure all at once can be too much. Wesley asks God only to show him as much of his sin as he can cope with at any one time.

The result is a prayer of petition and dedication (verse 2). If my time is in God's hand (Psalm 31:15), this brings the wisdom, power and love of God into my life. See how Wesley once more expresses our mutual relationship to God, as he moves from 'me' to God and back again. In the last line, with the phrase, 'And all thou art is mine', he consolidates the union of human and divine.

PRAYER
Loving God, in your mercy show me the dark side of my nature, that I may see where I hurt you, myself and my neighbour. Only you can do this. As you created me, so you in your wisdom, power and love can make me understand in a way that heals and does not destroy. Amen.

HSP (1742) CH 348 *HP 540

Thou hidden source of calm repose,
Thou all-sufficient love divine,
My help, and refuge from my foes,
Secure I am, if thou art mine:
And lo, from sin, and grief, and shame
I hide me, Jesus, in thy name.

Thy mighty name salvation is,
And keeps my happy soul above;
Comfort it brings, and power, and peace,
And joy, and everlasting love:
To me, with thy dear name, are given
Pardon, and holiness, and heaven.

The name of the LORD is a strong tower: the righteous runneth into it, and is safe.
Proverbs 18:10

Once more Wesley returns to the idea that the name of Jesus carries something of his very nature. A familiar pattern in Hebrew thought, it is familiar also in some traditions of Christian spirituality, where repeating the name 'Jesus' becomes a focus of prayer. Here, the strong tower image of Proverbs is combined with Peter's statement in Acts that apart from Jesus there is 'no other name under heaven given among mortals by which we must be saved' (Acts 4:12 RSV). To name this name is to receive the personal gift of security and happiness, joy and everlasting love, 'pardon and holiness and heaven'.

This last line echoes what Charles' brother John was teaching about the way of salvation. John writes: 'Our main doctrines, which include all the rest, are three: that of repentance, of faith, and of holiness. The first of these we account as it were, the porch of religion; the next, the door; the third is religion itself.'[1]

PRAYER
Hidden God, you are always a mystery and yet a calm resting place for me and for all people in every storm of life. Give me the trust and humility to turn to you for comfort in distress, and bless me with your everlasting love, that I may live my life joyfully. Amen.

---

*HSP 1749 RV 76 CH 201 HP 275 UMH 153

THE NAME OF JESUS (2)

Jesus, my all in all thou art:
My rest in toil, my ease in pain,
The medicine of my broken heart,
In war my peace, in loss my gain,
My smile beneath the tyrant's frown,
In shame my glory and my crown;

In want my plentiful supply,
In weakness my almighty power,
In bonds my perfect liberty,
My light in Satan's darkest hour,
In grief my joy unspeakable,
My life in death, my heaven in hell.

Christ is all, and in all.

Colossians 3:11

Yesterday's verses spoke of the name of Jesus, listing the generous gifts associated with that name. Today's portion of the hymn goes even further, addressing Jesus who is 'all in all'. In a great wave of skilfully balanced phrases Wesley gives a list of fourteen benefits contained within that 'all'. Each is biblical in origin. Poetry lovers will appreciate that in these verses what could be a dull catalogue comes alive with varied antitheses.

MEDITATION
Take some time to meditate on each line of these verses, pausing to recall difficult occasions in your own life which match those described in the poem's lines. When work has been too hard, when you have been in pain, when your heart has been broken, in what ways were you aware then of Christ's love reaching you? Did others help you as the agents of God's compassion?

---

*HSP (1749) RV 76 CH 201 HP 275 UMH 153

Father of Jesus Christ – my Lord,
My Saviour, and my Head –
I trust in thee, whose powerful word
Has raised him from the dead.

Faith in thy power thou seest I have,
For thou this faith hast wrought;
Dead souls thou callest from their grave,
And speakest worlds from nought.

In hope, against all human hope,
Self-desperate, I believe;
Thy quickening word shall raise me up,
Thou shalt thy Spirit give.

Faith, mighty faith, the promise sees,
And looks to that alone,
Laughs at impossibilities,
And cries, 'It shall be done!'

Then Abraham fell upon his face, and laughed, and said in his heart, Shall a child be born unto him that is an hundred years old? and shall Sarah, that is ninety years old, bear?. . . Sarah laughed within herself, saying, After I am waxed old shall I have pleasure, my lord being old also? And the LORD said unto Abraham, Is any thing too hard for the LORD?

Genesis 17:17, 18:12-14

In this hymn, Wesley is asking for what at first glance seems an impossibility – that out of frustrated efforts and disappointed hopes, he might experience a rebirth of his life through God's Spirit. But ours is the God of resurrection; and what could be more impossible than that? From the stories of the first Hebrews, he recalls the tale of elderly Abraham and Sarah, who are promised a son long after the age of child-bearing. Both Abraham and Sarah, on first receiving this word, laugh at the patent absurdity of the situation. Yet they also dare to believe that God is the God of impossible possibilities; and in Paul's words, 'in hope, against all human hope' (Romans 4:18) they experience the fulfilment of the promise, and become the spiritual ancestors of the people of God.

Faith does not require that we suspend our God-given reason; rather, it grounds itself in the faithfulness of God it has known in the past, and assumes that there are always unknown variables, even in a situation that seems hopeless. Often the mere energy that comes from knowing that we are doing the will of God can create changes in and around us.

PRAYER
Powerful God, give me the faith that laughs at impossibilities and cries, 'It shall be done!' And when things do not work out according to my plans, give me the faith to believe that you have something even better in store. Amen.

HSP (1742) *CH 350 HP 693

Jesus hath died that I might live,
Might live to God alone,
In him eternal life receive,
And be in spirit one.

Saviour, I thank thee for the grace,
The gift unspeakable!
And wait with arms of faith to embrace,
And all thy love to feel.

My soul breaks out in strong desire,
The perfect bliss to prove;
My longing soul is all on fire
To be dissolved in love.

Give me thyself – from every boast,
From every wish set free,
Let all I am in thee be lost;
But give thyself to me.

Thy gifts, alas! cannot suffice,
Unless thyself be given;
Thy presence makes my paradise,
And where thou art is heaven.

Whom have I in heaven but thee? and there is none upon earth that I desire beside thee.

Psalm 73:25

The desire to be dissolved in love is truly part of the mystical tradition – the yearning after God, the longing to be taken up in bliss and to feel things beyond all speech. Commentators suggest that the source of verse four may be the greatest of Catholic theologians, Thomas Aquinas. It is recorded that as he lay dying, in a vision Christ appeared before him and asked, 'Thou has written well of me, what shall thy reward be?' Thomas replied, 'Nothing but thyself.'

PRAYER
God, of your goodness give me yourself, for you are sufficient for me. I cannot properly ask anything less, to be worthy of you. If I were to ask less, I should always be in want. In you alone do I have all. *Julian of Norwich*

HSP (1742) *CH 403 HP 733

Glory, love, and praise, and honour,
For our food
Now bestowed
Render we the Donor.
Bounteous God, we now confess thee,
God, who thus
Blessest us,
Meet it is to bless thee.

Knows the ox his master's stable,
And shall we
Not know thee,
Nourished at thy table?
Yes, of all good gifts the Giver
Thee we own,
Thee alone
Magnify for ever.

Who giveth food to all flesh: for his mercy endureth forever. O give thanks unto the God of heaven: for his mercy endureth forever.

Psalm 136:25-26

This is one of a series of graces. It was probably for use in Charles Wesley's own family and the families of friends. The words are simple, the rhythm is catchy, and one can imagine that even small children could remember it. The simple analogy that begins verse two is drawn from the prophet Isaiah: 'The ox knoweth his owner, and the ass his master's crib: but Israel doth not know, my people doth not consider . . . They have forsaken the LORD' (Isaiah 1:3-4).

The poem starts with thanks to God for food, and then moves to appreciation of all gifts. Being truly grateful is a spiritual experience – one that has engaged the hearts of mystics and poets. It is sad that saying 'thank you', one of the earliest responses we teach to small children, often becomes just a formality for us in later life.

Thankfulness has to emerge from within us, not be imposed upon us. Being urged to be grateful can produce the opposite reaction. On the other hand, taking time to ponder our blessings may prove very fruitful and is a primary response to God.

MEDITATION
At the beginning of your time of personal prayer, recollect the events of today or yesterday for which you are grateful.

Graces (1746?) RV 66 *HP 35

Thankful for our every blessing
Let us sing
Christ the Spring,
Never, never ceasing.
Source of all our gifts and graces
Christ we own,
Christ alone
Calls for all our praises.

He dispels our sin and sadness,
Life imparts,
Cheers our hearts,
Fills with food and gladness.
Who himself for all hath given,
Us he feeds,
Us he leads
To a feast in heaven.

[God] did good, and gave us rain from heaven, and fruitful seasons, filling our hearts with food and gladness.

Acts 14:17

The occasion recalled by the biblical text underlying this poem was the embarrassing situation in which the apostles found themselves after Paul had healed a lame man in Lystra, a town now in modern Turkey. They were greeted as messengers of the gods; Paul, the messenger of Hermes and Barnabas of Zeus. Refusing devotion to themselves, they declared to the people their message of the one true God.

The poem is a grace – probably for families – set to a lilting rhythm that would help both young and old to remember it as a poem or song. The earlier grace gives thanks to God; with equal enthusiasm, this one focuses on Christ. The tone is joyful and there is a foretaste of the great banquet in the last line. In the gospels, feasts are tangible reminders of generosity in a world of scarcity, and also carry overtones of joy in the life hereafter.

MEDITATION
Say this grace aloud in the quiet of your room, and then perhaps use it on other occasions. In your daily prayer time take some time to write down what you are thankful for: people, events, good experiences, the natural world and so on. Make this the beginning of a Book of Remembrance which you add to from time to time.

Graces (1746?) RV 67 *HP 35

Parent of good, whose plenteous grace
O'er all thy creatures flows,
Humbly we ask thy power to bless
The food thy love bestows.

Life of the world, our souls to feed
Thyself descend from high;
Grant us of thee, the living bread,
To eat and never die.

Jesus said to them, 'I am the bread of life. Whoever comes to me will never be hungry, and whoever believes in me will never be thirsty.'

John 6:35 (NRSV)

The first verse gives thanks to God our loving parent, mother and father, who feeds not only human beings but all of creation. The phrase 'parent of good' is from the praise of Adam and Eve in Milton's *Paradise Lost*:

> These are thy glorious works, Parent of good,
> Almighty, thine this universal frame,
> Thus wondrous fair; thyself how wondrous then! (*PL* 5:153-55)

In the second verse of Wesley's hymn we are reminded that we do not live by bread alone; we need spiritual nourishment also. Christ, 'the life of the world', is the living bread.

But what of those who have no food? People all around us in our cities and in the wider world are hungry today. The basic cause is greed and unequal distribution of God's gifts, which permits the rich to have too much, while the poor have too little. If we understand that God cares for all creation, animals and plants and the whole environment, does that change the way we live?

PRAYER
Compassionate God, forgive me for receiving great benefits and forgetting to say thank you; forgive me when I have been preoccupied with the needs of myself and my immediate family. In your great love for all creation, show me how I can be a partner in your world. You who are the bread of life, feed me and all your children with your living bread. Amen.

HSP (1739) *PW 1, 189-90

Being of beings, God of love,
To thee our hearts we raise;
Thy all-sustaining power we prove,
And gladly sing thy praise.

Thine, wholly thine, we pant to be,
Our sacrifice receive;
Made, and preserved, and saved by thee,
To thee ourselves we give.

Heavenward our every wish aspires;
For all thy mercies' store,
The sole return thy love requires
Is that we ask for more.

For more we ask; we open then
Our hearts to embrace thy will;
Turn, and beget us, Lord, again,
With all thy fullness fill.

Come, Holy Ghost, the Saviour's love
Shed in our hearts abroad;
So shall we ever live, and move,
And be with Christ in God.

As the hart panteth after the water brooks, so panteth my soul after thee, O God.
Psalm 42:1

This hymn starts and ends with the God 'in whom we live and move and have our being' (Acts 17:28). Originally intended to be sung as a grace, Wesley turns this expression of gratitude for physical food into a prayer for spiritual sustenance. As we marvel at the prodigal generosity that wants only to give still more, we are drawn into the very essence of the love of God, on whom our whole being depends.

PRAYER
Loving, creator God, from whom I come, and to whom I shall go, give me the gift of knowing that I am part of you and you are part of me, all the hours of my days and all the days of my years, through Jesus Christ our Lord. Amen.

*HP (1739) HP 690

My God, I am thine;
What a comfort divine,
What a blessing to know that my Jesus is mine!
In the heavenly Lamb
Thrice happy I am,
And my heart it doth dance at the sound of his name.

True pleasures abound
In the rapturous sound;
And whoever hath found it hath paradise found.
My Jesus to know,
As rejoicing I go
To my life everlasting, 'tis heaven below.

Yet onward I haste
To the heavenly feast:
That, that is the fullness; but this is the taste;
And this shall I prove,
Till with joy I remove
To the heaven of heavens in Jesus's love.

The LORD is my strength, and my shield; my heart hath trusted in him, and I am helped: therefore my heart danceth for joy, and in my song will I praise him.

Psalm 28:7 (BCP)

'For believers rejoicing' says the caption at the head of the section of the 1780 hymn book where this hymn was set, and the record of those who have found delight in this exuberant hymn is a long one. Numerous tales are told of early Methodists who quoted parts of this at stressful moments in their lives. The dance-like rhythm confirms that joy, not gloom, was a feature of their faith.

C. S. Lewis, in his book *Surprised by Joy*, tells of the few times in his life when transcendent joy broke through the everyday world. These rare moments were so important that they changed his life. Other people may have similar experiences more frequently, but often joy is a word reserved for the out-of-the-ordinary experiences – the heart-dancing ones. Yet this buoyancy of inner joy and delight in the friendship of Christ can, according to Wesley, last a lifetime, and will continue in the heavenly banquet.

PRAYER
Loving God, turn our frowns upside down, and give us joy. Amen.

HSP (1749) CH 197 [2:5-6 And feel his blood flow, 'Tis life everlasting] *HP 563

O heavenly King, look down from above;
Assist us to sing thy mercy and love:
So sweetly o'erflowing, so plenteous the store,
Thou still art bestowing, and giving us more.

Our Father and Lord, almighty art thou;
Preserved by thy word, we worship thee now;
The bountiful donor of all we enjoy,
Our tongues, to thine honour, and lives we employ.

But O above all thy kindness we praise,
From sin and from thrall which saves the lost race;
Thy Son thou hast given a world to redeem,
And bring us to heaven whose trust is in him.

Wherefore of thy love we sing and rejoice,
With angels above we lift up our voice;
Thy love each believer shall gladly adore,
For ever and ever, when time is no more.

The LORD is my strength and my shield; my heart trusted in him, and I am helped: therefore my heart greatly rejoiceth; and with my song will I praise him.

Psalm 28:7

Readers familiar with the *Book of Common Prayer* will recognise that this hymn is based in large part on the prayer of General Thanksgiving. Though the kingly image may have less meaning for us in an age when monarchs have only symbolic power, and though we think more these days of heaven 'within' rather than 'above' us, the idea that we need the help of God within us to enable us to breathe our praise and express our gratitude is still an important one to grasp.

PRAYER
Lord, you have given so much to me,
Give one thing more, a grateful heart. *George Herbert*

---

*HSP (1742) RV 26 CH 191 HP 504

Jesus, with kind compassion see
Two souls who would be one in thee
If now accepted in thy sight,
Our childlike, simple hearts unite,
And grant us while on earth to prove
The noblest joys of heavenly love.

Before thy glorious eyes we spread
The wish which doth from thee proceed,
Our love from earthly dross refine,
Holy, angelical, divine,
O let it its great Author show,
And back to the pure fountain flow.

A drop of that unbounded sea,
O God, absorb it into thee,
While both our souls with restless strife
Spring up into eternal life,
And lost in endless rapture prove
Thy whole immensity of love.

'Those who drink of the water that I will give them will never be thirsty. The water that I will give will become in them a spring of water gushing up to eternal life'.
John 4:14 (NRSV)

The courtship of Charles Wesley and Sally Gwynne began with a 'love at first sight' meeting at her home in Wales in the summer of 1747, and continued by correspondence over the next six months as he travelled in Ireland. Letters included hymns which were intended to be sung by the lovers as a way of remembering their love. This is one of those love poems, adapted later for congregational singing.

The deepest concern of Charles, apart from practical considerations such as the approval of her parents, was that the marriage would not distract him from the love of God. 'O that it may bring us nearer and nearer to God, till we are both swallowed up in the immensity of his love,' he wrote.[1]

PRAYER
May those who are joined in the bonds of matrimony so live together that their love may enrich our common life and become a sign of your faithfulness.[2] Amen.
Anglican Church of Canada

---

*MS HSP (1749) CH 499 RV 143

The table of my heart prepare,
(Such power belongs to thee alone)
And write, O God, thy precepts there,
To show thou still canst write in stone;
So shall my pure obedience prove
All things are possible to love.

Father, instruct my docile heart,
Apt to instruct I then shall be;
I then shall all thy words impart,
And teach (as taught myself by thee)
My children in their earliest days,
To know, and live the life of grace.

These words, which I command thee this day, shall be in thine heart: And thou shalt teach them diligently unto thy children.

Deuteronomy 6:6-7

As he meditated on his responsibility as a father for the faith formation of his children, Charles Wesley could hardly fail to recall the disciplined practice of his mother Susanna in their Epworth home. Many of her views on child raising would not commend themselves in our age, with its radically different understanding of the nature of children and how best to educate them. On the other hand, from a letter she wrote in December 1711 to her husband Samuel during one of his lengthy absences, we learn that in addition to daily family devotions and teaching, she sought to give each child weekly personal time for intimate conversation on matters of faith.

The Wesleys' sense of this spiritual duty of parents toward their children owes much to the Jewish understanding of faith formation. The stories that teach the generosity of God and the way of faithful response must be passed on personally, to each new generation. Conscious of his personal inadequacy for this responsibility – which of us is not? – Charles asks for the gift promised by the prophets Jeremiah (31:33) and Ezekiel (36:26-27), that he may be motivated from within by a love for God's way that will communicate itself to his children in and through all that he teaches of the good life.

PRAYER
Gracious Spirit, may the heart of what I give these children in my care be my own experience of your generous love, that they too may come 'to know and live the life of grace'. Amen.

---

*SH (1762)

Jesus, in earth and heaven the same,
Accept a parent's vow;
To thee, baptised into thy name,
I bring my children now.
Thy love permits, invites, commands
My offspring to be blessed;
Lay on them, Lord, thy gracious hands,
And hide them in thy breast.

And they were bringing children to him, that he might touch them; and the disciples rebuked them. But when Jesus saw it he was indignant, and said to them, 'Let the children come to me, do not hinder them; for to such belongs the kingdom of God.'
Mark 10:13-14 (RSV)

From all accounts it seems that Charles was a devoted parent who took seriously and yet joyfully his responsibilities as a father. In this verse he sets the scene by declaring that the Christ who walked this earth is the same Christ to whom we pray. The Christ who took children on his knee and blessed them will still hold them, hug them and love them. Lines five to six, 'Thy love permits, invites, commands/My offspring to be blessed', reinforce the biblical story – parents were first allowed to come, then children were invited, and finally the disciples were commanded not to interfere.

Whether our church baptises or dedicates children, it welcomes them. The message that they are important to God has been shown to us in this little incident in the life of Christ. It also suggests that Christ must have been a person whom children liked. What does it say about us when we ignore or reject children around us? Perhaps we are missing out on the kingdom of heaven. What does it say about the priorities of our society and our world, when so many children are hungry and homeless and dying?

PRAYER SUGGESTION
Ask for a special blessing for the children you love and care about – those in your own family, those in your neighbourhood and those whose names you do not know, but whose needs are made known to you through the media.

*PW 10, 322

CHILDREN ON LOAN

Lord of all, with pure intent,
From his tenderest infancy,
In thy temple I present
Whom I first received from thee;
Through thy well-beloved Son
Mine acknowledge for thine own.

[Hannah said to Eli:] For this child I prayed; and the LORD hath given me my petition which I asked of him: Therefore also I have lent him to the LORD; as long as he liveth he shall be lent to the LORD.

1 Samuel 1:27-28

Unlike his brother John, Charles was a family man, writing tenderly to his wife when he was away from home, encouraging his daughter to learn poetry, and watching with a careful eye the musical genius of his two young sons, Charles and Samuel. But his first devotion was to God, and so, like Hannah with young Samuel in the temple, like Mary who took the young Jesus to the temple, Charles offers his child back to God with the words, 'Mine acknowledge for thine own.'

Many people have been attracted by the poem of Kahlil Gibran which starts: 'Your children are not your children, they are sons and daughters of life's longing for itself.'[1] This echoes the words said by parents in the baptismal service in the 1936 Methodist *Book of Offices*, 'We come here to acknowledge that this our child belongs to God and to receive him/her again from the hands of God.' Acknowledging children as a gift on loan, for a while only, allows them to be free to be owned by no one, and yet truly loved for who they are.

PRAYER
Parent of us all, give us grace to trust our children to your care as we hold their fragile lives in our own frail hands. Amen.

---

*PW 11, 119-20

Lord, that I may learn of thee,
Give me true simplicity;
Wean my soul, and keep it low,
Willing thee alone to know.

Let me cast myself aside,
All that feeds my knowing pride;
Not to man, but God submit,
Lay my reasonings at thy feet;

Of my boasted wisdom spoiled,
Docile, helpless, as a child,
Only seeing in thy light,
Only walking in thy might.

Then infuse the teaching grace,
Spirit of truth and righteousness;
Knowledge, love divine, impart,
Life eternal to my heart.

Whom shall he teach knowledge? and whom shall he make to understand doctrine? them that are weaned.

Isaiah 28:9

Striking a balance between a sense of self-worth and humility is not easy. This hymn speaks of being filled by God's truth rather than our own. Simplicity of heart suggests a childlike openness – the state which Jesus told us is the entrance to the kingdom.

Thomas à Kempis' popular book, *The Imitation of Christ,* was written at a time when scholastic learning was preoccupied with such subtleties that for many it became a hindrance rather than a help to the Christian faith. This passage on learning echoes something of the hymn's meaning:

> A humble knowledge of thyself is a surer way to God than a deep search after learning. Yet learning is not to be blamed, not the mere knowledge of anything whatsoever, for that is good in itself, and ordained by God; but a good conscience and a virtuous life are always to be preferred before it. But because many endeavour rather to get knowledge than to live well, they are often deceived, and reap either none or but little fruit.

PRAYER
More than all learning, I need your wisdom, O God. Give me an understanding heart. Amen.

---

*SH (1762) CH 293 HP 737

GENTLE JESUS

Gentle Jesus, meek and mild,
Look upon a little child,
Pity my simplicity,
Suffer me to come to thee.

Put thy hands upon my head,
Let me in thy arms be stayed,
Let me lean upon thy breast,
Lull me, lull me, Lord, to rest.

Hold me fast in thy embrace,
Let me see thy smiling face,
Give me, Lord, thy blessing give,
Pray for me, and I shall live.

Loving Jesu, gentle Lamb,
In thy gracious hands I am:
Make me, Saviour, what thou art;
Live thyself within my heart.

And they brought unto him also infants, that he would touch them; but when his disciples saw it, they rebuked them. But Jesus called them unto him, and said: Suffer little children to come unto me, and forbid them not: for of such is the kingdom of God.

Luke 18:15-16

Used in various versions as a bedtime prayer by generations of children, this simple, profound poem – originally fourteen verses – was written by Charles Wesley before he had children of his own. His family life later became very dear to him. Change in the meaning of words like 'meek' and 'pity' has made this poem less popular as a prayer for children today, but there remain images that would be comforting to a small child. The protective hands, the loving arms rocking the child to sleep ('lull me, lull me' is the repetitive base of a lullaby), and a face smiling with love – all evoke in the child a sense of security and responsive love.

PRAYER SUGGESTION
The last four lines speak for all of us, of every age. Repeat them now, as a prayer for this day.

---

*HSP (1742) RV 27 MHB 842

JESUS, THE GOOD SHEPHERD (1) 347

Jesus the good Shepherd is,
  Jesus died the sheep to save;
He is mine and I am his,
  All I want in him I have:
Life, and health, and rest, and food,
All the plenitude of God.

Jesus loves and guards his own;
  Me in verdant pastures feeds,
Makes me quietly lie down,
  By the streams of comfort leads:
Following him where'er he goes,
Silent joy my heart o'erflows.

He in sickness makes me whole,
  Guides into the paths of peace;
He revives my fainting soul,
  Stablishes in righteousness;
Who for me vouchsafed to die,
Loves me still – I know not why!

The LORD is my shepherd; I shall not want.

Psalm 23:1

People who have grown up in non-pastoral settings have tried to find other images, more familiar than that of a shepherd, to represent the loving care and guidance of God. 'The Lord is my pacemaker,' wrote one Japanese poet. 'The Lord is my probation officer,' wrote a young British offender.

For Jesus himself both the psalm and its pastoral setting would have been familiar from his childhood. So it is not surprising that John's gospel uses the image of the good shepherd to describe Jesus' vocation. Charles Wesley skilfully weaves together the psalmist's poem and the work and life of Jesus in whom we find all the fullness of God.

MEDITATION
Try writing your own paraphrase of the twenty-third psalm, using an image of protection that is real for you: The Lord is my . . .

AM (1800) *PW 8, 46-47 HP 263

Unappalled by guilty fear,
Through the mortal vale I go;
My eternal life is near,
Thee my life in death I know;
Bless thy chastening, cheering rod,
Die into the arms of God!

Till that welcome hour I see,
Thou before my foes dost feed;
Bidd'st me sit and feast with thee,
Pourest thy oil upon my head;
Givest me all I ask, and more,
Makest my cup of joy run o'er.

Love divine shall still embrace,
Love shall keep me to the end;
Surely all my happy days
I shall in thy temple spend,
Till I to thy house remove,
Thy eternal house above!

Yea, though I walk through the valley of the shadow of death, I will fear no evil: for thou art with me; thy rod and thy staff they comfort me. Thou preparest a table before me in the presence of mine enemies: thou anointest my head with oil; my cup runneth over. Surely goodness and mercy shall follow me all the days of my life: and I will dwell in the house of the Lord for ever.

Psalm 23:4-6

There are several ways of reading verse four of this psalm. The 'valley of the shadow of death' may refer to the foreshadowing of our own death. Or it may refer to the shadow cast over our lives when we are bereaved. The death of those we love is for many of us a more grievous prospect than our own death. Wesley reads the psalm as referring principally to the impending threat of our personal death, even referring to it as a 'welcome hour'. But life before death is also fully enjoyed when one shares with Jesus in the feast of life. The third verse of the hymn is a particularly happy rendering of the last verse of the psalm.

PRAYER
God of goodness and mercy, your whole nature is summed up in that one word 'love'. Help us to be more conscious of the love that ever surrounds us, from our first day to our last. Through Jesus Christ our Lord. Amen.

AM (1800) *PW 8, 46-47 HP 263

Omnipresent God, whose aid
No one ever asked in vain,
Be this night about my bed,
Every evil thought restrain;
Lay thy hand upon my soul,
God of my unguarded hours;
All my enemies control,
Hell and earth and nature's powers.

Loose me from the chains of sense,
Set me from the body free;
Draw with stronger influence
My unfettered soul to thee!
In me, Lord, thyself reveal,
Fill me with a sweet surprise;
Let me thee when waking feel,
Let me in thine image rise.

Let me of thy life partake,
Thy own holiness impart;
O that I might sweetly wake
With my Saviour in my heart!
O that I might know thee mine!
O that I might thee receive!
Only live the life divine!
Only to thy glory live!

As for me, I will behold thy face in righteousness: I shall be satisfied, when I awake, with thy likeness.

Psalm 17:15

Fear of the night goes back to our childhood, when nights seemed long and monsters lurked in dark corners. Fears still persist, even when the childhood monsters are gone. Wesley speaks of the 'unguarded hours' when we relax even our powers of self-control. Our thoughts may rove where they will, for good or ill. The night can also be the loneliest time of all; in half-sleep all the worries of the day can crowd in upon us, so that we feel trapped in a vicious circle of anxiety. The hymn asks that in this time of vulnerability when all our defences are down, God may be a sweet, surprising presence.

A TRADITIONAL PRAYER FROM INDIA

Dear Jesus, as a hen covers her chicks with her wings to keep them safe, do thou this night protect us under your golden wings. Amen.[1] *United Methodist Hymnal*

HSP (1749) *CH 278

350 FOR A TENDER CONSCIENCE

I want a principle within
Of watchful, godly fear,
A sensibility of sin,
A pain to feel it near.

I want the first approach to feel
Of pride or fond desire,
To catch the wandering of my will,
And quench the kindling fire.

That I from thee no more may part,
No more thy goodness grieve,
The filial awe, the fleshly heart,
The tender conscience, give.

Quick as the apple of an eye,
O God my conscience make;
Awake my soul when sin is nigh,
And keep it still awake.

You desire faithfulness in the inmost being, so teach me wisdom in my heart.
Psalm 51:6 (REB)

To understand this hymn more clearly, a little translation is needed. Words which have changed their meaning include 'want' (need), 'principle within' (inner guidance), 'fond' (foolish); 'quick' (sensitive) and the 'apple of the eye' 'the pupil of the eye'.

There was once a woman who, in 1960, was still being very careful to leave no light showing when she drew her curtains, because of wartime blackout restrictions which had in fact ended in 1945. Her conscience was still working on old information. Many of us suffer from an ill-informed conscience which causes us misplaced guilt.

So it is well to observe what Charles is saying in this poem. He needs a sensitive conscience about the things that really matter: the sin that hurts himself and his neighbour. If he fails to catch this sin early, he will ignore it later because, through habit, his heart will have become hardened into stone. Hence the line in verse three which asks for 'a fleshly heart' (Ezekiel 11:19) to bring him back to a sensitive awareness once again.

MEDITATION
Rewrite this hymn in your own words to be used later as a prayer.

---

*HSP (1749) [1:2 Of jealous, godly fear (UMH = watchful)] CH 299 HP 422 UMH 410

Jesu, my Truth, my Way,
My sure, unerring Light,
On thee my feeble steps I stay,
Which thou wilt lead aright.

My Wisdom and my Guide,
My Counsellor thou art;
O never let me leave thy side,
Or from thy paths depart!

Teach me the happy art
In all things to depend
On thee, who never wilt depart,
But love me to the end!

O make me all like thee,
Before I hence remove!
Settle, confirm and stablish me,
And build me up in love.

Jesus . . . having loved his own which were in the world, he loved them unto the end.
John 13:1

The mood of this simple, almost childlike prayer is one of rather fragile confidence. The third lines of both the first and last verse set this tone – the feeble steps, the need to be settled. This is a condition which many people know well, especially in busy, hurried lives. The centre does not hold and we become fragmented and unsure of ourselves and of God.

Charles' remedy is to stay close to Christ who is his personal truth, way, light, wisdom, counsellor and guide, and who loves him for all time. All these images can be a fruitful source of meditation. An American Quaker, Thomas R. Kelly, speaks of Christ drawing the mind like a needle to the polestar:

> Like the needle, the Inward Light becomes the truest guide of life . . . [and] urges by secret persuasion, to such an amazing Inward Life with him, so that, firmly cleaving to him, we always look out upon all the world through the sheen of the Inward Light, and react toward people spontaneously and joyously from the Inward Centre.[1]

PRAYER
Lord Jesus Christ, never leave me nor forsake me, for I need you from life's dawning to its end. Amen.

---

*HSP (1749) CH 424 [1:3 soul] HP 734

THE FLAME OF LOVE

O thou who camest from above,
  The pure celestial fire to impart,
Kindle a flame of sacred love
  On the mean altar of my heart!

There let it for thy glory burn
  With inextinguishable blaze,
And trembling to its source return,
  In humble prayer and fervent praise.

Jesus, confirm my heart's desire
  To work, and speak, and think for thee;
Still let me guard the holy fire,
  And still stir up thy gift in me –

Ready for all thy perfect will,
  My acts of faith and love repeat,
Till death thy endless mercies seal,
  And make my sacrifice complete.

The fire shall ever be burning upon the altar; it shall never go out.

Leviticus 6:13

This is one of the great hymns of Methodism. It is often sung to the tune 'Hereford', which was composed by Charles Wesley's grandson, Samuel Sebastian.

Scholars have discovered some twenty-five biblical references embedded in the hymn, but the images of altar, sacrifice, fire and heart are linked throughout. The starting point is the very practical instruction to Aaron the priest on how the newly liberated Israelites are to make the important ceremonial fire for burnt offerings. Charles, perhaps remembering the seventeenth century poet George Herbert's fine poem on the heart as an altar, asks that Christ light a flame on the altar of his heart. Note the very personal 'I', 'my', and 'me' throughout this hymn.

Sacred love is love in action, continually working and speaking for Christ and ready to do his will, whatever that may turn out to be. This sacrifice of our way of living does not end with death, for it is supported by the 'endless mercies' of the Christ who has conquered death and continues to love us in this world and the next.

PRAYER SUGGESTION
Read this through once or twice quietly as a prayer, asking for grace to make it your own.

---

*SH (1762) CH 318 HP 745 UMH 501

Jesus, my strength, my hope,
On thee I cast my care,
With humble confidence look up,
And know thou hear'st my prayer.
Give me on thee to wait,
Till I can all things do,
On thee, almighty to create,
Almighty to renew.

I want a godly fear,
A quick-discerning eye,
That looks to thee when sin is near,
And sees the tempter fly:
A spirit still prepared
And armed with jealous care,
For ever standing on its guard,
And watching unto prayer.

Wait on the LORD: be of good courage, and he shall strengthen thine heart: wait, I say, on the LORD.

Psalm 27:14

We live in an age of anxiety. Throughout the world unemployment is high, poverty and inequality seem to be increasing, and those who have jobs seem to be working longer hours and experiencing more stress as pressures mount. In the developing world, famine and civil war and injustice take their horrendous toll. Those of us who try to care for our neighbours feel overwhelmed by what has been called 'compassion fatigue'.

Charles Wesley turns to Christ for those inner spiritual resources which we need to cope with the sense of our own inadequacy and helplessness. The concept of 'waiting on God' means 'to place one's hope in God', the one who is our maker, and who, in Wesley's comforting phrase, is 'almighty to renew'. It is God who renews our energy, who shares our load.

MEDITATION
Ponder the strong phrases in the second verse, applying them to your own situation: 'a godly fear' – of what?; 'a quick-discerning eye' – to see what?; 'a spirit still prepared' – to do what?; 'armed with jealous care' – about what? Then 'keep watching unto prayer'.

---

*HSP (1742) CH 292 HP 680

A PATIENT SPIRIT

I want a true regard,
A single, steady aim,
Unmoved by threatening or reward,
To thee and thy great name;
A jealous, just concern
For thine immortal praise;
A pure desire that all may learn
And glorify thy grace.

I rest upon thy word;
The promise is for me;
My succour and salvation, Lord,
Shall surely come from thee:
But let me still abide,
Nor from my hope remove,
Till thou my patient spirit guide
Into thy perfect love.

[And Elijah said to God], I have been very jealous for the LORD God of hosts: for the children of Israel have forsaken thy covenant, thrown down thine altars, and slain thy prophets with the sword; and I, even I only, am left; and they seek my life to take it away.

1 Kings 19:10

Elijah has run away. He might well do so, for he has just killed four hundred and fifty prophets of Baal, the god of the Canaanites, in a dramatic confrontation on Mount Carmel. Queen Jezebel is after his life and now he hides in a cave and complains to God that he is the last one left to serve him.

Wesley uses this story as the basis for a more healthy response – that of praise to God and the desire to tell others of the grace of God. 'Jealous' can also be read as 'zealous', and Elijah was both. Christ calls us to a similar zeal as we follow his way of overcoming evil with good. We cannot do this without help, so the prayer in the last two lines of the hymn, the lovely image of the Spirit gently guiding us into perfect love, is one to make our own.

MEDITATION
Read 1 Kings 19:1-10, and try to imagine yourself in Elijah's shoes. What represents the cave in your life? When do you go there and why?

---

*HSP (1742) CH 292 HP 680

Light of the world, thy beams I bless;
On thee, bright Sun of Righteousness,
My faith has fixed its eye;
Guided by thee, through all I go,
Nor fear the ruin spread below,
For thou art always nigh.

I rest in thine almighty power;
The name of Jesus is a tower
That hides my life above;
Thou canst, thou wilt my keeper be;
My confidence is all in thee,
The faithful God of love.

Wherefore, in never-ceasing prayer,
My soul to thy continual care
I cheerfully commend;
Assured that thou through life wilt save,
And show thyself beyond the grave
My everlasting friend.

The name of the LORD is a strong tower: the righteous runneth into it, and is safe.
Proverbs 18:10

This hymn, with its images of 'light' and 'beams', of 'tower' and 'keeper' could call to mind the picture of a lighthouse, standing tall among the rocks and guiding the traveller through the stormy seas of life. Charles Wesley's original use of the word 'cheerfully' commend, rather than 'faithfully', as it was later amended, is typical of him. The spring of his confidence was one of joy – his keeper was his friend, from whom not even death would separate him.

MEDITATION
Ponder the last verse and repeat it quietly several times until you have learned it by heart. It will be a good antidote to all anxiety.

*HSP (1749) HP 681 [2:4 my helper 3:3 I faithfully 3:4 shalt save]

I know that my Redeemer lives,
And ever prays for me;
A token of his love he gives,
A pledge of liberty.

I find him lifting up my head,
He brings salvation near,
His presence makes me free indeed,
And he will soon appear.

Jesus, I hang upon thy word;
I steadfastly believe
Thou wilt return and claim me, Lord,
And to thyself receive.

Thy love I soon expect to find
In all its depth and height,
To comprehend the eternal mind,
And grasp the Infinite.

You, LORD, are my glory, you raise my head high.

Psalm 3:3 (REB)

Religion has not always been a liberating force in human lives. It can seem to be a chain for some people instead of being a force to set them free. Not so for Wesley. He lives in constant expectation that Christ is freeing him for new possibilities here and now. Aware of the limitations of mortality, he never lets go of the fervent hope that one day he will 'comprehend the eternal mind/And grasp the infinite'. More prosaic souls might consider this impossible, but saints and mystics have followed this quest with joy.

PRAYER
Mysterious God, you are always beyond my grasp and yet you are close to my heart, releasing me into the glorious liberty of all your children. Give me grace to trust your presence in my life, that I may walk without fear all my days. Through Jesus Christ our Lord. Amen.

HSP (1742) CH 373 *HP 731

Weary of all this wordy strife,
These notions, forms and modes, and names,
To thee, the Way, the Truth, the Life,
Whose love my simple heart inflames,
Divinely taught, at last I fly
With thee and thine, to live and die.

Forth from the midst of Babel brought,
Parties and sects I cast behind,
Enlarged my heart, and free my thought,
Where'er the latent truth I find,
The latent truth with joy to own,
And bow to Jesus' name alone.

My brethren, friends and kinsfolk those,
Who do my heavenly Father's will,
Who aim at perfect holiness,
And all thy counsels to fulfil,
Athirst to be whate'er thou art,
And love their God with all their heart.

[Jehu] saluted him, and said to him, Is thine heart right, as my heart is with thy heart? And Jehonadab answered, It is. If it be, give me thine hand.

2 Kings 10:15

John Wesley's sermon on 'The Catholic Spirit' was based on this unlikely text from 2 Kings. The age of the Wesleys, and of the Evangelical Revival, knew its share of religious controversy. Acrimonious debate marred the brothers' relationships with former Moravian and Calvinist colleagues, causing bitter and lasting divisions within the societies. Troubled by the harm these controversies were causing, John preached his eirenic sermon on 'The Catholic Spirit'. His plea for mutual respect and a recognition of fundamental unity between followers of Christ concluded with this hymn by Charles, echoing the words of Jesus that all who do the Father's will are one family of faith.

PRAYER

God of all, enlarge my heart and free my thought, that I may walk the royal way of universal love, until at last I am swallowed up in love for ever and ever. Amen.

---

*Catholick Spirit (1755) RV 146 [3:1 kinsmen]

358 A CHRIST-CENTRED HEART (1)

O for a heart to praise my God,
  A heart from sin set free,
A heart that always feels thy blood,
  So freely spilt for me;

A heart resigned, submissive, meek,
  My dear Redeemer's throne,
Where only Christ is heard to speak,
  Where Jesus reigns alone;

A humble, lowly, contrite heart,
  Believing, true and clean;
Which neither life nor death can part
  From him that dwells within.

Create in me a clean heart, O God; and renew a right spirit within me.
Psalm 51:10

I dwell in the high and holy place, and also with those who are contrite and humble in spirit, to revive the spirit of the humble, and to revive the heart of the contrite.
Isaiah 57:15 (NRSV)

The mood of these first three verses of an eight-verse hymn, though intense, is for Charles Wesley unusually calm. Including the word 'heart' in the first line of every stanza, he takes the psalmist's prayer for a clean heart and expands it into a prayer for a heart brought entirely under the rule of Christ. Readers familiar with the hymn will notice that in line six, the original words were 'my dear Redeemer'. John Wesley changed this in the 1780 hymnbook, preferring words which to him seemed less sentimental, 'my great Redeemer'. This form has prevailed in all later editions.

The heart which is truly submissive to the Redeemer's voice is then described in terms reminiscent of Isaiah's prophecy, that God will dwell with those who are of a humble and contrite spirit. Wesley, like the prophet, emphasises that the human heart can become the very dwelling-place of God, whose love is then so close to us that nothing can ever separate us from it.

PRAYER
Glorious God of all that is and all that is to be, I praise you with all my heart for all your goodness. Grant that I may praise you not only in my heart but with my whole life. Amen.

---

*HSP (1742) CH 334 RV 23 HP 536 UMH 417

A CHRIST-CENTRED HEART (2) 359

A heart in every thought renewed,
And full of love divine;
Perfect, and right, and pure, and good,
A copy, Lord, of thine!

Thy tender heart is still the same,
And melts at human woe;
Jesu, for thee distressed I am,
I want thy love to know.

Fruit of thy gracious lips, on me
Bestow that peace unknown,
The hidden manna, and the tree
Of life, and the white stone.

Thy nature, dearest Lord, impart,
Come quickly from above;
Write thy new name upon my heart,
Thy new, blest name of love.

To everyone who conquers I will give some of the hidden manna, and I will give a white stone, and on the white stone is written a new name that no one knows except the one who receives it.

Revelation 2:17 (NRSV)

After meditating in the first three verses on the qualities of a Christ-centred heart, Wesley expresses his own longing for a deeper union with Christ. He borrows the language of David's moving lament for his lost love, Jonathan (2 Samuel 1:26). Then Wesley turns to the promise in Revelation, made to those in Pergamos who remained faithful to Christ in spite of the evil surrounding them. They will be sustained, just as the people of Israel were in the wilderness, by the bread of heaven (manna) and they will be given a new name, engraved on a white stone, presumably a kind of passport of admission to a new kingdom.

PRAYER
Write your new name upon my heart, Lord Jesus, that I might share your compassion for all who grieve, and learn to love them with my whole being, seeking to heal and never to hurt my brothers and sisters. Sustain me by your grace and receive me into your kingdom. Amen.

---

*HSP (1742) CH 334 RV 23 HP 536 UMH 417

360 THE BEATIFIC SIGHT (1)

Come on, my partners in distress,
My comrades through the wilderness,
Who still your bodies feel;
Awhile forget your griefs and fears,
And look beyond the vale of tears
To that celestial hill.

Beyond the bounds of time and space,
Look forward to that happy place,
The saint's secure abode:
On faith's strong eagle-pinions rise,
And force your passage to the skies,
And scale the mount of God.

Who suffer for our Master here,
We shall before his face appear,
And by his side sit down;
To patient faith the prize is sure,
And all that to the end endure
The cross, shall wear the crown.

They that wait upon the LORD shall renew their strength; they shall mount up with wings as eagles; they shall run, and not be weary; and they shall walk, and not faint.
Isaiah 40:31

Although this may seem to be a hymn about heaven, it has a very earthly foundation. The 1740s saw violent opposition to 'Methodists'. They needed a sustaining vision. To help them endure personal attacks of the mob, injuries and frequent physical distress, they fixed their minds on their ultimate destination.

Note especially how the words 'beyond' and 'look' in verse one are picked up and developed at the start of verse two. The poem has fine Miltonic language, linking the image from Isaiah 40:31, 'they shall mount up with wings as eagles', with a fallen angel's pressure to move from hell; to 'force resistless way . . . to scale with upright wing against a higher foe' (*Paradise Lost, II* 62, 71-2).

This hymn is not in recent hymn books; perhaps the language is outdated. Perhaps not. We have only to think of the life and death of Bishop Oscar Romero and other modern martyrs to understand how they were held firm in their faith by the sense of solidarity with those who were partners in their distress.

PRAYER
Lord, we commend into your keeping those of our partners who are in distress at this time. Keep the light of hope burning before them. Through Christ our Lord. Amen.

---

*HSP (1745) RV 80 CH 324 MHB 487

THE BEATIFIC SIGHT (2)

Thrice blessèd bliss-inspiring Hope!
It lifts the fainting spirits up,
It brings to life the dead;
Our conflicts here shall soon be past,
And you and I ascend at last,
Triumphant with our Head.

That great mysterious Deity
We soon with open face shall see;
The beatific sight
Shall fill the heavenly courts with praise,
And wide diffuse the golden blaze
Of everlasting light.

The Father shining on his throne,
The glorious co-eternal Son
The Spirit, one and seven,
Conspire our rapture to complete,
And lo! we fall before his feet,
And silence heightens heaven.

In hope of that ecstatic pause,
Jesus, we now sustain thy cross,
And at thy footstool fall,
Till thou our hidden life reveal,
Till thou our ravished spirits fill,
And God is all in all.

Ye are dead, and your life is hid with Christ in God.

Colossians 3:3

This continues yesterday's study of the vision of heaven as a sustaining goal for those in conflict here on earth; it is fine poetry in the mystical, metaphysical tradition of Herbert and Donne.[1] Ponder especially the phrase 'silence heightens heaven'. See how Wesley follows this by the phrase 'ecstatic pause' – something reminiscent of the breathless silence which precedes the applause at the end of a fine orchestral concert.

MEDITATION
Meditate on any images here which expand your consciousness and give a sensation of adoration and praise. Try to put reason on hold for a while! Reflect particularly on the very last line.

---

*HSP (1749) RV 80 MHB 487

THE UNIVERSAL LOVE OF CHRIST (1)

Let earth and heaven agree,
Angels and men be joined,
To celebrate with me
The Saviour of mankind;
To adore the all-atoning Lamb,
And bless the sound of Jesus' name.

Jesus, transporting sound!
The joy of earth and heaven;
No other help is found,
No other name is given,
By which we can salvation have;
But Jesus came the world to save.

His name the sinner hears
And is from sin set free;
'Tis music in the ears,
'Tis life and victory;
New songs do now the lips employ,
And dances the glad heart for joy.

[They] said unto the woman, Now we believe, not because of thy saying: for we have heard him ourselves, and know that this is indeed the Christ, the Saviour of the world.
John 4:42

The title of this hymn, 'The Universal Love of Christ', is a fine starting point for the story of the encounter between Jesus and the Samaritan woman at Jacob's well. She is a foreigner and, as an apparently sexually promiscuous woman, would be regarded as an outcast from polite society. Jesus, however, treats her with a dignity which makes possible a dialogue of love, forgiveness and liberation. If ever we need a model for ministry it is here.

The overall framework of the hymn is one of praise and celebration in heaven and on earth. The name 'Jesus' works miracles of freedom – loosing in the poet an exuberance of delight that recalls the words of Psalm 28:7 in the *Book of Common Prayer*: 'My heart danceth for joy, and in my song I will praise God.'

PRAYER
Blessed be your holy Name, that I have found you my Saviour.
O I love you much, for I have much to be forgiven.
Susanna Wesley

---

*Hymns on God's Everlasting love (1742) RV 22 CH 33 [3:5-6 his lips . . . his glad heart]
HP 226

O unexampled love,
O all-redeeming grace!
How freely didst thou move
To save a fallen race!
What shall I do to make it known
What thou for all mankind hast done!

O for a trumpet-voice
On all the world to call,
To bid their hearts rejoice
In him who died for all!
For all my Lord was crucified,
For all, for all my Saviour died.

To serve thy blessed will,
Thy dying love to praise,
Thy counsel to fulfil
And minister thy grace,
Freely what I receive to give,
The life of heaven on earth I live.

Cry aloud, spare not, lift up thy voice like a trumpet.

Isaiah 58:1

This continues yesterday's hymn of praise to the name 'Jesus'. The biblical basis of the hymn is strongly built on by the language and imagery of Milton's *Paradise Lost,* a poem that from childhood had held a powerful grip on the imagination of both John and Charles Wesley. The dramatic conflict in Milton's poem between Satan and God, and Christ's intervention to save Adam and Eve, is the background to the first verse. Milton writes of Christ who:

Regardless of the bliss wherein he sat
Second to thee, offered himself to die
For man's offence. O unexampled love,
Love nowhere to be found less than divine! (*PL* III 408-111)

In verse two the poet calls for a trumpet, not to sound an alarm or warning (as in Isaiah) but to summon the people to a joyous festival as in the proclamation of the year of jubilee (Leviticus 25:9). The natural response then is service and praise.

PRAYER
Creator God, grant me the gift of communication, so that I might convey vividly to others the truth of who you are. What I know I have received of your grace, help me to give with integrity and a generous heart to others. Amen.

*Hymns on God's Everlasting Love (1742) RV 22 CH 33 HP 226

Rejoice for a brother deceased,
  Our loss is his infinite gain;
A soul out of prison released,
  And free from its bodily chain;
With songs let us follow his flight,
  And mount with his spirit above,
Escaped to the mansions of light,
  And lodged in the Eden of love.

Our brother the haven hath gained,
  Out-flying the tempest and wind,
His rest he hath sooner obtained,
  And left his companions behind;
Still tossed on a sea of distress,
  Hard toiling to make the blest shore,
Where all is assurance and peace,
  And sorrow and sin are no more.

There all the ship's company meet,
  Who sailed with the Saviour beneath,
With shouting each other they greet,
  And triumph o'er trouble and death:
The voyage of life's at an end,
  The mortal affliction is past;
The age that in heaven they spend
  For ever and ever shall last.

For me to live is Christ, and to die is gain.

Philippians 1:21

This hymn, a favourite of Charles Wesley himself, has been described as a 'typical death-triumph of the Methodist revival'.[1] It is thought to have been written in the year 1744 after the death of a Cardiff Methodist, whose final hours were a time of great joy for all present. Death here is seen as a release rather than a defeat.

The metaphor of the sailor coming home to shore, sustained through the last two verses, is a compelling one. The lively metre, too, counteracts feelings of sadness.

PRAYER
O God, from whom I come and to whom I shall one day journey home, save me from the fear of dying, and give me grace to let myself go one day into a larger life, through Jesus Christ. Amen.

Funeral Hymns (1746) *CH 48 MHB 973

Come, let us join our friends above
That have obtained the prize,
And on the eagle wings of love
To joy celestial rise:
Let all the saints terrestrial sing
With those to glory gone;
For all the servants of our King,
In earth and heaven, are one.

One family we dwell in him,
One church, above, beneath,
Though now divided by the stream,
The narrow stream of death:
One army of the living God,
To his command we bow;
Part of his host hath crossed the flood,
And part are crossing now.

Forgetting those things which are behind, and reaching forth unto those things which are before, I press toward the mark for the prize of the high calling of God in Christ Jesus.

Philippians 3:13-14

It is recorded that John Wesley not only thought this the 'sweetest hymn his brother ever wrote' but that a group of Methodists in Staffordshire were actually singing this hymn at the very time of Charles' death.[1] The sense of joy draws its imagery from the story of the Israelites, who, having wandered in the wilderness for forty years, are led by Joshua through the river Jordan on dry ground into the promised land (Joshua 3:4).

Some years ago, a doctor wrote an article with the title, 'Death as a constant companion'. He wrote gently of the naturalness of death, and how we try to avoid thinking about it in a world of medical 'cures'. Charles looks on death not only as a constant companion, but as a constant triumph, as his whole life moves towards the sight of the Master he serves. The stream to be crossed is narrow indeed, and part of the family is waiting on the other side.

PRAYER
Father of spirits, we have joy at this time in all who have faithfully lived, and in all who have peacefully died. We thank thee for all fair memories and all lively hopes, and for the dear, holy dead who make the distant heaven a home for our hearts.[2]
Methodist Book of Offices

---

*FH (1759) RV 93 HP 812

Jesus, the First and Last,
On thee my soul is cast:
Thou didst thy work begin
By blotting out my sin;
Thou wilt the root remove,
And perfect me in love.

Yet when the work is done,
The work is but begun:
Partaker of thy grace,
I long to see thy face;
The first I prove below,
The last I die to know.

I am Alpha and Omega, the first and the last.

Revelation 1:11

Christian perfection means being made perfect in love. It does not mean being perfect in the eyes of the world, a super-man or super-woman. It is not a state people can attain by their own efforts. It is a gift of God to those who want only the love of God for themselves and for others.

This cameo of a poem, a meditation on the passage in Revelation, is both simple and complex. The language is plain, the rhyme in couplets, the syntax straightforward, but there is an intricate play on words that recalls the poetry of the metaphysical poet, John Donne. The form of the poem reinforces the meaning and brings us, even in its brevity, to a sense of completion.

PRAYER
O Lord, the first and the last,
the beginning and the end;
you who were with us at our birth,
be with us through our life;
you who are with us throughout our life,
be with us at our death;
and because your mercy will not leave us then,
grant that we die not,
but rise to the life everlasting.
The Cambridge Bede Book

---

*SH (1762) HP 735

SELECT BIBLIOGRAPHY

Baker, Frank, ed. *Representative Verse of Charles Wesley,* London 1962.

Baker, Frank, *Charles Wesley's Verse. An Introduction,* 2nd ed. London 1988.

McMullen, Michael, ed. *Hearts Aflame. Prayers of Susanna, John and Charles Wesley,* London 1995.

Rattenbury, J. Ernest, *The Eucharistic Hymns of John and Charles Wesley,* London 1948.

Telford, John, *The New Methodist Hymn-Book Illustrated in History and Experience,* London 1941 (1934).

Watson, Richard and Trickett, Kenneth, *Companion to Hymns & Psalms,* Peterborough 1988.

Wesley, Charles, *The Unpublished Poetry of Charles Wesley,* ed. S. T. Kimbrough, Jr. & O. A. Beckerlegge, 3 vols. Nashville, TN 1988.

Wesley, John and Charles, *The Poetical Works of John and Charles Wesley, reprinted from the originals with the last corrections of the authors; together with The Poems of Charles Wesley not before published.* Collected and arranged by G. Osborn. 13 vols, London 1868-72.

Wesley, John and Charles, *The Works of John Wesley,* vol.7, *A Collection of Hymns for the Use of the People called Methodists,* ed. F. Hildebrandt & O. A. Beckerlegge, Oxford 1983.

Young, Carlton R. *Companion to the United Methodist Hymnal,* Nashville 1993.

The editors have endeavoured as best they could to identify and credit all the sources used by Elizabeth Hart in the preparation of this book. They ask the gracious indulgence of any author whose contribution may have been overlooked by them.

ABBREVIATIONS

AM	*Arminian Magazine*
CH	*A Collection of Hymns for the Use of the People called Methodists* (1780+)
CPH	*A Collection of Psalms and Hymns* (1737, 1738, 1741, 1743)
FH	*Hymns for the Use of Families* (1767)
HC	*Hymns for Children* (1763)
HGEL	*Hymns on God's Everlasting Love* (1741, 1742)
HGF	*Hymns on the Great Festivals, and other Occasions* (1746)
HIAM	*Hymns of Intercession for all Mankind* (1758)
HLR	*Hymns for our Lord's Resurrection* (1746)
HLS	*Hymns on the Lord's Supper* (1745)
HNYD	*Hymns for New Year's Day* (1750)
HP	*Hymns & Psalms,* Methodist Publishing House (1983)
HPT	*Hymns of Petition and Thanksgiving* (1746)
HSP	*Hymns and Sacred Poems* (1739, 1740, 1742, 1749)
HT	*Hymns on the Trinity* (1767)
HTTP	*Hymns for Times of Trouble and Persecution* (1744)
MHB	*The Methodist Hymn Book,* Methodist Publishing House (1933)
MS	Manuscript
NH	*Hymns for the Nativity of our Lord* (1744)
PH	*Psalms & Hymns* (1743)
PW	*The Poetical Works of John and Charles Wesley.* ed. G. Osborn
RH	*Hymns for those that seek and those that have Redemption* (1747)
RV	*Representative Verse of Charles Wesley.* ed. F. Baker
SH	*Short Hymns on Select Passages of the Holy Scriptures* (1762)
UMH	*United Methodist Hymnal* (1989)
UPCW	*The Unpublished Poetry of Charles Wesley.* ed. Kimbrough & Beckerlegge
VU	*Voices United,* United Church of Canada (1996)

INDEX OF FIRST LINES

INDEX OF BIBLICAL TEXT

INDEX OF SOURCES AND PERSONS QUOTED
other than Charles Wesley

REFERENCES

Extracts from the Authorized Version of the Bible (The King James Bible), the rights of which are vested in the Crown, are reproduced by permission of the Crown's Patentee, Cambridge University Press.

Extracts from the Revised Standard Version of the Bible are copyright 1971 by the Division of Christian Education of the National Council of the Churches of Christ in the USA.

Extracts from The Revised English Bible © 1989 Oxford and Cambridge University Presses.

Extracts from the New Revised Standard Version of the Bible are copyright 1989 by the Division of Christian Education of the National Council of the Churches of Christ in the USA.

Extracts from The Book of Common Prayer, the rights of which are vested in the Crown, are reproduced by permission of the Crown's Patentee, Cambridge University Press.

Methodist Publishing House gratefully acknowledges permission to use copyright items. Every effort has been made to trace copyright owners, but where we have been unsuccessful we would welcome information which would enable us to make appropriate acknowledgement in any reprint.

Meditation

9 [1]Dag Hammarskjöld, *Markings,* trs. W. H. Auden, Leif Sjöberg, Faber and Faber Ltd, 1966.

10 [1]*The Sermons of John Donne*, ed. Simpson and Potter, vol. 6, p 172.

26 [1]Thomas Hardy, 'The Oxen', *The Complete Poems,* Papermac.

31 [1]*Women Included*, Book of Services and Prayers, Saint Hilda Community, SPCK.

54 [1]Dietrich Bonhoeffer, *Letters and Papers from Prison,* The Enlarged Edition, SCM Press 1971, p 141-2.

55 [1]John Cosin, *A Collection of Private Devotions,* ed. Paul Stanwood, Oxford: Clarendon Press, 1967, p 81.

56 [1]*Oxford Book of Prayer,* (OUP) p 132.

57 [1]Beth Glick-Rieman, 'Growing Old', source unknown.
[2]Teilhard de Chardin, *Le Milieu Divin*, Collins 1960.

62 [1]John Wesley, *Letters*, 20 Jan 1787; 14 July 1748; 13 July 1774.

68 [1]Janet Morley, *All Desires Known,* SPCK, p 27. Permission applied for.

72 [1]Janet Morley, *All Desires Known,* SPCK, p 24. Permission applied for.

80 [1]Adapted from an Anglican Prayer of Exorcism, *Oxford Book of Prayer* (OUP), p 247.

82 [1]Prayer for the Service of the Lord's Supper, Draft Service p 83 *Services for Holy Communion* © Trustees for Methodist Church Purposes.

88 [1]William Arthur Cornaby, *Rambles in Central China*, London: Charles Kelly, 1896, p 28.

91 [1]Jean Vanier, *Eruption to Hope,* Toronto: Griffin House, 1971, p 46-7.

98 [1]Prayer by Robert H. Adams Jr. from *A Traveller's Prayer Book,* Copyright © 1965 by The Upper Room, Nashville TN. Adapted, 1983 WCC Publications, World Council of Churches, Geneva, Switzerland.

102 [1]Taizé Community, *Taizé Parables,* p 78.

111 [1]Dietrich Bonhoeffer, trans. Alan Gaunt © Stainer & Bell Ltd from *The Hymn Texts of Alan Gaunt.*

112 [1]J. Ernest Rattenbury, *The Eucharistic Hymns of John and Charles Wesley*, Epworth Press, p 23.

115 [1]The Iona Community Worship Book (Wild Goose Publications, The Iona Community, Glasgow, 1991). Used with permission.

119 [1]Prayer for Easter Day, Methodist Service Book, © 1975 Methodist Conference.

120 [1]From *The United Methodist Hymnal,* 1989.

127 [1]Holy Eucharist, *Book of Alternative Services,* Anglican Church of Canada, p 213. Permission applied for.

129 [1]Worship Book of the World Alliance of Reformed Churches, Seoul 1989. Permission applied for.

133 [1]Ordination Service, Methodist Service Book, © 1975 Methodist Conference.

134 [1]From *The United Methodist Hymnal,* by Laurence Hull Stookey. Copyright © 1989 by The United Methodist Publishing House.

144 [1]The Iona Community Worship Book (Wild Goose Publications, The Iona Community, Glasgow, 1991). Used with permission.

148 [1]Prayer for the Service of the Lord's Supper, Methodist Service Book, © 1975 Methodist Conference.

169 [1]Ernest Rattenbury, *Evangelical Doctrines of Charles Wesley's Hymns,* Epworth Press, p 258.
[2]Janet Morley, *All Desires Known,* SPCK, p 23. Permission applied for.

171 [1]Janet Morley, *All Desires Known,* SPCK, p 19. Permission applied for.

172 [1]A. M. Allchin and Esther de Waal, *Threshold of Light: Prayers and Praises from the Celtic Tradition,* Darton, Longmann and Todd 1986, p 50.

192 [1]The Covenant Service, Methodist Service Book, © 1975 Methodist Conference.

210 [1]Frank Baker, *Representative Verse of Charles Wesley,* London 1962 p 251.

211 [1]John Wesley, *Preface to Hymns for Children,* 1787, 1790.

215 [1]Brother Lawrence, *The Practice of the Presence of God,* Fourth conversation, 25th November 1667.

221 [1]'A Dakota Prayer' from *The Gift is Rich* by E. Russell Carter. Copyright © 1955 by Friendship Press, Inc. Used by permission.

234 [1]Sue Mosteller, *My Brother, My Sister,* Toronto: Griffin House, 1972, p 99.

237 [1]William Law, *A Serious Call to a Devout and Holy Life,* Chapter 18.

246 [1]African Prayer, source unknown.

247 [1]Adapted from the Carmina Gaedelica. The Iona Community Worship Book (Wild Goose Publications, The Iona Community, Glasgow, 1991). Used with permission.

254 [1]WAC Letter, 28th November 1898 (Meth. Miss. Archives).

260 [1]Prayer, © The Iona Community, 840 Govan Road, Glasgow G51 3UU, Scotland.

264 [1]William Arthur Cornaby, *In Touch With Reality,* London: Charles Kelly, 1905.

267 [1]Elaine Morgan, source unknown.

282 [1]Janet Morley, *All Desires Known*, SPCK, p 68. Permission applied for.

285 [1]Don Robertson, *BC Conference Call,* United Church of Canada, November 1992, p 17-18.

291 [1]Frank Baker, *Representative Verse,* p 251.

308 [1]Brother Lawrence, *The Practice of the Presence of God,* 2nd conversation, 26th September 1666.

309 [1]The Iona Community Worship Book (Wild Goose Publications, The Iona Community, Glasgow, 1991). Used with permission.

311 [1]Sallie McFague, *Models of God,* Philadelphia: Fortress, 1987, p 171.
[2]John Owen quoted in John Baillie, *A Diary of Readings,* OUP, 1955, Day 46.

313 [1]Dietrich Bonhoeffer, *Letters and Papers from Prison,* The Enlarged Edition, SCM Press, p 176.

319 [1]Book of Alternative Services, Anglican Church of Canada, p 439. Permission applied for.

331 [1]John Wesley, *Principles of a Methodist Farther Explained*, 1746, VI 4.

341 [1]Frank Baker, 'A Poet in Love – the Courtship of Charles Wesley, 1747-1749', Methodist History, 29, (1991) p 235-47.
[2]Service of Marriage, Book of Alternative Services, Anglican Church of Canada. Permission applied for.

344 [1]*The Prophet*, 'On Children'.

349 [1]A traditional prayer from India, from the *United Methodist Hymnal*, 1989.

351 [1]Thomas R. Kelly, *A Testament of Devotion,* New York: Harper, 1941, p 32.

361 [1]See especially E. M. Hodgson, 'Poetry in the Hymns of John and Charles Wesley', Proceedings of the Wesley Historical Society, 38 (1972), p 132.

364 [1]See Frank Baker, *Representative Verse of Charles Wesley,* London 1962, p 88.

365 [1]John Telford, The Methodist Hymn-Book Illustrated, 4th ed., Epworth Press, 1924, p 408.
[2]Methodist Book of Offices, © 1936 Methodist Conference.